Bureau Men, Settlement Women

STUDIES IN GOVERNMENT AND PUBLIC POLICY

Bureau Men,
Settlement Women

Constructing Public
Administration
in the Progressive Era

Camilla Stivers

University Press of Kansas

© 2000 by the University Press of Kansas

Published by the University Press of Kansas (Lawrence, Kansas 66049), which was organized by the Kansas Board of Regents and is operated and funded by Emporia State University, Fort Hays State University, Kansas State University, Pittsburg State University, the University of Kansas, and Wichita State University.

Library of Congress Cataloging-in-Publication Data

Stivers, Camilla.
    Bureau men, settlement women : constructing public administration in the progressive era / Camilla Stivers.
        p.   cm. — (Studies in government and public policy)
    Includes bibliographical references and index.
    ISBN 0-7006-1021-9
    1. Municipal government—United States—History. 2. Public administration—United States—History. 3. Women in public life—United States—History. 4. Progressivism (United States politics) 5. Sex role—United States—History. I. Title. II. Series.

JS323.S86 2000
352.16'0973—dc21   99-059853

British Library Cataloguing in Publication Data is available.

Printed in the United States of America

10 9 8 7 6 5 4 3 2 1

The paper used in this publication meets the minimum requirements of the American National Standard for Permanence of Paper for Printed Library Materials Z39.48-1984.

To Ralph

Contents

Preface

In the summer of 1984 I was a doctoral student, dutifully making my way through an enormous stack of classics, the required reading for Gary Wamsley's capstone seminar in public organization theory. About halfway through the term, I picked up what at first seemed to be just another dusty tome, Dwight Waldo's *The Administrative State*. Fifteen years later, I still recall my surprise and delight. Fresh, critical, disarmingly wise in the humble but piercing way I now recognize as characteristic of Waldo, *The Administrative State* said what no one else had said before and few have said since: that public administration, as conceived by its founders in the municipal research movement in the early twentieth century, was not simply a set of technical maxims for governmental efficiency but a full-blown normative theory of government. Waldo's insight changed the way I viewed the field and enormously increased my interest in being a part of it. In his twin admonitions, to think of public administration as a political philosophy and to think of it historically, I found my intellectual path.

This book reflects both these themes. It has seemed to me ever since reading Waldo that the field of public administration is more interesting and complex than most of its textbooks and scholarly research allow us to see. The continuing tension that Waldo recognized as central—between administrative effectiveness, on the one hand, and democracy, on the other—contains an inexhaustible supply of topics and makes room for a wide array of contending perspectives. But it is too often obscured by a single-minded search for "best practices" (contemporary jargon for "one best way"), for a science of administration that will resolve contradictions that, in my view, would be better left in place. As will be clear in what follows, it seems to me that there is little hope for a science of administration, given the subject matter's complex and value-ridden nature, but even if there were, I would not want one. I share the view of Hannah Arendt and others that when it comes to public questions, right answers drive out politics, which deals with issues that human beings are fated to disagree about but without which they would be thin creatures indeed. The way I tell the story of public administration's construction, then, reflects my own version of its political philosophy, which is, by definition, arguable.

I turn, as Waldo did, to its history in order to develop my understanding of why public administration has taken the rather narrow outlines it has. Like Waldo, I see science and business as crucial forces shaping the emergence of the field, but I add another element that lies within the first two: gender. During the Progressive Era, the first two decades of the twentieth century, both men and women took part in efforts to improve city governments and city life generally. But they did so in distinctive ways, based on widely shared agreements about proper roles for men and women in society. As a result of these expectations, women and men who shared broad reform goals translated those goals into quite different activities. To capture the difference in an oversimplified way, men set about trying to make the city run like a business, and women aimed to make the city more like a home. As Waldo showed, in the absence of any knowledge about what women of the time were doing and what they might have contributed to the field's development, one can tell the story of public administration and tell it persuasively. But without considering women's activities, it is difficult to imagine an alternative other than, as Waldo wryly noted, the ancien régime. My project is aimed at calling into question this taken-for-granted quality, which permeates the field and keeps it from seeing what might be.

While my greatest intellectual debt is to Dwight Waldo, there have been other important influences. Without the opportunity to argue with and learn from Orion White, Lou Weschler, Mary Timney, Larry Terry, Jim Speight, Cynthia McSwain, Cheryl Simrell King, Kirk Hart, Ken Dolbeare, Terry Cooper, and Jennifer Alexander—although they may not discern themselves in what follows (may not even want to)—the book would not have been possible. More direct debts have also accrued. Suzanne Mettler, Barbara Bridgman Perkins, and David Rosenbloom read the entire manuscript in draft and made a wealth of insightful comments that (when I followed their directions carefully enough) sharpened the argument considerably. Hindy Lauer Schachter's criticism of a preliminary version kept me on my toes as I continued to work. Students and faculty at The Evergreen State College, Cleveland State University, the University of Akron, Virginia Tech, and the Maxwell School listened, argued, and made helpful suggestions. Renee Nank and Steve Salmi, research assistants at Cleveland State, tracked down a lot of fugitive material, served as great sounding boards, and made many tasks easier because of their energy, good sense, and good humor. Fred Woodward of the University Press of Kansas encouraged me and waited patiently during the many months beyond my original estimate that it took to complete the project. Hui Sheng and David Mammen at the Institute of Public Administration (IPA) in New York City provided me with a desk, gave me access to the treasure trove of documents in the IPA's storage area, and hosted a brown-bag lunch discussion for IPA board members that resulted in a very helpful early sounding of the viability of my approach. Sally Coleman Selden at the Maxwell School of Syracuse University persuaded the university library to open its archives on a Saturday, helped me search through the boxes, organized discussions and social activities around my visit, put me up, and made sure that all the material I needed got photocopied and sent to me—all with her characteristic intelligence, energy, and cheer. The staff of the Social Welfare History Archives at the University of Minnesota was unfailingly helpful. Ruth-Ellen Boettscher Joeres, who has been my friend for thirty years, gave me a home away from home for the month I spent in Minnesota and all the affection and support that only friendship of such long standing and solidity is able to produce.

My greatest debt is to my husband, Ralph Hummel, who makes every day seem world enough and time. The book is dedicated to him, in smallest acknowledgment of things owed but impossible either to calculate or to express.

1

Finding a Usable Past

In 1905, a brash young man named Henry Bruere walked the streets of Manhattan armed with a camera. Bruere was part of a group of educated reformers who were interested in exposing what they viewed as the incompetence of New York City's government. Comparing the ruts and potholes he saw with city repair records that painted a glowing picture of street maintenance, Bruere and his organization published an exposé called "How Manhattan Is Governed." The report hit New York like a bombshell and led to the forced resignation of the Manhattan borough president, the first time a city official had been removed for sheer mismanagement rather than corruption.

From the efforts of well-to-do reformers like Henry Bruere to document the facts of municipal government came the applied academic field of public administration, devoted to training professional administrators and to developing systematic knowledge about governmental administrative structures and processes. As the twentieth century drew to a close, American public administration had become well established in academia, with undergraduate and graduate training offered at dozens of universities, and scholarly journals filled with its theory and research. Although academics often argue about whether their field is organized enough conceptually to constitute a full-fledged discipline, what began as a rather ad hoc effort, a small part of a much larger social dynamic, has become institutionalized in its own right.

Despite its intellectual roots in an era marked by immense political and economic change—one that has been the focus of hundreds of books and articles—American public administration has been strikingly inattentive to its emergence from the activities of a particular group of Progressive reformers. Many popular texts say nothing at all about the field's history; others settle for "a ritual mention" of Woodrow Wilson, whose 1887 essay is generally accepted as the founding document in American public administration, "followed by a jump to the present time with no historical analysis at all."[1] The few conscious efforts to tell the story trace public administration to "the stir-up about scandal, waste, and politics in the cities around the turn of the century"[2] and, more particularly, to the municipal research bureau movement that Henry Bruere helped pioneer. But these narratives are often couched simplistically in terms of a struggle between the forces of evil ("machine politics," "the bosses") and the champions of good ("reformers," "science"), a black-and-white analysis outmoded among historians more than two decades ago.[3] A typical account of the birth of public administration paints this picture:

> Cities were under control of political cliques and bosses who used their power more for their own advantage than for providing livable communities for their constituents. . . . City governments were in some ways a laboratory for sordid and despotic practices not illuminated by the searchlight of national publicity. . . . Little wonder that cities, for the most part, were dreary and dangerous places in which to live. . . . They suffered from poor transportation, miserable housing, inadequate sanitation, limited or no recreational facilities. Libraries were non-existent. Schools deteriorated with untrained teachers. . . . The foregoing conditions and forces in New York City provided a fertile setting for change that ultimately brought into flower the profession of public administration.[4]

In contrast, Progressive historiography is filled with lively debate and conflicting interpretation that expose most such judgments as unwarranted, yet relatively little of this more complex and interesting material has found its way into public administration literature. "All in all," comments Barry D. Karl, "historians have tended to take the history of public administration in terms which satisfied the practicing ideologues in the field . . . : that it was essentially a methodological field posing no threat to the traditional political structure . . . ; that it was a user of social science rather than a formulator of it."[5]

The purpose of this book is to tell the story of public administration's construction in a way that calls into question the field's rather taken-for-granted methodological quality and puts it back into its historical context, a framework in which science, business, and gender are equally important and in which its political dimensions are made clear. The story is significant in several respects. As I suggest, finding what one of its early scholars called "a usable past" for public administration entails the recovery of "aspects . . . which now lie buried"—broader historical, intellectual, and gender dynamics that show how factors that shaped one field also influenced and were shaped by forces at work in other areas.[6] The men of the municipal research bureaus, quintessential Progressives in many ways, have not been thoroughly studied by historians of the period, nor have urbanists exhausted the subject of their impact on the shape and dynamics of city governments. Although a few political scientists have taken note, perhaps because public administration is an applied field, political science seems to have underestimated the role of public administration's birth in American political development.

As I argue, gender is an important element in the story of how public administration came to define itself. Juxtaposing the activities of "bureau men" with those of settlement residents and members of women's reform clubs puts both into a broader context and highlights aspects that might otherwise go unnoticed; scholars of women's studies may therefore find the story of interest. The same is true in the consideration of public administration and social work in light of each other, as professions whose concerns at first overlapped and might have coalesced even further, but ended up separating.

In addition, public administration's story illustrates more generally how particular circumstances constrain and enable the formation of a body of thought. In this respect, it may appeal to those who have an interest in intellectual history. The construction of a discipline, by selecting, concentrating, and refining ideas and practices at work in the existing society, brings into sharp relief certain aspects of that society and casts others into shadow. Choices on the part of intellectuals, particularly in social science, about what is important or meaningful in the social dynamics around them set in motion patterns of thought that become important conceptual currency. Circulated in public, these concepts become means by which, for good or ill, people interpret the circumstances of their lives and decide what it is possible to do or worth doing.

Finally, decisions early in the twentieth century about what public administration might be and how one should study or practice it put in place conceptual boundaries and set in motion intellectual dynamics that persist in the field to this day. They have become so taken for granted, however, that they are little noticed by those who teach or study administration, let alone by those actively engaged in it. Such decisions have broader implications than the simple construction of a founding narrative, for, as Stephen Toulmin points out, "The beliefs that shape our historical foresight represent . . . our . . . horizons of expectation . . . limits to the field of action in which, at the moment, we see it as possible or feasible to change human affairs, and so to decide which of our most cherished practical goals can be realized in fact."[7] The story of public administration's development, in other words, has practical consequences. It contributes to our sense of the place of administration in American governance and political life, the questions and issues that are the substance of scholarly dialogue, the conventional wisdom in administrative agencies, the substance of the latest cutting-edge reform, and our sense of what it might be possible to think, say, and do about administrative governance in the future.

Americans today—especially those in public life—cast their understanding of the political and administrative present and their hope for its future partly in terms of ideas that animated the small group of municipal reformers in the early 1900s who took up the cause of correct administrative procedures and proper training for city government administrators. Most contemporary proposals for improving the workings of public bureaucracies—for example, "reinventing government"—reach the same diagnoses and offer the same nostrums as those on which the early administrative reformers relied. In context, such proposals reveal the same interests as those of an earlier era and thus can be understood, despite their rhetoric, not as strikingly original ideas but as part of a long-standing pattern. Public administration's history displays an abiding commitment to science, businesslike management, and masculinity, constitutive preferences that have not only described but also shaped the workaday reality in public agencies. The sources of this pattern require exploration.

THE PROGRESSIVE ERA

In the United States, the last quarter of the nineteenth century witnessed enough fundamental economic change and political unrest to make Teddy Roosevelt exclaim to the country, "We stand at Armageddon and we battle for the Lord."[8] The industrializing economy spawned corporations the scale of which dwarfed even the federal government. "The capital . . . raised to organize the billion-dollar steel trust in 1901 was enough to pay the costs of all functions of the federal government for almost two years." Large corporations far outweighed state governments; one large railroad employed 18,000 people, while the commonwealth of Massachusetts had only 6,000 employees.[9]

Railroads and the telegraph wove a national web that linked once insulated communities. More and more people lived in cities swollen by massive influxes of immigrants and afflicted by all the problems and pathologies that rapid growth and overcrowding produce. By the 1890s, the population on New York's Lower East Side was packed some 290,000 to the square mile, the densest in the world.[10] Urban working people and farmers alike struggled with and protested the economic pressures exerted on them, while cycles of boom and bust made rich and poor feel equally vulnerable to unpredictable ruin (although of course they were not).

In the midst of such starkly visible forces, quieter but just as fundamental changes were taking place. A new middle class developed, composed of small businessmen, technicians, managers, clerical and sales personnel, and professionals— not only the traditional independent physician, attorney, or clergyman, but salaried specialists in administration, social work, teaching, agriculture, and economics. Located between big-money capitalists and the laboring (or starving) masses, members of this new class, increasingly organized in trade associations and professional organizations, sought to bring order to a society threatened with chaos and, in so doing, create a niche for themselves in that society. Here among the middling sort, as the century turned, sprouted the admiration for planning, management, efficiency, science, and stability that made up the characteristic Progressive. Their answer to society's ills was systemization instituted by educated but objective experts, people whose only agenda was not economic self-interest but the simple desire to make themselves useful in restoring social harmony by tempering the worst effects of capitalism. Or so the new professionals saw themselves.[11]

The times spawned two impulses, one in the direction of social justice and improving the lives of the unfortunate, and the other toward rationalizing and regulating organizational, institutional, and societal processes.[12] These are the two faces of Progressive reform. Historians disagree about the relative weight of each, but rarely about their dual presence. The warmest-hearted reformer's concern for the poor recognized the need to help efficiently, while the most calculated plan to improve accounting methods presented itself as in aid of some social betterment goal. Yet the blend was sometimes more, sometimes less balanced, depending on the circumstances and the players. In public administration, the two impulses became increasingly uncomfortable with and finally estranged from each other. What occurred can be seen as a divorce of substantive intent from instrumental method. In municipal reform discourse, a gradual but inexorable shift in focus occurred, from meaningful outcome to correct procedure. Among public-oriented professionals, the question of how to govern scientifically and efficiently gradually effaced the question of which things were worth doing and whether they helped those who needed help. In turn, what could once be seen as the desire, however variable in scope, to work real change became diluted by the need to legitimate itself in terms of political and administrative rationality. A point was reached where people bent on meaningful change found themselves having to settle for relatively minor improvement or, worse, were no longer able to tell the difference between the two.

As this account shows, out of the eventual separation of substantive purpose and procedural means in municipal reform emerged the field of public administration as a self-defined intellectual enterprise and a practice self-consciously professional in aspiration and style if not in universal regard. Today, the field of public administration, particularly its professional curricula, occupies itself largely with scientific and businesslike administrative procedures, such as budgeting, personnel processes, management information, and employee supervision, and gives relatively little weight to broader questions of public purpose. As the concluding chapter suggests, throughout the twentieth century, proposals to improve administrative agencies repeated the litany of scientific and businesslike efficiency first intoned in the Progressive Era, as if there had been nothing more substantive then or since on which to base an understanding of public administration. These dynamics prompted the questions that animate this study:

1. To what extent did the conceptual and strategic choices made by public administration's founder-organizers open up certain arenas of thought and activity and foreclose others?
2. What factors played a role in the way the field came to define itself at this crucial inciting moment?
3. What factors, neglected or ignored at the time and since, could have resulted in a different founding story, one that made possible a continued intermingling of purpose and procedure?

The story told here attempts to recover fateful choices and lost opportunities in the construction of public administration. Existing narratives, as a rule, take for granted the altruism of the men of the bureaus of municipal research who instigated the first training programs to prepare professional administrators, as well as their success in reforming municipal administration and thus presumably blunting, if not banishing entirely, the impact of machine politics on city governments. Since the first two decades of the twentieth century, a great deal of interesting detail in the emergence of public administration has been lost to view. With it has disappeared a sense of the contingency that marks intellectual history, and the extent to which what now appears inevitable was once the stuff of argument, struggle, and deliberate campaign.

As the earlier example suggests, most of the field's accounts paint a somewhat cartoonlike picture. In that picture, until the bureaus of municipal research came along, American cities were stewpots of corruption and inefficiency. By reforming administrative procedures, the heroic knights of the bureaus struck at the Achilles' heel of the machine bosses and toppled them inexorably and in rather short order. The men of the bureaus, in contrast to city politicians and municipal workers, were selfless experts who saw the public good and brought it about.[13] Today, the narrative concludes, the professional education and scholarly work that developed from their research projects and training programs can be seen, if not always as unproblematically effective as their progenitors, certainly as a happy blend of dedication and knowledge.

This cartoon has obscured important elements and misled scholars, administrators, and students of public administration about the roots of their own intellectual or practical work. Behind it lies a much more interesting reality. While it may be, as one of the few efforts to recount the history suggests, that "the [municipal research] bureau demonstrated the value of the analytical approach in solving policy and administrative problems,"[14] those in attendance at the demonstration varied in their reactions to it. Suffused with a faith in science, in the power of facts to sway people's minds, the bureau men never understood why the world somehow failed to fall in line. Quintessential expert rationalizers and systemizers, they could not acknowledge how fundamentally public life entails the nonrational and the nonsystematic, or where the appropriate boundaries of their expertise lay.

Historians of the Progressive period have debated at length the issue of what motivated reformers such as the men of the municipal research bureaus, but they agree that in general the impetus was a blend of altruism and self-interest. In 1964, Samuel Hays took previous observers to task for taking municipal reformers at their word: that is, for putting too much weight on the reformers' own accounts of their motives and values and not enough on the extent to which their efforts furthered and were supported by big business interests.[15] Recently, Hays's emphasis on the influence of economics has been challenged by Finegold[16] and others, on the basis that Progressives were ideologically motivated. For an understanding of the development of public administration, it seems important to look both at the

ideas and values by which relevant reformers were guided and at the material interests shaping and being supported by their efforts. The first are important because,
as this book aims to show, the field of public administration still evolves largely
within the intellectual framework the bureau men crafted; the second count because
they enable a sense of the framework's tangible implications. Awareness of the economic and political interests served by early public administration makes it more
difficult to take for granted the founders' idea of their enterprise as neutral science.
Today, the bureau men's reliance on an ideology of scientific method as key to the
improvement of municipal government still provides the field's conceptual center
of gravity and the context within which, even when they reject it, public administrationists assess the legitimacy of their own work. In addition, the world's failure
to accept science as the unquestioned source of public wisdom continues to serve
as an object lesson in the variety of paths by which others—politicians, citizens—
determine the proper role and effectiveness of administration in governance.

In general, then, this account leaves aside the question of whether self-interest
or concern for the public good more strongly motivated municipal reformers, concentrating instead on the intellectual framework they built, its place in their reform
work, and the interests it served. But the origin of the focus for their theoretical and
practical efforts needs specific attention. Given the complex and colorful array of
reforming activities that are today viewed as characteristically Progressive, why
does public administration see itself as having germinated solely from the efforts
of a particular group of well-to-do men associated with the bureaus of municipal
research, rather than from broader and more diverse origins? As the bureau work
developed, why did it narrow its concerns from a rationale that blended social welfare with administrative efficiency to one bent much more exclusively on efficient
method for its own sake? Why did the bureau men concentrate to such an extent on
proper governmental budgeting, accounting, and organizational structure and lose
sight of the substance of government policy? How did public administration education come to be seen as a matter of training scientific managers for the public sector? Why, indeed, did the new academic field emerge as "public administration"
and not as "public service," which might have encompassed both the purposes of
government and its effective practice?

THE INFLUENCE OF GENDER

A number of factors contribute to building a plausible account. The present narrative adds to existing interpretations the buried fact that women played a distinctive
and significant part in the development of ideas about the proper role of government and the place of administration in it. Just as they shared in the practical work
of constructing a modern bureaucratic state, so, too, women and the concerns that
animated their activities could have been part of the story the field of public administration came to tell about its origins. That they are not requires explanation, since

so much of their work embodied the same dedication to more effective government as their male counterparts. To understand why women have been left out of the story, my account introduces the role of turn-of-the-century gender typifications and suggests that gender played a leading part in the construction of the field of public administration.

As Joan Wallach Scott has argued, use of the term "gender" implies that, rather than being a marginal element, "relations between the sexes are a primary aspect of social organization"; that individuals' sense of themselves as *men* or *women* are "in large part culturally determined" rather than biological or an outgrowth of individual personality; and that differences between the sexes display and reinforce a hierarchical organization that privileges masculinity. In other words, gender is not simply window dressing but a definitive element in social life, one that has power implications. For this reason, a gender analysis is a critical analysis. It points to how gender dynamics import sex-related expectations into arenas that otherwise have nothing to do with sex, thus giving pride of place to masculinity. Scott notes that throughout history "emergent rulers have legitimized domination, strength, central authority, and ruling power as masculine (enemies, outsiders, subversives, weakness as feminine) and made that code literal in laws (forbidding women's political participation, outlawing abortion, prohibiting wage-earning by mothers, imposing female dress codes) that put women in their place." Gender shapes the dynamics of public life just as it does in private.[17]

During the time when public administration evolved, the link between masculinity and public power is clearly visible. In the early twentieth century, Americans acted in terms of sharp divisions between the societal roles of women and men that had developed over the course of the nineteenth century. Expectations about what was proper for women and men to do were perhaps more rigid and more divergent than they have ever been in American life. These gender-based presumptions were as vividly reflected in public life as they were in the household. Public administration, like other social phenomena, emerged in this gendered context and was shaped by it in significant ways.

Nineteenth-century electoral politics was a masculine realm. The paradigmatic citizen was the free, white, self-supporting man who joined with his fellows in open-air rallies and saloon gatherings.[18] Party politics, the only kind that counted, was a kind of rough-and-tumble white male club. Partisan display in hundreds of towns and villages not only functioned as entertainment but also conferred important symbolic approval on candidates nominated at party conventions. Membership in the community depended on the expression of party preference through concrete political involvement.[19] The masculine rhetoric surrounding the political arena was striking: Metaphors of warfare, cockfighting, and boxing abounded. "Editors derided opponents as 'grandmas' and 'eunuchs.' Campaign speakers found themselves dismissed as feeble, weak, and shrill. . . . Conspicuously masculine rhetoric also accompanied pole raisings, in which men affixed a party banner to a post and installed it in a prominent location. Men on both sides proudly reported the length of their poles and the quickness with which they raised them. Local partisans accused each other of not being able to raise their poles, or in one case of 'failure to keep it in an upright position.' "[20]

Denied the vote from the country's founding moment, women had to content themselves with indirect involvement in politics, practicing what became known as "republican motherhood" by upholding moral values in the home and preparing their sons to practice citizenship.[21] Even though they could not vote, however, during most of the nineteenth century, women performed an important legitimating role in party politics by imparting "beauty, virtue and refinement" to political gatherings and thus raising them above their crassly masculine dynamics: "The 'angel of the home' legitimized the machinery of politics, and the machine validated the angel." Masculine politics relied on the presence of femininity; sex-related differences were called on to legitimate arrangements that otherwise had nothing to do with sexuality. Male politics constituted itself on the simultaneous presence and exclusion of women.[22]

A profound political realignment at the end of the century, however, upset the neat reciprocal arrangement that had made room for women in the political arena. The social destabilization threatened by Populism, in which women played a prominent and visible role, led middle-class men of the North to abandon their long-standing claims of protecting laborers and recast their politics in terms of social control. The source of civic order was now located more in the private household than in the public square; women's campaign work became restricted, and female orators and partisan clubs declined.[23]

During the nineteenth century, however, women's role as vessel and guardian of virtue had given them another opening into the public sphere, that is, charitable work and involvement in causes such as temperance and abolition. Public life needed the motherly efforts of women to temper the effects of masculine competitiveness and acquisitiveness, or so female reformers had argued and society had come to accept. As the century drew to a close and the problems associated with industrial capitalism and urban life worsened, women who were increasingly restricted from partisan political work turned to activities directed at improving municipal services, ameliorating poverty, and calling for social and regulatory policies. Women referred to such work as "public motherhood" and "municipal housekeeping." As Lisa D. Brush has suggested, growing reliance on maternal values as the basis of their political strategy may have been a case of "feminism for hard times." Barred more and more firmly from partisan activities, women had little choice but to assert their difference as an advantage—to advance claims to political voice on the basis of characteristics thought to be uniquely theirs.[24]

Given that party politics was a defining feature of nineteenth-century masculinity, reform men faced a difficult balancing act. Like their female counterparts, they were interested in expanding their influence over the public sphere. Beginning with the mugwump civil service reformers of the 1870s, they aimed to reduce the power of political machines by advocating the need for nonpartisan expertise in city government. But by distancing themselves from party politics and asserting the value of expertise in public life, male reformers risked appearing unmanly. Party loyalists, painted by reformers as ignorant and selfish, and threatened with loss of power, retaliated by castigating reformers as "namby-pamby, goody-goody gentlemen" who "sip cold tea," "political hermaphrodites," "the third sex of politics," "effeminate without being either masculine or feminine," "Miss Nancys," and "man milliners." As Richard Hofstadter notes, "To be active in politics was a man's business, whereas to be engaged in reform movements meant constant association with aggressive, reforming, moralizing women"—clearly not a happy prospect. Politicians intended to suggest that theirs was the "hard, masculine sphere of business and politics," one for which reformers were unfit. By styling themselves as nonpartisan and unselfish, reformers "suggested not purity but a lack of self, a lack of capacity for grappling with reality, a lack of assertion, of masculinity."[25] Reformers were trying to introduce what virtually everyone thought of as a female element—morality—into political life. In so doing, they risked associating themselves with weakness rather than strength. They therefore had to construct an image of themselves and a rationale for their approach that counteracted the portrait painted by machine loyalists and legitimated the power they sought to arrogate to themselves. As I suggest, municipal government reformers, especially the men of the research bureaus, did so by means of a masculinized rhetoric that melded science and business around the idea of efficiency.

The story of the construction of public administration unfolded within this gendered context, and certain aspects of it can be understood adequately only when gender is taken into account. During the Progressive period, reform work was visibly bifurcated along gender lines. There were separate reform clubs for men and for women. A majority of the settlement houses set up in poor neighborhoods were led and populated by women, and women were in the forefront of social welfare policy advocacy. The efficiency movement dedicated to rationalizing governmental structures and processes was almost exclusively male, as were the jewels in its crown, the municipal research bureaus. Although there were a few females among the professional staffs of the bureaus, such as Philadelphia's Dr. Neva Deardorff, most bureaus employed women only in clerical capacities, and women trustees were rare.[26]

Despite these divisions, in the early years of the twentieth century, male and female municipal reformers interacted with one another and collaborated on a variety of activities. Both men and women, whether they worked together or separately, explained their efforts in terms that variably blended "feminine" concern for social betterment with "masculine" commitment to efficiency. But as party politicians heaped scorn on reform men (particularly in reaction to their early successes) and wealthy supporters demanded less controversial activity more consistent with business interests, reformers turned away from concern for the conditions of people's lives, which was tainted with femininity, and toward ideas and rhetoric derived from indisputably male realms: science, business, and executive command and control.[27] As the impetus toward professionalization strengthened, men and women who shared a commitment to public service found themselves organizing into separate professions—the men in public administration, the women in social work. These professional boundaries were never complete. There were always a number of men prominent in social work and at least a few women who insinuated themselves into the provinces of public administration. But in general, the two professions grew up with memberships largely segregated on the basis of gender. Strikingly, however, both masculine public administration and feminine social work, as they professionalized, found themselves relying on rhetorical strategies that sought to suppress any hint of the womanly, and both did so through assertions of scientific efficiency.

GENDER, SCIENCE, AND BUSINESS

Even today, to call an enterprise "scientific" or "businesslike" is typically to give it a stamp of approval. To question, then, rather than to take for granted, why the bureau men would want their work to be considered scientific and businesslike requires conscious effort.

Why did science take pride of place at the heart of their ideology? I suggest that it was at least partly because of the deep cultural link in Western society between science and masculinity. Arguing that their approach was scientific enabled the bureau reformers to evade charges of deficient masculinity lodged by party politicians. Science also proved to be a solid basis on which to construct an understanding of government as a business and in so doing keep wealthy supporters happy. The purported objectivity of science and the frank self-interest of the business world do not at first blush appear to mesh easily, but since in concept and practice both were male realms, the bureau men's ideology was able to blend them, using notions of efficiency and scientific management. Science also furnished a rationale for the bureau men's advocacy of executive power. Science would show the one right way to manage government; implementing its findings meant concentrating power in the chief executive, rather than leaving decisions up to irrational and unpredictable legislative wrangling. Masculine images of command and control, centered in the chief executive and justified by scientific expertise, proved the final element in the bureau men's ideology. But was science really all that masculine? Recent analyses suggest that it was.

In 1938, Virginia Woolf observed, "Science it would seem is not sexless; she is a man, a father and infected too."[28] But extensive scholarly study illuminating the masculinity of science had to wait until the so-called second wave of feminism in the 1960s. Beginning with the documentation of sexual segregation in the practice of science, scholars quickly moved to a consideration of the extent to which the very notion of science is constructed on the basis of gender. In Scott's terms, they analyzed it as an instance of the use of sex differences to legitimate an enterprise that has nothing to do with sexuality. Carolyn Merchant's *The Death of Nature*, published in 1980, outlined the age-old connection between women and nature and argued that modern science aimed to dominate nature in the same way that, historically, men had dominated women.[29] In 1985, Evelyn Fox Keller's *Reflections on Gender and Science* declared that science is "made rather than born." Keller, a mathematical physicist, argued that founding fathers of modern science such as Francis Bacon relied on an explicitly gendered language in which the "virile" seeker after knowledge had the capacity to conquer a feminine Nature and make her his slave. Keller suggested that "'laws of nature' are more than simple expressions of the results of objective inquiry or of political and social pressures; they must also be read for their personal—and by tradition, masculine—content. [Feminist analysis] uncovers, in short, *the personal investment scientists make in impersonality;* the anonymity of the picture they produce is revealed as itself a kind of signature."[30] Merchant, Keller, and philosopher Sandra Harding brought to center stage pervasive gender-based dichotomies in both popular and scholarly science, such as hard versus soft data, the rigor of natural science versus the hoped-for relevance of social science, reason versus intuition, "as well as familiar appeals to the 'penetrating thrust of an argument,' 'seminal ideas,' and the like."[31] They pointed to how a seemingly impersonal objectivity masks the commitment to masculinity in science.

In 1992, historian of science and technology David F. Noble reviewed nearly two millennia in the development of Western ideas of knowledge and science. He found that "Western science evolved only half human, in a world without women." Noble argues that the masculinity of science was "no mere artifact of sexist history; throughout most of its evolution, the culture of science has not simply excluded women, it has been defined in defiance of women and in their absence."[32] Rooted in the struggle of Latin Christendom to establish itself as the source of orthodoxy, the culture of Western science grew out of the identification of religious heresy with women and the parallel barring of women from the universities established under church auspices. Not until late in the nineteenth century, Noble demonstrates, were women finally able to gain permanent access to universities and mainstream science. He argues that the doors to the academy remained open this time, while earlier efforts had failed, because of the demands of capitalism for a trained industrial workforce. These requirements supported the call for democratization of education, which made the exclusion of women increasingly difficult to justify on either pragmatic or moral grounds. As Noble points out, just as science became identified with industrial prosperity—a development that helps explain why the bureau men could link science with business—women identified science with freedom and equality both in the academy and in the world of work. Pioneering women's colleges such as Vassar, Wellesley, and Mt. Holyoke emphasized science in their curricula and prided themselves on their scientific atmospheres, where women could prepare themselves for careers that, unfortunately, turned out to be more difficult to achieve than to imagine. As new professions of science and engineering organized themselves, they consciously "refashioned the universities, and science itself, in their own more exclusive, and exclusively male, image." Success in professionalization came to be predicated on "a renewed distance from the undisciplined enthusiasm, impassioned iconoclasm, and supposed latent hysteria of women."[33]

The view of science as the way to industrial prosperity linked it with another equally masculine realm: business. Engineering, out of which the profession of business management developed, had styled itself as a priesthood of material development—echoing ideas about the male conquest of female Nature, "of the power of mind over matter." Henry Gantt, a pioneer in the field, described the engineer as "a man of few opinions and many facts, few words and many deeds."[34] Advocates of professionalism in business painted it in masculine colors, emphasizing tough-mindedness and heroism. As Karl points out, "The acceptance of business leadership in the half-century before the 1930s was based on an adulation of strength, a vital force which was, in its emergence as a myth, the transformation of the rugged frontiersman into the financier."[35] The idea of efficiency proved the crucial ingredient in completing the masculinity of the business manager: "An efficient person was an effective person, and that characterization brought with it a long shadow of latent associations and predispositions, a turning toward hard work and away from feeling, toward discipline and away from sympathy, toward masculinity and away from femininity."[36]

The cultural power of science and business in the early twentieth century was sought by both men and women, but its effects were different for the male profession of public administration than for the largely female domain of social work. Social welfare reformers and social workers were pressed by the cultural value assigned to masculine science and efficiency and men's disproportionate power in society to try to preserve their commitment to feminine ideas of social justice and caring while persuading the world of their devotion to practicality, hardheadedness, system, and minimum cost. In contrast, public administration's masculine ideology of science and business evolved to justify the actions of its overwhelmingly male membership; there was no need to resolve the kind of contradiction that faced social workers, only—by claiming neutral expertise—to prove itself free of moralizing femininity. Paradoxically, the image of scientific neutrality made public administration appear gender-free. The profession of public administration could comfortably assume the guise of ungendered objectivity it has worn ever since.[37]

THE DEVELOPMENT OF PUBLIC ADMINISTRATION

The reading of public administration's history offered here maintains, first, that the "feminine" activities of women's clubs and social welfare reformers represent public administration's buried heritage, an entire panoply of concerns that the developing field sometimes consciously rejected, sometimes simply lost sight of. Available histories in public administration neglect the fact that the expansion of social welfare and other governmental programs and the administrative processes to support them—the development of an administrative *state,* in fact—were mainly the result not of the bureau men's science but of advocacy based on the results of practical experiments: pilot projects, in effect, conducted by settlement house residents and clubwomen. Second, my narrative suggests that gender played a constitutive role in the field's construction, that is, the tension between masculinity and femininity revealed in the ideas of public administration's founders is central to the shape the field assumed. The extent to which the developing field focused increasingly on a narrower understanding of scientific, efficient administration can be traced at least in part to gender typifications and dynamics that favored masculine ideas and activities over those thought to be feminine. During the crucial decade and a half when the research bureau movement crystallized out of municipal reform, when its ideology took shape, its institutions solidified, and its training programs were organized, there was a noticeable shift away from the sense that administrative efficiency was important in order to provide services and programs and toward a concern for efficient management per se and for the executive power to bring it about. But the preference for efficiency, for scientific and businesslike public management, was rooted deep in the urgency of the bureau men's need for legitimacy, their need to show the world that, despite being nonpartisan experts, their masculinity was unquestionable. Given their desire to be judged on the basis of hard facts, the outcome was foreordained.

Meanwhile, in the realm of social work, settlement residents advocated substantive measures aimed at meeting human needs within an increasingly business-oriented public sphere. As a group, they never lost sight of the conditions of people's lives and the role governments might play to make them better, but social welfare advocates were unable to institutionalize these concerns within the social work profession. Instead, older ideas of scientific charity out of which casework evolved became the core. Despite the proliferation of scientific case managers and methodologies, there continued to be those who debated about, worked for, and eventually won ameliorative and redistributive legislation. But the field as a whole turned as resolutely toward science in the search for professional status as did public administration. In juxtaposition, social work and public administration reveal the long-lasting costs of such a turn.

In public administration, administrative means eclipsed policy ends, or came to be seen as ends. Scientific investigation of public agency structures and procedures and the preparation of businesslike public managers became public administration's reasons for being. Even though the victories they won had come about politically, through pressure tactics, negotiations, relationship building, and compromise, early public administrationists credited pure science ("facts") for their gains. They debated the one best budgeting method, personnel policy, or pattern of supervision, as questions about the proper substance of governmental activity receded toward the field's peripheral vision. Public administrationists even told themselves that the place of administration in governance depended precisely on noninvolvement with matters of purpose; a public manager's role was to execute orders determined by the legislature, not to play a part in determining the substance of those orders. Always more ideology than reality, what became known as the "politics-administration dichotomy" assumed conceptual center stage in the field. Ever since, as roundly as it is periodically rejected, it is resuscitated just as regularly, newly window-dressed, to persuade the skeptical that tenured, unelected managers have a legitimate part in democratic governance, one based on managerial expertise rather than on political acumen.

In telling the story of the construction of public administration during the Progressive period, my account focuses principally on the New York Bureau of Municipal Research, founded in 1907. Confining the story to this one organization is justified, because it was the center from which the entire bureau movement sprang, and with it training programs for public administrators. Men of the New York Bureau fanned out across the country, many times at the request of people in other cities who had heard about their work, to offer not only investigative skills on particular administrative matters but also guidance in setting up similar bureaus. The entire bureau movement had a center of gravity and a clear ideological wellspring in New York; thus the ideas and actions of this relatively small number of men had far broader significance and lasting impact than might have been possible if New York had been their only arena. The New York Bureau became, in effect, the central organ in municipal research for the entire United States, simply by coming first and then being seized on by others as an intellectual source. As a trustee of the New York Bureau exclaimed, "Just because municipal research concerns itself with methods rather than with men, just because it operates impersonally through discovering and publishing facts, it promises to be as successful in one place as another."[38] Similarly, the Training School for Public Service, organized by the New York Bureau in 1911, became the model for all other training programs for public managers. When it moved wholesale to Syracuse University in 1924, the training school metamorphosed into the Maxwell School for Citizenship and Public Service, the oldest continuous university program in public administration. Thus conceptual and practical choices made by the training school organizers carried more than normal weight in the development of the field.

Chapter 2 tells the story of the organization and development of the New York Bureau of Municipal Research, of what the bureau men did, how their work was received, and how they thought about it. Chapter 3 begins to set the bureau men in a larger framework. It reviews the reforming efforts of settlement house residents and women's club members, whose work represents a "feminine" approach in which commitment to improving living conditions, especially those of the poor, was the animating impulse and efficient methods were seen as instrumental to its achievement. Chapter 4 outlines the philosophy of government and administration reflected in the writings and work of the men of the New York Bureau. The discussion compares the bureau philosophy with the thinking of social welfare reformers on the same topics to demonstrate how the bureau men's ideas, out of which the field of public administration developed, constitute only one aspect of a much more varied array. Chapter 5 focuses on the New York Bureau's training school and on how the drive to become a profession, or at least to assume aspects of professionalism, shaped the thinking and activities of the bureau movement partisans. The parallel process in social work, again, puts public administration into context and suggests that the two professions were alike in rejecting the substantive emphasis on societal change in favor of a quest for legitimacy based on science and business. Throughout, an effort is made to compare the particulars of the New York Bureau case to parallel ideas and developments among reform women. My aim is to foreground aspects of public administration thinking too often taken for granted, sharpen the sense that the construction of public administration could have happened otherwise, and suggest ways in which social welfare activities carried on mainly by women could have influenced its evolution. Thus reform women, active in clubs and settlement houses, developed their own notions of how to understand urban problems, improve municipal governments, get rid of or temper the effects of bossism, manage public agencies, conduct relationships with citizens, and professionalize their practice. The intent is, by bringing the two arenas of municipal reform work into juxtaposition, not only to question unnoticed assumptions in public administration and to tell the story in ways that recover the part women played in it but also to reveal gender as a primary element in the field's construction. Set side by side, clear differences in values and reform approaches are visible between bureau men and reform women:

Bureau Men	Reform Women
City as business	City as home
Structural reforms	Improved living conditions
New methods	New programs
Focus on system	Focus on caring
Science as objective, efficient	Science as connected, experiential
Persona: expert	Persona: neighbor
Citizenship as oversight	Citizenship as involvement
Favorite administrative recommendations:	Favorite administrative recommendations:
Systematize (budgeting)	Humanize processes
Centralize (executive control)	Link agencies to people
Neutralize (politics-administration dichotomy)	Use discretionary judgment (no politics-administration dichotomy)

Throughout, I argue that the distinctive contributions represented in the women's perspective have been, if not entirely lost to public administration, at a continuing disadvantage. But they might yet be revivified and moved to center stage. The book concludes with reflections on the persistence of the bureau men's ideas in the field of public administration and what implications this analysis may hold for its future.

For all its recent preoccupation with reinventing itself, American public administration has been reluctant to take the necessary first step that a true reinvention entails: a reflective step backward into its history. "Origin stories have consequences. . . . They give . . . meaning, name effective causes, and fix the odds on the future."[39] The perspective this book adopts is that public administration's continuing neglect of its past reduces the likelihood of an effective future, one in which purpose joins practice[40] and in which Waldo's "efficiency for what?" question replaces the search for one best way as the field's most fundamental foundation.[41]

2

The New York Bureau
of Municipal Research

By the time of the founding of the New York Bureau of Municipal Research in 1907, the municipal reform movement was in full swing. Municipal research was to become one of the movement's most ardent expressions. As E. L. Godkin, editor of *The Nation,* proclaimed, prominent men were rallying to municipal reform out of concern that "the passionate pursuit of equality of conditions on which the multitude seems now entering" was a fundamental threat to society.[1] The political implications of municipal reform strategies like the research bureaus were clearer at the time than many scholars and students of public administration seem aware of today.

Conditions in which Godkin's multitude lived in America's cities were shocking enough. Between 1890 and 1924, about 23 million people came to the United States from eastern Europe and southern Italy. About three-quarters entered through the port of New York, many of them settling on the Lower East Side. The immigrants were packed into noisome tenements and exploited in factories and sweatshops. Settlement leader Lillian Wald observed that the very "words 'East Side' suggested an alarming picture of something strange and alien, a vast crowded area, a foreign city."[2] Muckraker Jacob Riis described the way "the other half" lived in terms that left educated people little room for uncertainty about the immigrants' destitution and desperation:

> [A case] that came to my notice some months ago in a Seventh Ward tenement was typical enough. . . . There were nine in the family: husband, wife, an aged grandmother, and six children. . . . All nine lived in two rooms, one about ten feet square that served as parlor, bedroom, and eating room, the other a small half-room made into a kitchen. The rent was seven dollars and a half a month, more than a week's wages for the husband and father, who was the only breadwinner. . . . That day the mother had thrown herself out of the window, and

was carried up from the street dead. She was "discouraged," said some of the other women from the tenement.

And again: "Well do I recollect the visit of a health inspector to one of these tenements on a July day when the thermometer outside was climbing high in the nineties; but inside, in that awful room, with half a dozen persons washing, cooking, and sorting rags, lay a dying baby alongside the stove, where the doctor's thermometer ran up to 115! Perishing for the want of a breath of fresh air in this city of untold charities!"[3]

Most of the immigrants could not afford a steam-heated apartment or one lit by electricity; kerosene was used for light and coal for cooking. The typical family spent 30 percent of its earnings on rent, 40 percent on food, and the remainder on fuel, light, clothing, medical care, and everything else. Twelve- to fourteen-hour workdays were common, and employers often cheated workers out of their meager wages, fined them for lateness, refused to let them go to the bathroom, and charged them for materials such as needles. In the rush season, garment workers sometimes stayed on the job forty or fifty hours. " 'You don't mean at one sitting, do you?' a settlement house investigator asked a man who had done it many times. 'Yes,' he replied, 'it is a common thing.' "[4]

Confronted with immigrant workers' efforts, through political machines, to lift themselves and their cities out of squalor and neglect, well-to-do reformers' strategies were frankly partisan at first. In New York, in order to beat Tammany Hall, the Democratic machine, "fusion" tickets united Republicans with members of nonpartisan good government groups and Progressive Democratic social reformers. The fusion strategy elected as mayors William B. Strong in 1894 and Seth Low in 1901, but each was turned out at the next election. With their candidate in office, coalition members fell to wrangling over specific policies and were unable to deliver the tangible goods that might have preserved the broad support that had won victory for their candidate.[5] Some reformers began to wonder whether a different, less overtly political strategy might be more effective.

Telling the story of the construction of public administration requires the examination of one facet of the new nonpartisan thrust in municipal reform: the rise of municipal research bureaus. Beginning in 1905, groups of well-to-do men established privately sponsored organizations to look into municipal administrative practices.[6] They intended to use systematic investigation rather than electoral politics as their chief strategy for gaining control of city governments. The bureau movement, as it came to be called, was one expression of the municipal reform preference for nonpartisan approaches and of the particular political, economic, and social context in which reform unfolded.[7] Yet the bureau movement had a distinctive character. Its origins lay in New York City, and its center of gravity remained there. The New York Bureau of Municipal Research eventually served as the birthplace of public administration as a field of study. An understanding of how and why the New York Bureau was organized and the context within which it pursued its work can illuminate how something that came to be called "public administration" took the shape it did.

As the nineteenth century drew to a close, James Bryce's *American Commonwealth* exclaimed that "the government of cities is the one conspicuous failure of the United States,"[8] and a new generation of well-to-do activists, spiritual if not literal children of the mugwump civil service reformers of the 1870s and 1880s, took Bryce's assessment as their rallying cry. Municipal government seemed to them the one great unsettled national question, writ large because of the tremendous growth of cities, the severity of the problems afflicting them, and the conspicuous hold political machines had over them.[9]

The 1890s was a crucial decade in American politics. These years heralded a transformation from what Stephen Skowronek has called the government of courts and parties to what became known as the administrative state. Throughout much of the nineteenth century, political parties had fostered public activity within an American system fractionated by a constitutional structure dependent on separated powers and checks and balances. "Party organizations bound the national government to each locale and linked the many discrete units of government horizontally across the territory. This brought a measure of cohesion . . . and standardization." Party machinery also served as a mechanism for poor and working-class white men to participate in politics and sometimes as a career ladder as well. Meanwhile, courts produced binding answers to issues of relations between state and society, filling a vacuum left by the absence of anything but a rudimentary administrative capacity.[10]

During the courts-and-parties period, governments acted principally as conduits for the distribution of resources and privileges to individuals and groups: land, charters and franchises, tax exemptions, the privilege of charging tolls on roads and bridges, public works subsidies, government jobs, and so on. "Forever giving things away, governments were laggard in regulating the economic activities they subsidized." Parties shaped the distribution of goods just as they turned out the electorate.[11]

In the closing decade of the nineteenth century, the Populist movement mobilized southern blacks, poor whites, struggling farmers, and a visible cadre of women around proposals that sought to redress some of the harshest consequences of free-market capitalism. Populism, along with immigrant support for city machines and urban voters' flirtations with socialism, convinced elites that continued reliance on parties as the guiding political mechanism threatened chaos. Reformers who eventually rallied under the banner of Progressivism took a variety of tacks to restore order, assert social control, and harmonize conflicting interests, including the imposition of measures to restrict the franchise—voter registration, poll taxes—as well as steps to strengthen governments' administrative and regulatory capacities.

In cities, antimachine sentiment was the node from which the reform impulse sprang among the well-to-do. And indeed, the New York machine, Tammany Hall,

had always reflected, since its beginnings in 1786, an aversion to upper-class privilege and a belief in the virtue of the common man. Several recent scholars have
shown that throughout the nineteenth century, wealthy men of affairs remained
deeply involved in party leadership, although after about 1840 they were unlikely
to hold elective office.[12] Nevertheless, Tammany Hall's political culture always
centered around working-class and poor neighborhood institutions, especially
saloons, which functioned as virtual social clubs.[13] After the conviction and impris-
onment of Tammany boss William Marcy Tweed in 1871, the machine appeared
mortally wounded to some reformers. In the 1880s, however, Tammany adopted a
strategy aimed at broadening its base, including supporting fusion candidates,
recruiting respected businessmen as sachems, and putting together ethnically mixed
tickets.[14] With other neighborhood organizations such as churches, unions, improvement associations, and charitable organizations, Tammany forged a new cadre of
effective neighborhood-based leaders that constituted an explicit challenge to the
city's better sort. Reform was directed not only at corruption, then, but also at a
government that favored the expression of local interests—immigrant neighborhood needs and services—over citywide business and professional interests.[15]
Because of the party machinery's roots in local neighborhoods, reformers increasingly styled themselves as "nonpartisan," particularly as fusion with one party or
another produced only limited results.

During the late nineteenth century, concern grew among the upper middle
class over the power of the working class in the city council and the party organization. In reality, in New York as well as in a number of other large cities, this
threat was limited, because the city's elite had considerable formal and informal
power that could not be dislodged simply by the election of working-class aldermen. In the wake of the Tweed scandal, much of New York City's fiscal authority
had been transferred from the aldermen to a Board of Estimate and Apportionment.
Under the reform charter of 1873, the board consisted of the mayor, the comptroller, the president of the Board of Aldermen, and the president of the Department of Taxes and Assessments. By 1901, the board had become the city's chief
budget-making and financial body, rudimentary as those functions were. Its members, even the ones aligned with Tammany, were generally old-stock white Protes-
tants of means. The aldermen's chief power was control over the awarding of utility
franchises and right-of-way privileges. Early in the twentieth century, however, the
Board of Estimate and Apportionment acquired financial authority over highways,
sewers, and public buildings and gained the power to amend or repeal franchises
granted by aldermen. Aldermen provided services to residents of their districts,
where they held unquestioned status, but they had to battle for reelection every two
years and frequently found themselves voted out of office, a threat that spurred the
personal loyalism and election-day shenanigans that offended the reform-minded.[16]

Meanwhile, the upper classes had their own bastions of power, particularly
independent boards that governed schools, parks, libraries, and the sinking fund.
Many of these boards had their own funding and taxing authority. Sometimes

whole functions were turned over to elite private organizations, as in the case of the Charity Organization Society of New York, which handled the few services directed at the poor. In addition, feeling themselves blocked from elected office, upper-class men increasingly organized in extragovernmental bodies such as the Chamber of Commerce, the Board of Trade, civic leagues, and other good government organizations, which advocated structural reforms, pressed for legislation, and endorsed reform candidates. As Leonard White's study of city managers commented, "The opposition to bad government usually comes to a head in the local chamber of commerce."[17] Finally, of course, a city government hard-pressed to cope with the increasing demands of a fast-growing jurisdiction could not afford to let too great a gulf grow up between itself and the city's wealthy, who were an important source of property tax revenues and some of whom—J. P. Morgan, for example—could single-handedly rescue the city from financial ruin during inevitable downward plunges in the economy.[18]

Thus, in New York as in cities across the country, reform attempts to restructure city governments, such as by increasing the mayor's power or installing a city manager, reducing the number of elective offices (the much-vaunted "short ballot"), and weakening the neighborhood-based authority of the aldermen, amounted to preserving the power of the well-to-do, especially solid businessmen. Municipal reformers pushed the idea that city government was business, not politics, an idea intended to make nonpartisanship legitimate as well as to render government susceptible to direct business and professional influence and less dependent on the unpredictable, informal arrangements characteristic of machine politics.[19]

Recent studies suggest that the failure of city governments so much decried by reformers was more a matter of perception than of undisputed fact. American cities averaged two to three times the water and sewer line mileage of German cities, more flush toilets and bathtubs than Germany or Great Britain, more paved streets (though the quality was admittedly variable), more extensive streetcar systems, larger and better fire departments, and disease control that was as good as or better than that in many European cities. These infrastructures had been put in place during the 1870s and 1880s, the heyday of laissez-faire political rhetoric, and were largely the product of party machine quid pro quo politics, which, for all its distastefulness in the eyes of the better-off, functioned in ways that rudimentary city governments otherwise would have been unable to. Moreover, despite charges leveled by bureau men, by 1900, many city government agencies were already becoming professionalized. "Especially in the large cities, . . . permanency of personnel and reliance on expertise were becoming significant characteristics . . . of city government generally."[20] This was particularly true in the case of libraries, public health, education, fire departments, and engineering offices. George B. McClellan, mayor of New York at the time of the founding of the New York Bureau of Municipal Research, commented in his memoirs: "That the government of the city of New York functions smoothly and, take it all in all, very well, despite district leader commissioners and deputy commissioners under Tammany, and despite incompetent theorists under 'reform,' is because each department has a permanent official, who is usually called the chief engineer, who really runs it. These men are able and efficient, are well paid, and deserve every cent that they receive."[21] Thus, in contrast to reformers' outcries, late-nineteenth-century political machines were reasonably successful at meeting the rising service expectations of city residents and keeping taxes in check; what they lacked was an ideology that would legitimate them in the eyes of elites.[22]

Two failures in turn-of-the-century municipal government have withstood revisionist scrutiny: the police department, which largely deserved the reformers' diatribes about favoritism and payroll padding, and the absence of anything approaching adequate charity and social welfare services, particularly in contrast to European cities.[23] In rhetoric, male reform groups, including members of the research bureau movement, cast all city agencies as afflicted with the kind and level of corruption and nonprofessionalism that seem to have been true only in the case of the police. The inadequacy of the municipal government workforce became the bureau men's rallying cry. The need to make agency procedures more efficient and scientific and its managers more professional became the lever that would, if not dislodge Tammany Hall entirely, then lift the educated into positions of greater influence over municipal government.

As Samuel Hays has observed, the Progressive Era was a time when causes or movements animated whole groups of people concerned about social conditions.[24] Municipal reform itself was a movement, as were scientific management, the efficiency movement, and the research bureau movement. Each was devoted partly or wholly to the improvement of municipal government structures and procedures; all were spurred by the prospect of rationalizing and systematizing public life. Meanwhile, social welfare reformers, most of them women, were galvanized toward their own version of city betterment, which, though it did not ignore administration, focused more directly on problems associated with poverty generally and the needs of immigrants in particular. Although these two versions of reform shared a commitment to making cities more livable, they translated this broad goal into quite different ideologies, strategies, and activities. This chapter tells the story of the New York Bureau's development, chapter 3 compares this story with the work of the social welfare reformers, and chapter 4 offers connections and contrasts between the two reform impulses.

THE MUNICIPAL REFORM MOVEMENT

Rather suddenly between 1889 and 1895, the municipal reform movement assumed national prominence, as reformers from individual cities began to sense the advantages of information exchange and joint effort. In 1894, leaders of New York's City Club and the Philadelphia Municipal League organized the first National Conference on Good City Government, which led to the formation of the National Municipal League. Over the next few years, the league formulated what became known as its "municipal program," a set of reform priorities focused on insulating cities from rural-dominated state legislatures and strengthening city government powers. As Delos Wilcox declared, the program's aim was to "formulate the best American theory as to the right organization of government," not "to insure good administration but to give an opportunity for it."[25] The principles set forth in the municipal program included home rule for cities, the need for expert administration, and concentration and centralization of authority, with an emphasis on the mayor and comptroller.

While the National Municipal League assumed its central place in municipal reform, in individual cities, a panoply of civic organizations took up various aspects of city betterment. Reformers chose to organize themselves in extragovernmental associations because what they saw as their own higher motives did not fit very well within the political party's quid pro quo dynamic. In many cases, too, reformers felt ill at ease among party regulars who were not of their class. In 1895, for example, James C. Carter, president of New York's City Club, explained that the club provided an opportunity for "perfectly familiar and unrestrained intercourse among a body of men of similar tastes and views."[26] Members of the City Reform Club, organized in 1882 by the young Theodore Roosevelt, were "wealthy business or professional men, well-educated, Protestant in religion, and from native-stock families."[27] Membership in the best clubs was of course restricted to males: "Including women . . . would have openly invited the derisive label of 'man milliners.' "[28] The American Political Science Association, established in 1903 and populated in its early years by members of reform clubs, held obligatory "smokers" for the "gentlemen" of the association and reserved its leadership positions for males.[29]

The civic group embodied the reform shift away from both electoral politics and civil service reform. Disillusioned over the failure of the mugwump attempt to put "good men" in government, reformers took up a new strategy, one emphasizing not only nonpartisanship but also the importance of sound administration guided by a strong executive. They maintained that continuous surveillance, pressure, and assistance on the part of informed citizens would change the ways of city officials. Even bad men, if properly guided, could practice good government. Civic groups would provide disinterested and expert advice and thus not only help hard-pressed administrators but also secure a place for themselves in governance. "Though marching with the people, the progressive reformers clearly marched at their head."[30] Some associations took a broad-spectrum approach; others concentrated on particular urban needs, such as outdoor recreation, kindergartens, crime prevention, transit reform, public education, or charity work. Many prominent reformers belonged to several such organizations, and these interlocking memberships helped to weave the civic groups together in a more or less united bloc.[31] For example, Steven Diner's study of Chicago reformers notes: "Of 169 [prominent] men, 113 were members of the City Club, 55 belonged to the Union League

Club, 45 to the Chicago Club, and 36 to the Commercial Club. Of the 46 women, 35 belonged to the Women's City Club, and 22 were members of the Chicago Women's Club."[32] Each club was sure to have many members who also belonged to other reform organizations.

Although each reform organization had its particular values and approaches, the cause of municipal reform was permeated with the idea that the city was essentially like a business and ought to be run along business lines: "[T]he comparison of government to a business corporation appeared repeatedly in the writings of the political reformers. It was not only the corporation's commercial efficiency, with its suggestions for tax cutting, that the reformers had in mind but also the corporation's singleness of purpose and the discipline and effectiveness this singleness permitted."[33] Reformers saw city government not as a political mechanism for dealing with conflicting interests but as an administrative entity for finding and carrying out the best policy to deal with particular urban problems—hence their enthusiasm for nonpartisan elections and proper administrative procedures.[34] The People's Reform League of New York, organized in 1890 by a small group of reformers, took as its motto, "Municipal government is business and not politics."[35] If city government was business, the need for efficiency and the expertise that educated reformers could provide was self-evident. Thus, although few big businessmen were directly involved in municipal reform, the movement served their needs by adopting a business ideology in which, despite talk of democratization, the model for good city government was not the New England town meeting but the private for-profit corporation.[36]

In the process of making municipal governments businesslike, reformers met the needs of corporate capitalists for stability, predictability, and efficiency in the face of threats posed by militant unions, immigration, and incipient socialism. Municipal officials saw the efforts of civic groups as important support for their work, even, in some cases, as useful buffers that protected agencies from more radical pressure groups. While there was tension between the reformers and their administrative "clients," and disputes between them occasionally made headlines, there was more cooperation than animosity.

In fact, cooperation became the reformers' explicit aim. According to William Welch, for example, "More can be accomplished by the quiet intelligent and well-directed efforts of individuals and of such organizations as societies for city improvement which do not directly antagonize those who wield political power."[37] Defeat at the polls had meant exclusion from direct power; by turning to civic group activism, the reformers had influence that was less subject to sudden reversals. City officials saw that even modest accommodations to the reformers' suggestions could temper their criticism, while taking a hard line might arouse the citizenry-at-large, an alarming prospect for officials and reformers alike. Despite a great deal of reform rhetoric about shining the light of science on a government operating in darkness, both public administrators and civic activists favored working out their relationships outside the limelight.[38] R. Fulton Cutting, one of the founders of the New York

Bureau of Municipal Research, said in 1906 that civic group reform was "much more practical" than previous efforts because it abandoned the impossible goal of dislodging the machines in favor of "methods that are lower and promise more."[39]

Despite this new realism, reformers never abandoned an ideology that couched their efforts in terms of "democratization" and "progress." More rational, efficient government was self-evidently more moral, the product not of particular interests but of universal impulses and truths. The reform battle was a conflict between "evil men who must be driven from power, and good men who must be activated politically to secure control of municipal affairs."[40]

Municipal reformers only infrequently expressed a gendered understanding of their work or the values that animated it. But they had inherited from the mugwump civil service reformers the accusations of insufficient manhood leveled by party politicians—names like Miss Nancy, man milliner, and political flirt. Mugwumps had been said to part their hair down the middle and ride sidesaddle. In contrast, a party man was unmistakably a "thoroughbred stallion." It was clear that "the man who proposed to tame, cleanse, or elevate public life by means of his own special code of purity violated role stereotypes as brashly as the suffragist who asked for a woman's place in politics."[41] Given these dynamics, municipal reformers struggled to define themselves in terms that sustained images of manhood in the face not only of politicians' insults but also of slurs from men of their own kind. Theodore Roosevelt, despite being a founder of the first reform club in New York, had said that reformers were "not robust or powerful men. . . . They avenged themselves for an uneasy subconsciousness of their own shortcomings by sitting in cloistered—or rather, pleasantly upholstered—seclusion, and sneering at and lying about men who made them feel uncomfortable." Henry James's novel *The Bostonians* characterized reformers as "long-haired men and short-haired women."[42] Male reformers hoped to turn aside such insinuations by clothing their activities in unmistakably masculine garb—science, efficiency, and executive command and control—a move that would ultimately unite traditional notions of masculinity such as virility and aggression with "overt middle-class respectability."[43]

A similar strategy was already at work among the ranks of adherents of what came to be called scientific management. Men such as Frederick Taylor, Henry Gantt, Frank Gilbreth, and Charles Ferguson styled themselves "a conspiracy of men of science, engineers, chemists, land and sea tamers and general masters of arts and of materials—a fellowship at deadly enmity with all parasites and pretenders," a group that would be a "little ruthless and unscrupulous on the side of civilization." The image of the man of science "cleaving the Gordian knot of politics with one swift blow" was common around the turn of the century. "Science" suggested disinterestedness and rigor, and "management" was allied with ideas of mastery, firm guidance, and constraint. The scientific manager would be "the man in control of affairs."[44] These ideas, couched in a clearly masculine rhetoric, proved irresistible in the work of municipal reform, though their function as a defense against femininity was rarely acknowledged.

FOUNDING OF THE NEW YORK BUREAU

In 1903, George B. McClellan, a party man from a respectable family (his father was the noted Civil War general), was elected mayor of New York on the Tammany-backed ticket. Somewhat shaken by reform victories at the polls in 1894 and 1901, Tammany boss Charles Murphy, together with McClellan, offered the city several significant gestures in the direction of reform: a new water system, street repairs, subways, and improvements in city administrative processes. McClellan and Murphy did not see eye to eye on many aspects of city government, but McClellan was determined to work with the Tammany boss because, the mayor said later, " It was impossible to keep clear of politics if I were to accomplish results."[45] McClellan's comment reflects the status of mayors in early-twentieth-century municipal governments. Bosses themselves almost never sought the office because it was a "position of little power, but great responsibility, especially as the focus of discontent with the functioning of the city government."[46] Given the lack of power in the mayor's office, McClellan felt that depending directly on public opinion for support was too risky, because it was virtually impossible "to arouse public opinion on any issue short of one involving a great question of public morals."[47]

Occasionally, McClellan challenged some of Murphy's more blatant favoritisms. Once, without McClellan's okay, Murphy gave a contract to a Tammany ward leader to put advertisements on the fences surrounding the construction site of the New York Public Library. The contractor stood to net $50,000 a year from the ads, while the city would get nothing. McClellan ordered Murphy to tell the contractor to paint over the signs, or McClellan would have it done and the contractor could sue if he wanted to. Another time, McClellan discovered that certain Civil Service Commission members never went to their offices. After a warning, the mayor removed the offending members, much to Murphy's consternation. In 1905, McClellan broke with Tammany entirely.[48]

McClellan took up the cause of administrative reform with noticeable vigor, appointing an advisory commission on finance and accounting to look into financial methods and practices in municipal agencies. Frank Goodnow, professor of administrative law and author of *Politics and Administration;* E. R. A. Seligman, professor of political economy at Columbia University; and Frederick W. Cleveland, professor of finance at New York University, were among those appointed to the commission. The investigation immediately ran into difficulties, including the woefully confused state of New York's accounting system and stonewalling on the part of agency personnel, many of whom owed their jobs to Tammany.[49]

Meanwhile, among civic reformers, the idea of systematic investigation into city administration was beginning to jell. William H. Allen, head of the New York branch of the Association for Improving the Conditions of the Poor (AICP), wanted to apply the association's philosophy of efficient charity to governmental processes. According to a profile of Allen in the leading reform journal at the time, Allen campaigned to let the public know more about public baths. Twenty thousand children were taken to the baths and taught that they were for their use. A number of unnecessary employees were let go, and the hours of operation were extended. In 1901, the AICP asserted that it could run a public bathhouse for 30 percent less than the amount a Tammany politician had requested for the purpose.[50]

Meanwhile, Frederick Cleveland had begun to think about a way to institutionalize his efforts to improve municipal accounting: "an independent agency, supported by citizens, which would be equipped to obtain information about the management of public affairs."[51] Allen and Cleveland had completed their dissertations in the same year under economist Simon Patten at the Wharton School of the University of Pennsylvania. Cleveland, a specialist in municipal accounting, had come into contact with AICP leaders when he revised the organization's accounts and reporting systems.[52] It is likely that the difficulties encountered by the mayoral commission on which Cleveland was serving pushed him further toward the notion of an independent investigative organization.[53] At any rate, Allen suggested to R. Fulton Cutting, president of the AICP board and head of the Citizens' Union, an organ of reform politics, that improving administrative methods was a better approach to governmental reform than continued fruitless efforts to dislodge Tammany Hall at the polls. Allen argued that savings could be realized if a nonpartisan agency studied administrative processes and came up with ideas for more efficient management of resources. Cutting, who was interested in keeping alive reformers' energies in years when there were no political campaigns, agreed to put up $1,000 a month for twelve months to give the idea a try. The Bureau of City Betterment (BCB) was established in 1905 as an arm of the Citizens' Union.[54]

Allen selected as director of the BCB Henry Bruere, a University of Chicago graduate, former settlement house resident, and former welfare secretary for Chicago's McCormick Works (later International Harvester Company).[55] Years later, Bruere recalled that he was hired to "carry out Allen's idea that progress in the Municipal Government . . . must be a continuous effort expressing a citizen determination based on facts and employing a method of organization and management and skills which were developed in private enterprise and business, to improve public administration." Bruere said that he made an impression on Allen by the efficient way he had learned to put stamps on letters.[56]

The new BCB director focused his initial attention on the office of the Manhattan borough president and its responsibility for street paving, sewers, and public baths. President Ahearn, however, denied the fledgling investigator access to his office records. Bruere decided to study what could be observed outside rather than go through a protracted lawsuit, so he set about trying to compare available repair records with the actual condition of Manhattan streets. Bruere and his assistants documented many instances of streets that were supposed to have been repaired but were still in terrible condition.[57] Bruere published his findings, including photographs, in a pamphlet entitled "How Manhattan Is Governed." The measured tone of the introduction ("The purpose of the inquiry . . . was, first, to ascertain the facts respecting [Ahearn's] administration and, second, to suggest its improvement along specific lines") belied the severity of its criticism.[58] Pointing out that the power of Ahearn's office gave him a tremendous opportunity to serve the public, the investigators set forth in detail how that opportunity was being wasted as a result of incompetence and inefficiency in various public works, including streets, sewers, and public baths.

The report caused considerable furor. Ahearn filed a libel suit against Cutting as chairman of the BCB board of trustees. Mayor McClellan, who was not averse to making things uncomfortable for a Tammany man like Ahearn (his memoirs refer to Ahearn as a "near illiterate, completely under Murphy's thumb"), appointed reformer John Purroy Mitchel as special corporation counsel to look into the discrepancies.[59] Mitchel was impressed with Bruere, and the two struck up a long-lasting association. Together they prepared a report, which they submitted to George McAneny, president of the City Club, with the request that McAneny, in his capacity as a private citizen, submit the report to Governor Charles Evans Hughes.[60] After holding hearings, Hughes removed borough president Ahearn for inefficiency, even though no evidence of personal corruption could be found. "Hughes said it was no excuse that Ahearn did not know about the holes in the streets, as he claimed; he was paid to know."[61] Elated BCB officials cited the governor's action as the first time an American elected official had been removed for incompetence rather than actual wrongdoing.

As the aftermath of the Ahearn investigation unfolded, Bruere and his assistants continued investigating "citizen complaints" about various city departments and making "detailed inquiry into certain phases of the municipal business," results of which were routinely furnished to the press. For example, the BCB investigated charges of "wasted water," departmental payrolls for what were said to be unauthorized salary increases, the Department of Street Cleaning, and the Police Department. Bruere said that the BCB was "an experiment in the direction of achieving greater efficiency in city administration through the agency of publicity."[62]

Bruere's peripatetic efforts soon brought him to the attention of Hermann Biggs, the public health legend who was then New York's medical health officer. Biggs's department was faced with a host of growing public health problems, including high infant death rates, tuberculosis and other communicable diseases, impure drugs, smoke, litter, and contaminated milk. He was interested in finding a better way of justifying annual funding requests to the Board of Estimate and Apportionment. Every year, the health department, like other departments, would routinely present inflated requests in anticipation of reductions. The board, knowing the requests to be inflated, would arbitrarily but just as routinely slash them, in the case of the health department, from 18 to 42 percent. Frequently, agencies would find themselves unable to get through the year on the funds they had been allocated, and the city would make up the difference by issuing special revenue bonds.[63]

Biggs invited Bruere to help him develop a way of justifying his requests that would result in more predictable and larger allocations of funds. For Bruere, this was a welcome chance to demonstrate the value of a systematic agency budget.

The health department was an ideal test case because of the critical nature of public health problems and because "the department of health was in position to make out a clear case before any jury; it had definite work to do and could clearly describe why that work should be done."[64] The outcome of their work was the first itemized municipal agency budget in the United States, which so impressed the board and the aldermen that they passed separate resolutions requiring all city agencies to prepare annual budgets. The budget document made the case for funds in terms that could have been lifted from a late-twentieth-century equivalent: "How much sickness the department of health will prevent next year and how many lives it will save depends very largely upon the amount of money you grant that department. The department of health is striving towards a complete control of the health of the city—towards the complete prevention of preventable diseases and preventable death. How nearly this end is to be reached in 1907 is a question of dollars and cents. Briefly, it is a question of how much health the city can afford to buy."[65]

While these initial BCB successes were unfolding, Mayor McClellan's own investigative commission found itself mired in agency resistance and confusion and turned to the BCB for help. Bruere worked with Frederick Cleveland to analyze the city's confused business records. The resulting report castigated city departments for having no uniform system of accounts, for "purposeless restatement of the same facts and . . . useless waste of effort. . . . Records kept for giving information to creditors . . . [are] not much short of chaotic. . . . Several hundred accounts [were found] concerning whose meaning the city's accountants themselves have little or no knowledge."[66] His collaboration with Bruere prompted Cleveland to draft a memo to Allen calling for the organization of an independent "bureau of municipal research"[67]—that is, one separate from the Citizens' Union, which engaged in electoral politics. Allen and others succeeded in getting Cutting, John D. Rockefeller, and Andrew Carnegie to put up the necessary initial funds, and the New York Bureau of Municipal Research was incorporated in April 1907. At its first board meeting on May 8, E. R. A. Seligman of Columbia University was elected chairman, Frank Tucker of the AICP vice-chairman, Allen secretary, and Cutting treasurer. Other founding board members included the City Club's George McAneny (also a journalist and later president of the borough of Manhattan) and Richard Watson Gilder, tenement house reformer and editor of *The Century.* They were joined a month later by Albert A. Shaw, editor of *American Monthly Review of Reviews* and chairman of the Rockefeller General Education Board, and Carroll D. Wright, president of Clark College and former U.S. commissioner of labor. Other early board members included Henry S. Pritchett, president of the Carnegie Foundation, and Frank A. Vanderlip of National City Bank. Although Bruere was appointed the bureau's initial director, Allen, Bruere, and Cleveland functioned as codirectors almost from the beginning and were so appointed formally in 1909.

The articles of incorporation outlined the purposes of the new bureau:

- to promote efficient and economical municipal government;
- to promote the adoption of scientific methods of accounting and of reporting the details of municipal business, with a view to facilitating the work of public officials;
- to secure constructive publicity in matters pertaining to municipal problems;
- to collect, to classify, to analyze, to corelate [*sic*], to interpret, and to publish facts as to the administration of municipal government.[68]

Bruere later said that the aim of the bureau was "the substitution of effective processes for wasteful methods, of businesslike practice for confusion," a reflection of the bureau men's insistence that their purpose was not investigating corruption but simply helping agency personnel to do their jobs better.[69] But perhaps inevitably, because their first project had resulted in the removal of a city official, the bureau men tended to be seen by Tammany stalwarts as busybodies and snoopers. Mayor McClellan's memoirs present this picture:

> There was a citizens' organization called the Bureau of Municipal Research of which an able and agreeable young man named Henry Bruere was the head. Its purpose was the uncovering of graft in the city government. I . . . preferred to keep its good will and use it to help Mitchel in his work. One day Bruere came to me and said that he strongly suspected that [the Department of Water Supply, Gas, and Electricity] was honeycombed with graft and that he would like to investigate it. I told him to go ahead. . . . Some months later Bruere and Mitchel came to me and announced that the investigation of the department was completed. Mitchel said, "Mr. Mayor, we have very bad news for you." I was terribly shocked. "What's wrong?" I asked. "That's just the trouble," replied Mitchel. "There's nothing wrong."[70]

According to a 1908 newspaper account, Bruere and Cleveland directed the actual investigating work, with Bruere making the initial contacts with city officials and Cleveland supervising the work of implementing improved methods. Allen, meanwhile, was responsible for "the publicity end . . . carrying forward the propaganda of municipal research with persistence and vigor." Allen was said to be in touch with the mayors and comptrollers of the hundred largest cities.[71] Allen's idea of the bureau's work was to "give statistics flesh and blood. . . . The Bureau," he said, "will be an outpost for social workers . . . a unifying force [for] good government."[72]

William Allen had studied at the University of Chicago and in Leipzig and Berlin before pursuing a Ph.D. in economics at the University of Pennsylvania. His mentor Simon Patten advised him to "help the other fellow" but not to live in a settlement house, commenting somewhat cryptically, "Be orthodox in other people's specialties and you can be as heterodox as you please in your own." This advice Allen later ignored.[73] He took a job at the State Charities Aid Association of New Jersey that required him to visit insane asylums and poorhouses all over the state. This was Allen's introduction to fact collection as a mechanism to improve the management of institutions. He said that the lesson he learned was that "you couldn't get answers out of books. You had to think and feel as you went along." After two years, Allen transferred to the AICP. He played the role of the crusader in bureau activities, with a zeal that brought him into conflict with those who did not share his views. Bruere called Allen "a person of very rapid cerebration . . . extremely conscious of the authenticity of his own convictions . . . a great believer in the eloquence of facts." He saw Allen as the idea man and himself as the one who opened doors and exerted leverage to get things done.[74]

Bruere had studied economics and sociology at the University of Chicago, where he heard lectures by Thorstein Veblen, Wesley Mitchell, and Charles Zueblin. He recalled that Zueblin taught him that "living in a community is a pleasurable thing to do if you do it with intelligence and decency and social participation. . . . A good citizen . . . exerts himself in cooperation with right-minded persons for good ends." Bruere characterized his teachers as laying "a platform . . . on which we are building a new kind of America." He admitted that his level of involvement with the ideas of his professors was not very deep. "They were all able men. I didn't think much about them; I just respected them."[75]

Bruere seems to have been something of a young man on the make. From his beginnings as a social worker and settlement house resident in Boston, he went on to cultivate connections with the wealthy and powerful, including Chicago's McCormick family. Bruere apparently had a talent for being in the right place at the right time, forming relationships with men such as Cleveland and Mitchel that furthered his career. When Mitchel was elected mayor in 1913 on a reform ticket, he appointed Bruere city chamberlain. As a 1914 newspaper account maintained, "The constructive spirit of the Ahearn investigation opened for Mr. Bruere the doors of practically all of the municipal departments." The article complimented Bruere on avoiding "the attitude of the detective and prosecutor," an approach that set him apart from Allen, although the two appear to have gotten along relatively well.[76] Barry Karl has called Bruere a "guide of the wealthy," in contrast to Cleveland, who "was concerned with the purest form of practical efficiency, the rationalization of accounting systems."[77] Bruere lacked both Cleveland's penchant for technical detail and Allen's zeal. His temperament seems to have made him something of a mediator and diplomat.[78]

Cleveland, the most seasoned of the three at the time of the inauguration of the bureau (Allen was thirty-three, Bruere twenty-five, Cleveland forty-two), maintained the posture of the accounting expert throughout the early years of the bureau, until his resignation in 1917. Cleveland had graduated from DePauw University and received his Ph.D. in economics at the University of Pennsylvania's Wharton School in 1900, which pioneered the idea of management as a procedural science (in contrast to rival Harvard's case study approach).[79] At Wharton, Cleveland joined William Allen under Simon Patten's tutelage. Patten taught them that in the new economy of sustained abundance, the masses had to be educated for consumption. Patten used frankly gendered language in which Puritanism and historical concreteness were "womanly," free-market capitalism and abstract reasoning "manly." He advocated a synthesis between the two principles.[80] Both Cleveland and Allen were influenced by Patten's economics of abundance to view government not in the old distributive sense but as an instrument to fill public needs. Cleveland also owed much to Charles Waldo Haskins, a pioneer in the accounting profession, who saw accountancy as the "hub of the universe of commerce, trade, and finance," an idea Cleveland adapted to public affairs in the notion of scientific budgeting as the hub of governance.[81]

More single-mindedly than his two coleaders, Cleveland believed in a scientific approach to public administration, one grounded in professional expertise. According to Raymond Fosdick, a fellow reformer, Cleveland had "a rather involved" way of speaking that was "often baffling to a person interested in the simple facts of a case." His insistence on objectivity eventually brought him into irreconcilable conflict with Allen, the popularizer and advocate, even though the two had been good enough friends for each to name a son after the other.[82] His attention to detail and concern for organization are reflected in the newspaper clipping file he maintained, still available among bureau records, which preserves not only favorable but also highly critical and even hostile press coverage, some of which showed Cleveland personally in an unflattering light. Irene Rubin suggests that Cleveland's perspective shifted during the bureau's early years, from a concern for the relationship between good methods and the ends of government to one focused much more narrowly on technical procedure.[83] Since Cleveland outlasted both Allen and Bruere at the bureau, defeating Allen in the controversy that erupted between them, his perspective may have had the greatest impact on evolving ideas about public administration. At any rate, the New York Bureau's philosophy did shift markedly during its formative first decade, from a perspective that at least expressed an interest in using government to better the conditions of people's lives (one they shared with the "feminine" social welfare reformers) to a more purely masculine agenda that restricted itself to scientific and business efficiency.

FOUNDING VISIONS

In 1907, William Allen's *Efficient Democracy* declared: "A man may be a walking dictionary, living encyclopedia, bacteria wizard, or virtue personified, and yet not intelligent as to government."[84] Allen argued that intelligence in government was a matter not of goodness but of efficiency, that is, of a scientific approach that would reveal the essential facts on which democratic government could be based. "Goodness," of course, was a quality that at the time was directly associated with women, who were considered the embodiment of virtue in society. To reject goodness for efficiency was implicitly to turn from femininity to masculinity. The book presented a proposal for the establishment of an "Institute for Municipal Research," which would serve as a "mechanism for learning and publishing the facts of social life and public administration" (ix). Facts would enable the public to exert intelligent control over administrative processes.

Efficient Democracy is perhaps the clearest available statement of the municipal reformers' new nonelectoral approach to governmental improvement. Allen's argument is that it is a waste of time to strive for "goodness" in city officials, because goodness cannot be objectively measured, whereas efficiency can be. Using as illustration the work of the AICP's Robert M. Hartley, Allen demonstrated how efficient administrative processes would make the desire to do good more effective in government, as Hartley's work had shown it to be in private charity. For example, the association's "friendly visitors" (the equivalent of today's caseworkers) had to follow an established protocol for determining which families in need to visit and how often. Because they had to use a particular form requiring them to plan their work systematically,

> they were saved a vast amount of tape that was no less red because wasted. The energy formerly spent on deciding not to visit a family could now be spent on deciding what to do for the family visited. After learning that they could not keep an orderly pad and do disorderly work, and that the little feminine devices to keep up appearances would be quickly disclosed to the questioning supervisor, they stopped trying to make columns even by putting names where there was room . . . and began seriously to take advantage of the saving that came from system. (162–64)

Allen argued that, rather than turning the visitor into an administrative automaton, this sort of system actually put a premium on the exercise of her judgment, because the result could be compared with facts about the conditions her work was trying to relieve. Her performance was judged not by what she meant to do but by what she achieved. This argument reflects the frank advocacy of masculine efficiency measures to control feminine irrationality, a theme that had sounded in scientific charity circles since the Civil War (see chapter 4)—circles in which Allen had moved during his time with the State Charities Aid Association of New Jersey and the AICP.

In applying the lessons learned from efficient charity work to governmental reform, Allen held that the trick was to tap the resources of the relatively small percentage of citizens who were sincerely motivated to improve government. As it was, he argued, "battle-scarred soldiers of the common good" were wearing themselves out "flit[ting] from one important subject to another" because they lacked the information to make their advocacy effective. Allen recommended that the dedicated few devote themselves to finding and publishing facts about governmental performance that would "enlighten and convince public opinion." In another effort to show how masculine efficiency surpassed sentimental female efforts, Allen contrasted systematic fact-finding with the worthy but small-scale efforts of the settlement houses, whose residents were providing "three shower baths" instead of working to set up a municipal bathhouse capable of handling "9,000 tenement residents a day," or teaching English to "a dozen Swedish maids" instead of doing something about "200,000 children behind in their school grade." The efforts of the enlightened few, Allen argued, would be put to better use by making a fact-based case for governmental provision of such services: "The ultimate efficient state will stigmatise post-budget expressions of virtuous indignation as a weak substitute for intelligent ante-budget demands and arguments" (274).

The culmination of Allen's argument in support of efficient democracy was his proposal for the establishment of an Institute for Municipal Research, which would coordinate the fact-finding and advocacy process, helping the various charitable societies work together and present a "solid front to the city" (278). The institute, in Allen's vision, would furnish leaders and the public at large with the "facts necessary to sound judgment regarding problems of municipal government or the acts and pretensions of officials and candidates" (281). It would take on analysis of annual municipal budgets and departmental organization and work, focusing specifically on comparing the amount spent with the results achieved.

Allen also suggested that sociological research would be necessary to develop knowledge about the causes and extent of city problems such as crime and disease, knowledge that would demonstrate the need for city government action. Calling government the most important agency for benevolence, Allen held that treating the results of problems was less effective than coming to understand and remedy the causes. Existing benevolent organizations did not have the resources for such investigations.

Overall, Allen's brief for what became the Bureau of Municipal Research made the point that fact-finding would make government more effective: not only would research bring problems to light and describe their causes, but analysis of agency processes would enable them to use knowledge of problems to carry out solutions. Although Allen emphasized efficiency in the narrow sense of cost saving, he placed it in a broader context within which, by supporting effective action, it served government's role as the largest benevolent society, the one charged more than any other with making the lives of city residents better. In his reminiscences, Allen claimed that "the governmental research movement was not a penny-saving or penny-pinching proposition at all. It was a movement to make democracy a living, vital thing, because it showed how people could get done what all the time they really wanted to get done but didn't know how."[85]

Henry Bruere's writings show a similarly instrumental understanding of efficiency. In an article published in the 1909 *Proceedings of the American Political Science Association,* Bruere characterized the Bureau of Municipal Research as "seeking to awaken popular intelligence, not about political principles, but with respect to current acts and omissions of governmental agencies."[86] He described the bureau's method as scientific analysis of government, publication of facts, and correction of governmental defects. Acknowledging that the bureau's efforts to date had resulted in the removal of incompetent city officials, Bruere maintained that the bureau took "no special interest in the mere fact that enormous waste occurs in the conduct of municipal business" but that it was "keenly interested in the fact that community needs are not filled . . . , that death, disease, distress, ignorance and crime are increased as a direct consequence of this waste." The bureau's efforts were aimed at preventing or reducing waste so that community improvement could be promoted more effectively.[87]

Several years later, Bruere was continuing to promote the idea that municipal research was aimed at efficiency for the sake of "progressive social welfare," substituting for the haphazard voluntary efforts a "city-wide, community planned and community executed program of citizen well-being."[88] In other words, masculine order and system would replace the work of volunteers, virtually all of whom were women. Bruere said that although the idea was widespread that efficiency in government meant only a focus on promoting business methods, the real value of efficiency efforts would be measured by accomplishments, such as reducing infant mortality rates or the number of families relying on charity. "No city government . . . can achieve efficiency . . . merely by bringing about precision, orderliness and economy in the performance of existing tasks."[89] Similarly, in his 1912 book on commission government, Bruere maintained that if the aim of efficiency were simply lower taxes and economical performance, the adoption of business methods would be enough; but the promotion of community welfare required the city to understand the "social and economic requirements" of its community and equip itself to take the lead in fulfilling these conditions: "Before government services are extended to meet the demands of progressiveness, it is obviously desirable to have present activities efficiently conducted. The efficiency movement has therefore addressed itself to bringing city business methods up to the level of the best private methods."[90]

Fact-finding would bring to light the gap between community needs and existing services and identify opportunities where the exercise of efficiency would make existing resources go further. Again Bruere argued that the necessary initial emphasis by bureau reformers on governmental accounting, purchasing, timekeeping, and so on masked a real concern for the objectives and results of governmental activity. He set forth a vision of a populace awakened by fact-finding to new awareness of community: "The thousands who hang on straps in streetcars and subways, drink badly filtered water, work in unsanitary factories, suffer from overcrowding, and haunt the streets for work in times of unemployment, are developing a 'consciousness of kind,' a solidarity of interest, which will make effective the demand for expertness and efficiency in municipal administration."[91]

Of the three founding leaders, the accountant Frederick Cleveland put the most consistent emphasis on efficiency, but even he sometimes acknowledged the larger context: "The demand for efficiency must go farther than to require that the government shall get a dollar for every dollar spent; it must constitute a demand that the government is doing the thing most needed, is conserving those ends and purposes which can not be adequately reached through private undertakings."[92] In a

1912 speech to the Efficiency Society, he advocated educating the public by means of accurate information about governmental processes and using savings to support additional government programs in health and public works. Good financial reporting would enable citizens to hold government responsible for spending its resources wisely.[93] In *Organized Democracy,* published in 1913, Cleveland stressed the social purpose of government, which required that economy be practiced to promote health, education, law and order, transportation, and other functions necessary to the public good.[94]

Jonathan Kahn argues that the founding visions on which the bureau based its early work were shaped in important ways by two scandals that erupted in 1905, over corruption in gas and electric franchises and in the life insurance industry. These scandals and the ensuing state-level investigation heightened public anxiety about corporate use of public power and legitimated new government activism in regulation, administration, and planning. According to Kahn, although legislation passed in response to the scandals helped restore public confidence in business, a deficit in public trust in government remained, one that the Bureau of Municipal Research was able to fill. The bureau's use of oversight and publicity helped rebuild public support for government and channeled that support in directions that preempted any fundamental challenge to the existing governmental structure.[95]

THE BUREAU'S WORK AND ITS IMPACT

Looking back on the early years of the New York Bureau, it seems likely that Henry Bruere was correct: the bureau's emphasis on efficient procedures must have made it difficult for observers—let alone agency personnel who were the target of the bureau's advice—to treat rather vague statements about community well-being and social welfare with the same seriousness they were forced to accord more tangible efficiency moves. In the same way, most of the bureau's actual activities did not address the substantive improvement in city living conditions that its founders' writings promised.

From the beginning, the work of the research bureaus concentrated on administrative structures and processes, including the development of budgeting and accounting methods; standardization of personnel procedures such as time sheets, job descriptions, work routines, and performance assessments; design of organizational charts; improvement in purchasing and inventory control; and systematization of records in all areas of government. As the new bureau's activities moved into full swing, concentration on ferreting out instances of inefficiency and on designing new forms, structures, and accounting procedures shaped not only public understanding but also the researchers' self-understanding of what their real intentions were. Although bureau leaders maintained that their purpose was not "to seek out misconduct" but "to study the conditions and methods that continually generate such conduct, with a view to securing new and scientific machinery to prevent it," this was a distinction whose subtlety was lost on many observers.[96] Contemporaries of the bureau men, especially agency rank-and-file employees and machine politicians, put more weight on what municipal researchers did than on what they said. Deeds had a more immediate and tangible impact than declarations of intent. And indeed, tensions that inhabited the bureau men's intentions over time could not be sustained. Their insistence on efficient procedures as the means to make government a force for improving city life inexorably drove the latter concern toward the periphery.

In a 1912 progress report, "Six Years of Municipal Research for Greater New York," bureau officials compiled a list of "a few larger benefits of municipal research for New York City."[97] The list was almost exclusively made up of improvements in administrative procedures. At the top was the bureau's success in removing borough president Ahearn for incompetence and waste; succeeding items included "reorganization of the department of finance," "time sheets and service records as the basis for auditing payrolls," "budget reform," "an increase of $2,000,000 a year in revenues due to the reorganization of water collection methods," and "system and economy substituted for waste and chaos in the repairs and stores methods of the water department and in the purchasing and repair methods of the police department." The list of accomplishments included the establishment of a Bureau of Child Hygiene in the Department of Health, but nowhere did the report make the explicit argument that setting up such a bureau had been possible only because enough funds had been freed through administrative efficiency. Nor did the report mention bureau efforts to develop new ways of mapping tuberculosis cases or its study of tenement conditions.[98] Instead, the emphasis throughout was on cost saving for its own sake:

- The time consumed from the receipt of vouchers to payment has decreased by 50%. . . .
- A furnace intended for $3 coal is fed $3 coal and not $5 coal. . . .
- $150 a week for four years saved by Bellevue [Hospital] in standardizing the amount of linen gauze to be used in surgical operations. . . .
- Waste cinders and ashes are used for making walls in Richmond. . . .
- [Water] meters are read systematically under conditions that insure an honest reading. . . .
- $20,000 was saved on an order for $30,000 for fireworks.[99]

Minutes of bureau board meetings during this early period also contain frequent references to projects aimed at uncovering either waste or corruption and to progress made in securing the cooperation of municipal officials in these efforts. For example, the minutes for May 15, 1907, include a list of planned investigative projects:

- Borough of Manhattan: Complete investigation in progress
- Department of Health: Frame system of recording and accounting

- Department of Parks: Administrative methods
- Board of Aldermen: Continue assistance to members
- Department of Finance: Co-operate in securing new budget
- Tenement Department: Analysis of available records; study of methods
- Department of Docks: Now being investigated by Mr. Sikes

On June 19, 1907, there was a reference to "hearty cooperation" received from the heads of Docks and Ferries, Water Supply, and Gas and Electricity on studies of their departments. On February 4, 1908, "Mr. Tucker held that the Bureau must encourage city officials by allowing them to claim credit for the meritorious changes." On April 8, 1908: "Too little cooperation has been received from the department of finance, which has been represented by practically only one man qualified to supervise accounts, his assistant being inexperienced and apparently desirous of obstructing installation. Both had been at times hypercritical of details."[100]

Although municipal researchers regularly downplayed the importance of publishing their findings in order to shine a light on agency waste, fraud, and abuse, it was a central part of their strategy. Fellow researcher Myrtile Cerf, for example, commented: "In New York, the improvements in service were effected by publicity given conditions found after investigation, thereby forcing the department head in some instances to correct the evil pointed out where aid could not be secured solely upon suggestion."[101] A 1911 newspaper article on the Philadelphia bureau, the second to be formed and a direct outgrowth of work by the New York Bureau, called the latter "a body of investigators of civic evils" that had faced "the blustering wrath of many local city officials."[102]

The bureau's emphasis on investigating city agencies and on instituting efficient procedures met with unsurprising skepticism if not outright stalling or stonewalling on the part of agency personnel. In addition, many projects ran into the inevitable unforeseen difficulties that face any attempt to reshape the basic processes in an organization, and these difficulties just as inevitably found their way into the newspapers. The Department of Finance project became especially troublesome, as efforts to systematize record keeping interrupted the usual flow of work, including the issuance of weekly paychecks to day laborers in various departments. Bureau men argued that eventually clerks and accountants would get used to the new system and blamed the late paychecks on "the rooted antipathy of old servants of the city" and on "insufficiency of assistance."[103] Tammany-backed papers, however, had a field day with the snafu, describing one of the reformers in pointedly gendered terms that reveal the machine loyalist's scorn for the effete "man milliner":

City Chamberlain Martin Wins Decisive Victory
over that Dear Henri Brue-ere in the Matter of Pay Warrants

The Bureau of Municipal Research is said to be at it again. . . . Henri's aesthetic tastes never did and never will like the system of pay warrants in vogue with Chamberlain Martin. It wasn't their color so much. . . . It was their open-heartedness—their inability to conceal—their brutal frankness in telling for what purposes they were drawn. So Henri evolved a voucher of his own—a dainty, perfumed thing, omitting altogether the purpose for which the city's money was to be paid. In place of the common, plebian "salaries" or "advertising" or the like Henri placed a key . . . for instance, "23" meant "refer to ledger 23," so that the Chamberlain's office would have to go to the Finance Department. . . . When this proposition was placed before Mr. Martin he thought some things he didn't mention aloud, being a gentleman, but he declined absolutely to accede to Henri's request. The latter, his hair rampant, fumed and almost slapped Mr. Martin on the wrist.[104]

Comptroller Herman Metz, who backed the bureau's efforts, found himself criticized in the press for aiding Republican muckraking efforts by Democratic stalwarts who were unable to overlook R. Fulton Cutting's ties to the Citizens' Union and its opposition to Tammany.[105] Metz and Mayor McClellan came into conflict over the issue. McClellan accepted the assurances of his agency staffers that the new forms devised by the bureau were bogging down administrative processes because they could be used on only one brand of typewriter; Metz, in return, called McClellan "a shorter, uglier word."[106] Behind-the-scenes negotiations eventually resolved the problem: McClellan announced on February 4 that all his department heads had agreed to cooperate with the new system, and bureau reformers publicly acknowledged that there might be good reasons why agency personnel would have trouble with it, assuring, "There shall be no punishment for unintentional offenders."[107]

Such controversies and their portrayal in the press ensured that bureau reformers would be regarded by many members of the public as elitist troublemakers. One friendly critic commented, "The 'bureau of municipal research crowd' have been a bit slow in finding [a saving] sense of humor [regarding their work] and have been . . . rather careless about allowing the reformer's instinctive provincialism of spirit to develop in the form of offhand and cocksure disparagement of proposals advanced by other thinkers."[108] A few days after it was announced that the pay warrant controversy had been resolved, Parks Department commissioner Henry Smith made a speech in which he "attacked the work of the Bureau of Municipal Research, calling it the 'Municipal Besmirch Society.' " Smith complained that the bureau was getting between him and the rest of city government: "If I want anything I have to go to the Unique Director or the Technical Director [of the bureau]. The system is a failure and they know it."[109] Tammany drew on the "Besmirch" idea in its political campaigns and even went so far as to stage an exhibit lampooning the bureau, complete with monkeys, a goat, a parrot, an elephant, and placards bearing likenesses of leaders of the "Bureau of Municipal Besmirch."[110] According to Tammany, the bureau was slandering city officials so that wealthy contributors could buy bonds at prices reduced in the face of the scandal.[111] Bureau officials expressed appreciation for the free publicity.

In 1912, at a meeting of the Woman's Forum, William Allen engaged in a debate with Reginald Pelham Bolton, head of the Washington Heights Taxpayers' Association. Their exchange reflects the suspicion met by defensiveness typical of the bureau's public relations during its first decade. Bolton charged that the bureau's investigative methods, coupled with a "habit of arrogating to themselves the credit for much of the work of improvement of conditions," had led to increasing hostility between it and city officials. In rebuttal, Allen "contrasted Bolton's wealth with his own modest means" and "asked anyone to inform him how he could maintain the friendliness of an official after telling him that he was a liar." Bolton shot back: "Is the Bureau the sole source of all truth?" Allen "denied trying to convey the impression that the Bureau could not be improved" and invited members of the Woman's Forum to conduct their own investigation of it.[112]

While such press accounts gradually shaped public perceptions regarding the bureau, reformers in other cities paid attention to its growing influence on city government and requested the New Yorkers to help them form their own research organizations. The first was Philadelphia, followed by Cincinnati, Chicago, Dayton, Milwaukee, Minneapolis, Akron, Toledo, Detroit, and others. Except for the Chicago and Milwaukee bureaus, most were privately organized and financed. New Yorkers joined the staffs of bureaus in Philadelphia, Cincinnati, and Chicago. The New Yorkers worked extensively with bureaus in other cities, providing technical assistance in the design of investigations and making their own staff available to conduct certain studies. These interlocking relationships gave the entire research bureau phenomenon a philosophical and methodological homogeneity it might not otherwise have had (see chapter 4).

THE INFLUENCE OF MONEY

From the beginning, the New York Bureau—like most pioneering nonprofit organizations—had to worry about financial support for its efforts. It came into existence as the result of gifts from wealthy men. R. Fulton Cutting provided the initial $12,000 to support the Bureau of City Betterment as an offshoot of the Citizens' Union. Then, as a result of Cutting's persuasiveness, Andrew Carnegie and John D. Rockefeller made possible the first year of the independent New York Bureau. The organizers were nothing if not ambitious. Early on, they anticipated the acquisition of a $10 million endowment, but fund-raising remained a constant struggle throughout the bureau's initial decade. Although the bureau eventually received a fair number of relatively small donations, in the $5 to $10 range, there were never enough of these to eliminate the need to court big donors and to make sure they remained happy with the bureau's work.[113] Inevitably, the interests of rich donors came into conflict with at least some of the bureau's activities, and when they did, the bureau found itself having to adjust in order to survive. Considering the story in light of the relative influence of gender, science, and business, it could be said that the feminine interest in social improvement nascent in the bureau's early work was snuffed out by masculine science nourished by the big-business interests that were such a crucial source of support.

In "A National Program to Improve Methods of Government," the bureau listed total contributions between January 1, 1906, and December 31, 1914, of $949,424. The biggest donor was Rockefeller, with a total of $125,400, followed by Cutting with $116,785, Carnegie with $55,000, Mrs. E. H. Harriman with $51,500, Kuhn Loeb Company with $41,000, J. P. Morgan and Company with $29,200, and Henry Phipps with $23,500.[114] These seven gifts represented nearly half the total support for the bureau during this period; when another five gifts of between $10,000 and $20,000 each are added in, the result constitutes about 54 percent of the bureau's resources.

Such heavy reliance on tangible expressions of goodwill from a few rich givers was always a sore point with bureau men. They argued that the influence of donors could not be seen in the results of bureau work: "It could not have done business for ten years without leaving evidence behind which would have destroyed its standing for impartial representation of facts."[115] Nevertheless, suspicion about the influence of wealthy donors on the bureau's work continued.

Much of the work of fund-raising fell to William Allen, who had styled himself as something of an expert on philanthropy. *Efficient Democracy* contained a chapter on "efficient philanthropy," and Allen published a book and several journal articles on the subject. He had a less than ideal temperament for the job of courting wealthy donors: a combination of sincere reforming zeal, which made him an effective advocate for the causes he believed in, with a limited ability to tolerate disagreement with his views. (A review of *Efficient Democracy* commented wryly that reading it felt somewhat like being taken onto Allen's knee for a patronizing lecture.[116]) As Allen's vision of the bureau expanded, his ambitions eventually brought him into conflict with more conservative forces.

In 1909, Allen published an article in *The Survey,* the major organ of communication among social reformers, entitled "Mr. Rockefeller's Greatest Gift."[117] The essay was a paean to Rockefeller's approach to giving away his spare millions. But Rockefeller did not part with his money without some concern over how it would be spent. Eventually, the extent of control exercised by the bureau's biggest donor triggered a controversy of crisis proportions between Allen on one side and Cleveland, joined with bureau board members, on the other. According to Allen, as a condition of his support, Rockefeller wanted to stop the public school reform work, an activity spearheaded by Allen, as well as to separate the bureau's training school (see chapter 5) from its research efforts, eliminate the weekly postcard publicity bulletins by which the bureau informed the public of its work, and stop the out-of-town activities of New York Bureau staffers, who were not only providing technical assistance to other bureaus but also doing research for a number of other city and state governments.[118] Allen finally resigned on October 5, 1914, in a letter one account characterized as a "fourteen inch sociological mortar."[119]

Allen maintained that trustees had urged him "not to make a moral issue out of a mere question of expediency" and to go along with Rockefeller's wish that the bureau get out of what Allen called "the fight to secure democratic, progressive, informed management of New York city's school system."[120]

Bureau trustees presented a united front to the press, maintaining that Rockefeller was not attempting to control the bureau and that the problem was Allen himself. One newspaper account, however, quoted one of "Dr. Allen's critics" as follows:

> This fight is an inner bureau fight. Dr. Allen and Frederick A. Cleveland, who now becomes the sole head of the bureau, differs [sic] as to its policy. Dr. Allen favored publicity. Under his direction the bureau issued bulletins semi-weekly or oftener of what the bureau was doing or intended doing.
>
> Mr. Rockefeller and others in the bureau did not believe in so much publicity. Mr. Rockefeller held that it was a bureau of research, not of bulletins. Two trustees resigned, it was said, because they thought there was too much publicity.
>
> Dr. Cleveland disagreed with Dr. Allen's idea of introducing a large number of young men into the work who had little or no former experience. There were also many other differences between the two men.[121]

As a result of events extending far beyond its boundaries, the New York Bureau's relationship with the Rockefeller Foundation brought it into the national limelight. Soon after Allen's resignation, he joined the staff of the U.S. Commission on Industrial Relations, which was looking into conditions surrounding strife between capital and labor. Commission chairman Frank P. Walsh had learned in October 1914 that John D. Rockefeller, Jr., who was by this time carrying out his father's directives about the use of the family fortune, had hired Mackenzie King to conduct a rival study of industrial relations. Fearing that Rockefeller was bent on undermining the commission's work, Walsh determined to investigate him along with other philanthropists, an aim whose appeal must have been irresistible to Allen. No sensible man, Walsh maintained, could believe that "research workers, publicists and teachers can be subsidized with money obtained from the exploitation of workers without being profoundly influenced in their point of view."[122]

R. Fulton Cutting testified before the commission on January 28, 1915, immediately following three days of testimony by John D. Rockefeller, Jr. The commission used Rockefeller's appearance as an opportunity to inquire into his role in the bitter coal mining strike in Colorado. Colorado Fuel and Iron Company, the largest coal company in the state and the target of United Mine Workers' organizing efforts, was 40 percent under Rockefeller control. From September 1913 through April 1914, southern Colorado had been racked by violence between strikers and company troops. In the notorious "Ludlow Massacre" on April 20, 1914, actions by National Guardsmen, called out by Colorado's governor, resulted in the fiery deaths of two women and eleven children. Under close questioning by Walsh,

Rockefeller maintained that he had no knowledge of working conditions in Colorado, such as the long hours, poor sanitation, company stores, company prohibitions on workers owning houses, and so on, nor had he spearheaded the company's resistance to unionization. Acting on Mackenzie King's advice, Rockefeller said that his conscience was aroused and his views on the moral duties of corporate directors had changed. He invited leaders of the United Mine Workers to meet with him in his offices at 26 Broadway.

The meeting took place on the same day as Cutting's testimony about the financing of the New York Bureau. Cutting was asked whether he sensed "undue influence" by philanthropists on the work of the organizations they financed. Cutting replied that this might happen if the foundations fell into the hands of "men with anything but lofty purpose."[123] He admitted that the bureau had changed its agenda along the lines Rockefeller wanted but insisted that "they had the change in mind before it was made a condition of the gift." The audience, which included the famous labor leader Mother Jones, was "listless" until the last question of the day: At the time Rockefeller had made his offer to the bureau of $20,000, "with the condition that out-of-town investigations be stopped, were your experts in Colorado investigating Judge Ben B. Lindsey?" Lindsey, famous as a pioneer in juvenile justice, had earlier testified in support of the miners. The implication of the question was that the bureau had been enlisted by Rockefeller to exert pressure on Lindsey. Cutting replied that bureau men probably were in Colorado at the time, as they were "making investigations in all parts of the country."[124]

On February 3, Frederick Cleveland submitted a statement to the commission, making public for the first time a list of the bureau's principal donors. Cleveland maintained that the bureau had been completely unbiased in its fact-based investigations until, during Cleveland's absence to serve on President Taft's Commission on Economy and Efficiency, Allen began to participate actively in the research work and became harshly critical of professional educators, a stance that brought him into conflict with the bureau's board of directors. Cleveland pointed out that Allen himself had repeatedly solicited Rockefeller's support and as late as December 1913 was still expressing hope that Rockefeller would come forth with an endowment for the bureau.

Cleveland's statement was aired on a day when the hearing board and its audience were gripped by the testimony of Mrs. Mary Petrucci, whose three children had died in the Ludlow fire. The headline of one account conveys something of the bizarre contrasts that marked the day's proceedings: "WOMEN TELL HORRORS OF COLORADO LABOR WAR . . . Miner's Wife Who Lost Three Children Testifies to Condition that Led to Call to Arms—Rockefeller Foundation Secretary [Jerome D.] Greene Says He Has Seen Rockefeller Twice in Five Years—Research Contributions."[125]

Cleveland testified in person on February 6, the last day of the New York hearings, as did Allen. Their remarks came on the same day as personal appearances by Andrew Carnegie and John D. Rockefeller, Sr., both of whom characterized their primary purpose in life as doing good for their fellow men. Carnegie's face "beamed delightedly when he told how pleased he was to know that behind his back his men always called him 'Andy.' "[126] He attributed his success to "always granting the demands of labor, however unreasonable."[127] The spectacle of two of the world's wealthiest men "raising their voices for 'steady work and good wages' for American workingmen" quite naturally stole the limelight from Cleveland's and Allen's mutual animadversions.[128] It is likely that the juxtaposition of bureau testimony denying the influence of wealthy donors with a rare opportunity for the public to hear directly from the likes of Carnegie and the Rockefellers did little to sever perceived connections between the bureau and the rich and powerful. The bureau continued to have money worries until the early 1920s, when it was reconstituted as the National Institute of Public Administration (see chapter 5).

THE BUREAU'S EVOLUTION

The extent to which the influence of Rockefeller or other large donors was responsible for the changing thrust of the bureau's efforts is a matter of interpretation rather than proof one way or another. It is not unreasonable to suppose that persons who give large amounts of money to an enterprise will expect to have at least some influence on the nature of the work. But the bureau's reliance on objective science as the foundation of its legitimacy must have made its representatives especially sensitive to charges of being influenced by money. After all, they had leveled this same charge against machine politicians. If not science, then what basis did the bureau men have for arguing that they had a better way of running government? Being cast as pawns of Rockefeller skirted the New York Bureau too close to the possibility that "science" meant knowledge that supported the interests of big-money capitalism.[129] From this perspective, Rockefeller's own insistence that the bureau confine itself to scientific research sounded the death knell to policy advocacy and direct involvement in activities to improve city living conditions.

Seen in this context, the position taken by Allen, which emphasized aggressive investigation and publicity, constituted a more fundamental threat to the research bureau phenomenon than it might have appeared at the time. Although a good part of the conflict between Allen and Cleveland can be seen as a clash between two monumental egos, and although both were elitists in the sense of believing that they had a lock on the truth, they embodied different philosophies about the relationship between knowledge and power. Not only was Allen readier than Cleveland to challenge existing economic and political arrangements, but he believed in the positive effect of making government defects public. Like most educated men of his era, he believed that few members of the public were either willing or able to take on the duties of reform. But he was willing to give the general public an opportunity to make up its own mind, especially if doing so would bring embarrassment to those Allen felt were abusing the public trust. For Allen, "science" was less a method than a rallying cry that enabled him to push substantive policies he believed promoted the improvement of city life. In this respect, despite his pugnaciousness, Allen's viewpoints, which consistently connected proper procedure with substantive outcomes, were the most "feminine" of any of the bureau men. Perhaps because of his social work background, he was committed to advocacy and uninterested in objectivity in the sense of dry neutrality. Cleveland, in contrast, was more cautious, less democratic, and much more attached to systematic procedure for its own sake. Allen's departure, then, as Cleveland took over as sole director, signaled the disappearance of any trace of a reform impulse that might have been understood at the time as feminine, as well as a growing conservatism on the part of the bureau. A more staid existence might have been expected, but as it happened, the bureau continued to find itself involved in controversy over its approach to governmental reform.

3
The Other Side of Reform

During the decades when male reform organizations were developing the municipal program and the founders of the research bureau movement were gearing up
to attack administrative inefficiency and corruption, other reform efforts also got
under way. Two are particularly relevant to an understanding of how the field of
public administration emerged. Their characteristic interests and reform strategies
overlapped and contrasted with those of the bureau men in ways that reveal the implicit boundaries that were beginning to congeal around a practice that would come
to be called "public administration." Well-to-do women, largely excluded from
men's reform clubs, formed their own organizations and attacked a wide range of
urban problems. At the same time, social welfare reformers, predominantly women,
founded settlement houses in city neighborhoods inhabited mostly by poor immigrants. Women's clubs and settlement residents took their own tack. Instead of concentrating on improving the structures and administrative processes of municipal
governments, as the research bureaus and other municipal reformers did, clubwomen and settlement folk launched a campaign aimed directly at improving living conditions in cities.

Municipal government reformers such as the men of the research bureaus
argued that rational structures and efficient procedures would contribute to the public good by reducing corruption and saving money. Although social welfare reformers also hated political corruption and recognized the value of efficiency, they
zeroed in on urban problems directly. They saw their work as an aspect of municipal reform, however, not something distinct from it. Settlement resident Helen
Campbell commented in 1898 that "the Social Settlement and Municipal Reform
are, in the nature of things, inseparable . . . the work of men and women together,"
a statement that suggests how early the gender dimensions of reform work became
visible.[1] Helena Dudley of Boston's Denison House argued that "if municipal work
only means direct influence in political matters, the Boston settlements can claim

little. If, however, general work for extending the advantages of the best life of the city to all citizens be meant, all settlement activities come under this head."[2] That women had to defend their place in the municipal reform arena suggests the masculinity of its image and the consequent need to justify an approach that focused on improving living conditions rather than on combating machine politics.

Clubwomen and women of the settlement houses typically attacked the problems of cities in what they thought of as women's ways. Clubwomen called their activities "municipal housekeeping," and the settlement philosophy, even when articulated by men, prominently displayed values that the distinctly gendered society of the time understood to be feminine. I point to gender dynamics not to suggest that biology predestines women and men to sharply different sorts of public work but to recapture aspects of reform thinking largely abandoned in the construction of public administration and to disclose the process that narrowed the array of concerns and approaches considered appropriate to the field.

An examination of municipal housekeeping is of interest because it shows how men and women, operating in gender-divided clubs and pursuing similar though not always identical problems, tackled them in ways that diverged on the basis of gender. Men and women could sometimes reach different diagnoses of the same problem and, accordingly, prescribe distinctive remedies. The municipal housekeeping in which clubwomen engaged offers evidence that the strategies of male reformers were not universally regarded, even among well-to-do people, as the only or the best way to address a given problem. Women, like men, took up the cause of civic improvement, but in a distinctive way. Eventually, women's clubs became important elements in a social welfare policy network that generated government programs that were important prototypes for later, more sweeping measures. In addition, the contrast between women's and men's club work suggests that men, like women, acted as much on the basis of socially generated preferences and expectations as out of supposedly objective analysis. The work of women's and men's reform clubs thus fills in the context within which the research bureaus did their work: a society that saw the world in distinctly gendered terms and acted accordingly.

The settlement movement, on the other hand, brought men and women together in common cause, sometimes in separate settlement houses but often working side by side in the same organization. Overall, women predominated in settlement work numerically as well as in terms of influence and leadership and were able to put a characteristically feminine stamp on it. Also, as this chapter shows, even though the settlement movement featured several prominent men and a significant proportion of firing-line male workers, its philosophy, values, and approaches corresponded closely with typifications of femininity widely if not universally subscribed to by both sexes. Nevertheless, men and women of the settlement movement shared its values and worked collaboratively if not always literally side by side. As I suggest, settlement work reflected a different set of concerns and efforts than those of research bureau activists. This is so even though both were undertaken with a declared interest in improving the quality of life in America's cities, and even though several of the men who led the research bureau movement had had settlement experience. Settlement work thus embodies and reveals a feminine side of municipal reform, but one in which both men and women joined. In many of its aspects, this work constitutes public administration's buried heritage: ideas and values that were carried from the settlement world into administrative reform efforts, ideas and values that could have become part of public administration but did not.

"DANTE IS DEAD"

Since the Federalist period, women had been associated with indirect practices of citizenship such as "republican motherhood," an ideology that invested women's domestic work as wives and mothers with public significance. Though barred from voting, women were said to practice citizenship by nurturing within the home important values such as responsibility and public-spiritedness, encouraging them in husbands and teaching them to sons. Women's citizenship was indirect: their wifely and motherly duties supported the societal framework and values that stabilized the social order and made men's more active citizenship viable.[3]

In the early decades of the nineteenth century, under the banner of republican motherhood, middle- and upper-class white women took on a quasi-public role as bearers and guardians of societal virtue. Gradually, this role gave them an opening into the public sphere, through the practice of voluntarism in charitable organizations. As Kathryn Kish Sklar notes, however, the ideology of republican motherhood only partly accounts for how women were able to sustain their presence in a public sphere to which they were widely considered alien.[4] Women's volunteer work resulted in the development of a network of autonomous institutions, including women's clubs, settlement houses, and other crusading organizations, such as the Women's Christian Temperance Union. These institutions enabled middle-class women to establish their independence from men's reform efforts and to define their own gender-specific goals. The institutionalization process, however, was made possible only because women were able to justify it as womanly despite its public nature. Men had no similar challenge. Manliness was already inherently linked to publicness.

From the beginning of their movement outside the home into benevolent activity in public, women defended the propriety of their involvement in charitable work as consistent with their appointed place in society. Far from being a contradiction to the link between women and domesticity, they argued, their charitable work was an evocation of "true womanhood." Although it represented a move into public space, their approach to social benevolence was uniquely their own and not an intrusion into activities defined as masculine, such as business and party politics. The centerpiece of true womanhood was woman's supposed moral superiority, her "piety, purity, submissiveness and domesticity."[5] The apparent gulf between women's moral excellence and the evils of society justified the movement of women into social betterment activities. Most well-to-do men accepted and even welcomed this rationale. In their eyes, women's charity work not only was consistent with women's role as guardians of societal virtue but also freed men for the self-interest, competitiveness, and cunning on which business and politics depended. Women ensured the continuity of virtue in the public sphere at a time when men increasingly came to equate politics with self-interest, abandoning the connection between political activity and virtue that the American civic republican tradition had once instantiated.[6]

As the nineteenth century drew to a close, and processes of industrialization and urbanization produced a host of social ills in America's cities, well-to-do women gradually expanded their work outside the home from charity into "municipal housekeeping." They began to look beyond person-to-person efforts such as visits to poor families bearing baskets of food and limitless supplies of good advice. They adopted the viewpoint that "the more civic work, the less need of philanthropy," the title of a 1912 article by Mrs. Imogen B. Oakley of the General Federation of Women's Clubs.[7] Women who had originally come together at club meetings to "discuss Dante and Browning over the teacups, at a meeting of their peers in some lady's drawing room," began to see the "unsightly heaps of rubbish [that] flanked the paths over which they had passed in their journeys thither: they began to realize that the one calling in which they were, as a body, proficient, that of housekeeping and homemaking, had its outdoor as well as its indoor application . . . [T]hey learned that well kept lawns were but the outer setting of well kept houses, and that back yards and back alleys had their places in the great science of home making."[8] When Sarah P. Decker was inaugurated in 1904 as president of the General Federation of Women's Clubs, she declared: "Ladies, you have chosen me as your leader. Well, I have an important piece of news for you. Dante is dead. He has been dead for several centuries, and I think it is time that we dropped the study of his inferno and turned attention to our own."[9]

Many clubs initially devoted a great deal of time and effort to "cleanup" days, purchasing trash buckets, giving prizes for backyard improvement, and trying to get rid of billboards. Next came beautification efforts involving tree planting, window boxes, and park benches. They soon began, however, to extend their idea of municipal housekeeping to broader aspects of civic affairs. They saw that "municipal organization had to do with things it was essential should be well done if their efforts as mothers were not to be negatived. The water pumped to their houses, the street, the alley, the school, the hospital, the street car, the park, are all powerful aids to the development of a healthy and enlightened family life, if they are well managed; but they are also agencies for evil, if poorly managed."[10] The "extension of the homemaking instinct" led clubwomen into campaigns for better sanitation, the clearing of alleys, improved garbage collection, the eradication of flies, street sweeping, medical inspection of children, tuberculin testing of cattle, playgrounds and recreational facilities, investigation of the treatment of juvenile offenders, child labor regulations, and better factory conditions generally. They advocated legislation or increased appropriations for civic improvements, sometimes even running for local office themselves.[11] As Mary Ritter Beard put it, "in years gone by, women would have stood by the tub or faucet and thanked bountiful providence for water of any amount or description; but now, as they stand there, their minds reach out through the long chain of circumstances that connect the faucet and tub with the gentlemen who sit in aldermanic conclave."[12]

Clubs began to report success in improving the quality of city life. Their members started up public bathhouses, turned schools into community centers, had incinerators installed, got city slaughterhouses cleaned up and meat inspected, and organized free medical clinics. A club in Fort Collins, Colorado, reported: "We have been the direct and sole agents in individual drinking cups in the schools." The Jamestown, North Dakota, club boasted: "The city council did everything we asked."[13] In New York, the Women's Health Protective League "made the first systematic investigation of the condition of city stables, of slaughter houses, of bakeries, and of garbage disposition, and . . . brought a continuing pressure to bear upon the Street Cleaning Department and upon the Board of Health to do their sworn duty."[14]

From such tangible steps, clubwomen expanded to the study of tax assessments, city planning, charter revision, and other municipal reform efforts in which men were already involved. Study led to advocacy and agitation. Clubwomen held the city responsible for functions already under its authority ("If schools are seen to be avenues of contagion, adequate school medical inspection is demanded by the clubs"[15]) and kept a critical eye on the city's level of performance, especially in areas traditionally considered women's work: "In humanitarian activities of the community, the almshouses, foundling asylums, and institutions for custodial care, women have seen that functions traditionally theirs were not invariably performed to their satisfaction by their male successors. Reason and sympathy have combined to force women to assert themselves."[16] Despite the skepticism or inattention of male politicians, the women persisted. As a Wisconsin clubmember said, "The woman movement is not popular here, so we are obliged to win our way."[17] Women won their way by studying problems and pressing officials for solutions; when politicians tried to "evade issues by talking learnedly of finance, the clubs, armed with information, are ready to bring them back to the point."[18] Women scrutinized proposed policies and testified at legislative and budget hearings. When local governments acceded to their demands and geared up new programs, women themselves became involved in their management. This was particularly true of new social welfare programs: "One can scarcely imagine . . . a court of domestic relations, a bureau of child hygiene, a hospital social service department, a recreation center, a juvenile court, being run without women."[19]

Spurred by the massive migration of southern blacks to big cities, urban black women undertook extensive institution-building efforts in their segregated neighborhoods. According to Darlene Clark Hine, by 1920, they had established in cities such as Cleveland, Detroit, Milwaukee, and Indianapolis homes for the aged, hospitals, nursing schools and colleges, orphanages, libraries, and gymnasiums.[20] Black women were almost always barred from clubs established by white women and therefore had to concentrate their work in black neighborhoods. Rarely did the activities of blacks and whites overlap. Black women generally had fewer resources at their command than whites, and there was less of a gulf between the helpers and the helped than was the case with white women.[21] Because of segregation, black women focused on founding and running institutions in their own communities, rather than pressing governments to take on new responsibilities. Therefore, their activities provide perhaps the clearest example of an alternative public sphere (see chapter 4). Barred from public life not only by their sex but also by Jim Crow laws that restricted African Americans from all manner of activities, black women constructed a network of institutions that met the needs of their communities and fulfilled ideas of public service and the common good that were said to ground the very polity that barred them from full membership in it.[22]

In 1890, four years before the founding of the National Municipal League, white clubwomen organized the General Federation of Women's Clubs, which drew together a vast network of local clubs. By 1896, it was estimated that 100,000 women were affiliated with the federation through their own organizations, and clubs in twenty-one states were united in state networks. The biennial meetings of the federation took up a wide variety of public issues. The 1896 meeting, for example, voted to study "forest conditions and resources and to further the highest interests of our several states in these respects."[23] At the 1898 meeting, for the first time the women approved a petition to be sent to Congress; it had to do with the protection of birds. This convention also adopted far-seeing resolutions recommending standards for woman and child labor and resolved that all clubs should study public sanitation. In 1900, the federation's convention dealt with industrial problems, conservation, and the merit system of the federal civil service, although this last issue was exhausted in a mere five minutes. In 1904, civil service was voted a major issue for the next biennium, but it was tied to improving conditions in state charitable institutions rather than to "honest and efficient government" per se.[24] By 1910, the cause of civil service was languishing in the clubs. The clubwomen's lack of interest seems to have been tied to the feeling that civil service reform was a male responsibility: "It borders on politics," one state report said, "and our men have spoken in no uncertain terms concerning it."[25] Women felt strongly that they had special skills and sensitivities to bring to civic improvement and were not particularly interested in tagging onto issues men already seemed to have covered. Municipal housekeeping, it appeared, could not be expanded indefinitely.

Clubwomen, in fact, argued that they played a special part in public life that men's clubs could not, namely, "the power to make, of any place in which [they] may happen to live, a home for all those who come there."[26] They argued that in countries where there was a real leisure class, well-to-do men did the reforming, but "in the United States men are caught up in business."[27] The social role assigned to women gave them a unique perspective on public problems. They suggested, in terms that sound surprisingly contemporary, that "although women under the same conditions as men would react the same, because their conditions have been different, their mind on politics will have its own viewpoint."[28] As Richard T. Ely, a noted reformer, observed: "[Women] are cold and unmoved when we [men] talk about municipal government as business, but when we bring forward the household ideal, they think of the children, and their powers are enlisted, and when they are once aroused you may be sure that something is going to happen!"[29]

Although men's and women's reform clubs often took up the same or similar problems, their approaches frequently differed. For one thing, not being voters, women had to employ what Robert Wiebe has called "a politics of indirection" that involved working through male officials and party members, with "women educating the public, men proposing the law, women arguing the case, men claiming the credit."[30] Men's and women's clubs also defined their goals and objectives differently and emphasized different aspects of urban reform. Men's clubs, preoccupied with the notion that the city was essentially a business corporation, tended to establish "good government" as their principal aim,[31] whereas women's clubs were more likely to speak in homely terms of improving the quality of community life. To differentiate themselves from party politics, which well-to-do men considered corrupt, men's clubs explicitly declared themselves to be nonpartisan. Not being voters, clubwomen apparently felt little need to assure people of their nonpartisan approach. Men's clubs also generally espoused business values, as when the City Club of New York described its aim as giving the city a "clean, business-like administration," and emphasized scientific investigation as their approach.[32] Similarly, "the common language of the [Chicago] City Club was business. The inherent morality of that language rested on concepts of responsibility and philanthropic duty."[33] In addition, men seemed more likely to characterize their activities in terms of investigation of, or watchfulness over, city affairs.[34] Women spoke of furnishing city government with "object lessons" from which it might learn.[35]

Women, as we have seen, talked in terms not of business but of making the city a home for all. Since homemaking was so firmly identified with womanhood, and since women's clubs used domesticity as a rationale for their entrance into the public sphere, their ideology points up the masculinity of men's business-oriented approach, a dimension that might otherwise go unremarked. Even when male reformers did not speak in specifically gendered terms, women's exclusion from business and the dichotomized ideologies of the two sexes highlighted the gender dimensions of their respective approaches. And frequently, male reformers did explicitly define their activities along gender lines. Arnaldo Testi notes that the new college-educated reformers defined reform as masculine in order to combat the anti-intellectualism of party work. They engaged in politics, but they distanced themselves from traditional party rites and loyalties. Direct relations to the administrative arm of government, such as those formed by municipal research bureaus and other groups determined to "cooperate" with government officials, enabled reformers in many cases to bypass the party structure. And administrative reform sometimes became an explicit part of the "strenuous life," as when Theodore Roosevelt held a conference at Harvard University in 1894 on "The Merit System and Manliness in Politics."[36]

Although men's and women's clubs undertook many of the same activities, the men's clubs characteristically conducted investigations of municipal corruption and inefficiency, such as probes by the City Club of Chicago into the city's police department and into municipal revenues. Men's clubs also emphasized legislation they were able to get passed or prevent from passing. The bulk of this legislation had to do with the revamping of governmental structures or with expenditures. The City Club of New York, for example, boasted of having "secured passage of the law extending the term of the mayor, comptroller, the borough presidents and the president of the board of aldermen from two to four years, thus doing away with political campaigns every two years and permitting each city administration to accomplish important public improvements and to carry out a definite policy."[37] The New York club defeated legislation that would have raised city employees' salaries and provided them with old-age pensions, "which would have involved a heavy and unnecessary burden upon the taxpayers of this city."[38] When women's clubs bragged about their accomplishments, they tended to point to improvements in health, sanitation, education, or other areas of social welfare, many of which did not require legislative action, and to speak of the quality of life rather than administrative reform or cost savings. At least in terms of imagery, women cleaned up city streets and playgrounds; men cleaned up governmental corruption.

Women also tended to understand some problems differently and to propose different solutions for them. For example, Maureen Flanagan's study comparing two Chicago reform clubs, one male and one female, reports that even though the two clubs were both composed of white, upper-middle-class people, the women's vision of city betterment differed from that of their male counterparts. One hot issue taken up by both sexes was garbage disposal, in particular, whether an existing garbage rendering plant should be taken over by the city government. The men's club consulted with outside experts and concentrated its investigation on what today would be called cost-benefit considerations. The men concluded that there was no evidence that city ownership would prove more efficient; therefore, the plant should remain in private hands. In contrast, the women studied the problem themselves. Mary McDowell of University Settlement, chair of the club's city waste committee, traveled to Europe to study alternative waste disposal methods.[39] The women's conclusions were based on the presumption that it was wrong to think of garbage disposal solely as a business. Rendering garbage required city residents to sort their refuse by hand, which the women believed was unhealthy. They recommended that garbage be incinerated instead. Their report argued: "The true measure . . . of efficiency . . . is not the financial returns . . . but the character of the service given."[40] The women's club favored municipal ownership and operation of garbage disposal on the basis that it would better serve the health and welfare of the city than private ownership, while the men argued that the good of the city would be served by maximizing private profit and minimizing government involvement.

Eventually, women's clubs expanded their work and policy advocacy from the local to the national level. After Hull House's Julia Lathrop became chief of the newly formed federal Children's Bureau in 1912, she established the bureau as the center of a network of women's organizations that included both settlement houses and clubs. Herself a member of the General Federation of Women's Clubs, Lathrop enlisted the clubs in a nationwide effort to improve the system of birth registration. Clubwomen went door to door to check the accuracy of existing records and lobbied for stronger registration laws and procedures. National women's groups formed child welfare committees linked to the bureau; this network supported policy advocacy that eventually resulted in passage of the first federal social welfare legislation, the Sheppard-Towner Act of 1921, which provided grants for states to set up clinics to disseminate health care advice to mothers before and after the birth of their babies.[41]

Although clubwomen based their activities on the accepted feminine social role, through their work, they came to see the difficulty of restricting their purview to traditionally female concerns. They continued to justify their activities as womanly, but over time, they broadened their scope considerably. "Women's problems" came eventually to include not only child welfare and education but also sanitation, transportation, wages, and hours of work—in other words, the full range of issues plaguing the cities of their day. They came to see women's problems as coextensive with human problems. At the same time, women grew increasingly restless under the limitations of a politics of indirection made necessary by their lack of the vote. As Mary Ritter Beard observed, women "first thought of working upon *him* to arouse *him* to a sense of *his* responsibilities. They went to see *him,* pointed out to *him* municipal needs, presented possible achievements, discussed with *him* party programs and the positions of various candidates and urged *him* to vote in harmony with the public welfare. Results were seldom satisfactory."[42] Realizing that women were too often ignored by politicians in search of votes, the General Federation of Women's Clubs finally approved in 1914 a resolution calling for women's suffrage. While clubwomen would continue to talk of "municipal housekeeping," they began to join the agitation for suffrage in the hope that, as voters, women would more readily win the attention of male politicians. As voters, however, women would no longer be able to justify their place in public life as special. Once they became theoretically equal, it became increasingly difficult to sell women's ideas as different, especially as morally superior (see chapter 4).

THE SETTLEMENT MOVEMENT

In the waning years of the nineteenth century, well-to-do men and women began to establish settlement houses in poor city neighborhoods. The first was Stanton

Coit's short-lived Neighborhood Guild on New York's Lower East Side, established in 1886. A year later, a small group of Smith College graduates founded the College Settlement Association. Other women's colleges quickly established chapters, but it took the women two years to open their first settlement house, also on the Lower East Side. That same year, Jane Addams and Ellen Gates Starr opened Hull House on South Halstead Street in Chicago. These early groups of settlers all seem to have been independently inspired by the example of London's Toynbee House, which had been established in 1884 on Christian Socialist principles to bring knowledge and enlightenment to the poor. Addams and Starr, Coit, and a number of other Americans had visited Toynbee House, where they were stirred by the social action possibilities of living and working with poor people. As news of the settlement idea spread, other houses sprang up. Coit's Neighborhood Guild was reorganized as University Settlement in 1891; in 1893, Lillian Wald established the Henry Street Settlement, also in New York. Among the six houses established between 1886 and 1891, there was a "settlement spirit" that led settlers with experience to assist others in establishing new houses.[43] By 1910, there were more than 400.

Although inspired by Toynbee House and other English settlements, from the first, the American settlers took a consciously different tack. They placed less emphasis on cultural uplift and more on teaching neighborhood residents practical skills. They were more interested than the English in using the settlement as a spur to wider social change. Finally, women played a much more important role in the American settlement movement. One English visitor commented: "The settlement conception in America is much wider than . . . here. It is not merely that the poor should be treated to Shakespeare readings, technical classes, free concerts, and charity organization fallacies [sic]. It is that every town should have at least one center of civic virtues. They are looked upon with pride by the trade unionists; their influence is always at the disposal of the champion of municipal reform; they have given public parks and playgrounds to cities."[44] Woods and Kennedy's *The Settlement Horizon* saw America's distinctive settlement spirit as compounded of religious fervor, "aspects toward unaffected human intercourse and outreaching mutual aid," the settlers' desire to put their higher education to good use, and a commitment to American political principles.[45]

American settlement house activities usually included amateur dramatics, singing groups, art classes, and the like, but from the first, the settlers saw their primary mission as the development of an understanding of the conditions and causes of poverty, especially by living with and learning from neighborhood residents themselves. By becoming neighbors of the poor, they would gradually become their friends; by sharing the experiences of the poor, they would be able to interpret neighborhood problems to those who currently did not understand them but might be able to make a difference.[46] They rejected the basic principle of charity work at the time, which was that poor people were poor because of individual character flaws. The settlement workers believed, instead, that most poor people were caught up in economic and political dynamics that dwarfed individual initiative and hard work. They believed that, as educated people, their role was to serve as the link between poor neighborhoods and the wider world. Looking back on her years in Greenwich Village, Mary Simkhovitch observed: "In the early 1900s sections of the city were more shut off from one another than now, as there were no subways and few automobiles, and the whole idea of 'neighborhood' was therefore more real."[47] Settlement workers documented problems and transmitted their findings to policy makers and other influential people, while establishing services and institutions that their communities wanted and needed. A brief review of some of their major accomplishments gives a sense of the magnitude of their impact:

- The first model public playground in the United States, "outside of the sand garden type," was established by Hull House in 1893.[48]
- The first juvenile court was instituted in 1899 through efforts centered at Hull House, with residents serving as the first probation officers, paid through private donations they raised themselves. Beginning with efforts on the part of Chicago clubwomen, who were shocked to learn that juveniles were routinely locked up with adult offenders, a committee drafted a bill that took nearly ten years to pass. Because the new law allocated no funds to pay the probation officers it authorized, the women raised the necessary funds. The first probation officer hired was a resident of Hull House. Not until eight years later did the county government finally assume responsibility for paying the salaries of probation officers.[49]
- Hull House was responsible for the first state government employment bureau. Concerned over the manner in which private employment bureaus were cheating naive immigrants, Hull House established its own employment bureau and lobbied the state government for the establishment of publicly funded bureaus.[50]
- Hull House pioneered in health and sanitation inspection. Residents investigated an unusual concentration of typhoid cases by inspecting 2,002 houses, supplemented with bacteriological research by Dr. Alice Hamilton, another Hull House resident. The published report prompted official inquiry into the activities of the Sanitary Bureau; eventually, five bureau workers were indicted for bribery, and four were charged with "inefficiency."[51] It is worth noting that this investigation predates Henry Bruere's scrutiny of municipal inefficiency in New York by several years.
- The first special-education classes in city schools were the result of efforts by the Henry Street Settlement in New York. Residents encouraged the work of Elizabeth Farrell, a local teacher interested in helping the retarded, and persuaded the Board of Education to permit her to teach a class of handicapped children and to provide funds for special equipment. In 1908, the board established a separate department for teaching the retarded.[52] In addition, Henry Street and its noted head resident, Lillian Wald, are famous for pioneering the visiting nurses program.

• New York's Greenwich House established a clinic for sick babies that eventually served as the catalyst for citywide care provided by the city government.[53]
• In 1908, Greenwich House's Congestion Committee sponsored an exhibit at the American Museum of Natural History on the harmful effects of overcrowding, which resulted in a State Commission on Congestion and the first meeting of the National City Planning Conference in 1910.
• University Settlement in New York set up a kindergarten, playground, library, vocational training classes, and summer school, all of which were eventually taken over by the city.

Settlement leaders pressed first local and then state and national governments to pay attention to conditions in poor neighborhoods and to adopt many of the measures they instigated. Mary Simkhovitch of College Settlement in New York reported: "In large cities, one settlement activity after another has been taken over by city government—training, kindergartens, playgrounds; public school functions; departments of health and of parks have expanded."[54] By 1914, George McAneny, president of the New York City Board of Aldermen, could say: "There is hardly a function of the settlement twenty years ago that has not passed into the hands of progressive city governments today. The settlement will always show the way, for it and the social worker represent the advance line of our progress."[55] Settlement leaders showed the way to governments by lobbying strenuously for new municipal ordinances and programs. They called for the regulation of housing and sanitation; they propagandized for closed sewers and adequate garbage collection; they argued for nurses in public schools, for school lunches, for use of school facilities after hours, for special-education classes. They called for minimum wage and maximum hour legislation, workers' compensation, and restrictions or outright prohibitions on child labor.[56]

Many settlement leaders joined with organized labor and other groups that were concerned about working conditions. Mary McDowell, who began her career teaching in the Hull House kindergarten and went on to head Chicago's University Settlement located "behind the stockyards," supported efforts to unionize meatpackers and made the settlement house a haven for workers and union leaders during the great strike of 1904.[57] Hull House was part of a network of organizations, including the Ladies Federal Union, that attacked conditions in the garment industry.[58] Frances Kellor of the College Settlement Association investigated profit-making employment agencies for women in Boston, Chicago, and New York, which led to several convictions. Kellor was later appointed chief investigator for New York State's Bureau of Industries and Immigration. Florence Kelley, associated first with Hull House and then with the Henry Street Settlement, served as Illinois' first factory inspector and later became head of the National Consumers' League, which tried to educate consumers to purchase only goods made under humane conditions.[59]

GENDER IN SETTLEMENT WORK

In contrast to British settlements, in the American settlement movement, women predominated numerically. Between 1886 and 1914, 60 percent of settlement residents were women. Most of these women were unmarried college graduates.[60] The median length of residence for all settlers was three years, but unmarried women spent an average of ten years in settlement work, and many remained for their entire adult lifetimes. For men, the more typical pattern was a short time in settlement residence during their twenties, then marriage and a career elsewhere.[61] Settlement house governing boards also reflected female majorities.[62]

There were structural factors contributing to these gender-based differences. In contrast to Britain, where male graduates of Oxford and Cambridge used settlement work as a predictable stepping-stone to careers in the civil service or electoral office, the U.S. civil service at this time was not considered attractive by elite American men; usually they felt compelled to leave settlement work after a short time to forge careers in the ministry, journalism, social work, or academia. Moreover, in British settlements, women were considered "helpers," having no college degrees and no prospect of career government service. American women with college degrees found settlement work to be a career opportunity they otherwise would have lacked. Although higher education was more open to them than to English women, as graduates, they had found little else to do except to return home, marry, and raise children. Encouraged by ideas of "true womanhood" to devote themselves to civic affairs, but barred from electoral politics, educated women found that settlement work represented a rare and welcome opportunity. Those who wanted to had a chance to gain entry into public posts because of the lack of a strong career civil service in the United States.[63]

Among settlement leaders in the United States, women were some of the most effective and well known. Jane Addams, Lillian Wald, Julia Lathrop, Florence Kelley, Grace and Edith Abbott, Mary McDowell, Mary Simkhovitch, and others were recognized leaders of the movement and in the forefront of its advocacy of social policies. Many went on to government service in positions that pioneered women's involvement in running public institutions. Strikingly, although some settlement houses were segregated by sex, a number led by women had both male and female members. One student of settlements comments that "men and women shared leadership positions in the first eight major settlements and the vast majority of the later leaders were women."[64] British Fabian socialist Beatrice Webb, who visited Hull House in 1898, wrote in her diary that "the residents consist in the main of strong-minded, energetic women, bustling about their various enterprises and professions, interspersed with earnest-faced, self-subordinating and mild-mannered men who slide from room to room apologetically." Among these "earnest but unprepossessing men" were Mackenzie King, later prime minister of Canada; the future cofounder of the University of California at Los Angeles; and George

Hooker, a journalist and longtime director of the Chicago City Club.[65] Albert J. Kennedy, himself a settlement pioneer, commented that compared to the "Hull-House stable," the young men of the settlements were "unwashed behind the ears."[66] Robert A. Woods, another American settlement leader, observed that in contrast to Britain, in the United States "there was a feeling that male settlement-house residents were, somehow, 'a group of exquisites.' "[67] Like other male reformers, men of the settlement houses endured the continuing suspicion that somehow their masculinity was deficient; they were unusual in their persistence in the face of such aspersions.

Women's settlements, according to Sklar, were "emphatically autonomous institutions. They permitted women reformers to draw upon male assistance without succumbing to their control. . . . Settlements served as a substitute for the political, professional, academic, and religious careers from which they were excluded by reason of their gender."[68] For women, then, settlement work became an opening into a form of public life they otherwise would have lacked, one they could justify, as had reforming clubwomen, as consistent with their appointed social role as guardians of public virtue. For men, settlement work represented a more equivocal choice, yet an apparently rewarding one.

THE SETTLEMENT VISION

Like clubwomen, women of the settlement movement often used metaphors of family and home, friendship and hospitality to characterize their activity, whereas the men of the movement tended to sound more like structural reformers, using terms like institution, ward, city, program, and career.[69] Overall, however, the settlers shared a moral vision that had a different emphasis than that of the administrative reformers. The men of the research bureaus and other structural reformers viewed government as a potential threat to individual liberty or as a service provider of last resort; settlement folk tended to see it as a potential guarantor of social rights. They were led to this position at least partly by their view of poverty as a social rather than an individual problem. If poverty were socially caused, then it had to be socially ameliorated, an enterprise in which government would have to play a crucial and leading role. Thus settlement residents and other women active in reform causes were more likely than their male counterparts in the research bureaus to interpret reform as involving expansion of government functions rather than their contraction in order to lower taxes and save money.

Holding the state directly responsible for social welfare, women of the settlements were able to interpret economy and efficiency in a less narrow way than male municipal reformers often did. Their concern for administrative reform was always tied to their recognition of the importance of policy implementation. Julia Lathrop, longtime resident of Hull House and the first woman to head a federal agency, commented: "The growing tendency to enact social legislation is crucial in its need of a new public conscience as to public administration."[70] Bureaucrats would have to be caring, in much the same way that parents were, if policies were to be successful. For example, probation systems should be kept out of politics and staffed by people who thought of themselves as mothers to the children under their supervision. When settlers advocated civil service reform, it was so that new policies would be more likely to improve daily life for city residents and workers. Sophonisba Breckinridge, a Hull House resident and pioneer in social work education, wrote in one of her textbooks that economy and efficiency meant something different "in their application to public welfare" than they did in business and industry: "In the latter fields the profit-seeking impulse makes the balance sheet the final criterion. In political and domestic organization, human well-being under conditions of justice, freedom, and equality, are the objects sought, and business administration can never be the guide to truly successful organization."[71]

Settlement women adopted this stance because, like clubwomen, they accepted the notion that women had a special place in society as guardians of public virtue, nurturers, and civic housekeepers. They argued that their role gave them the moral authority both to act directly and to advocate government action. As Jane Addams said, settlement women saw their work not as philanthropy but as fulfilling "the duties of good citizenship."[72] Their direct knowledge of urban conditions and the misery of poor people's lives issued a moral commandment that they felt compelled to heed. Commenting on the findings of an early-twentieth-century tenement house commission, Lillian Wald said: "Reading these things must bring a sense of fairness outraged. . . . Say to yourself, Is there a wrong in our midst, what can I do? Do I owe reparation?"[73] In addition, they saw the problems of the poor as affecting all of society. Julia Lathrop defended the Childrens' Bureau investigation of infant mortality on the grounds that it was "fundamental to social welfare, of popular interest, and [served] a real human need."[74]

Like clubwomen, settlement women believed that while men's interests diverged and conflicted with one another, women of all classes converged on the basis of maternal values. Therefore, women reformers had a strong sense of community. Dr. Alice Hamilton, occupational health and safety pioneer and longtime resident of Hull House, said that living in a settlement made it impossible "to divide people into sections and file them away in labelled cubby-holes."[75] The settlements saw their most central responsibility as the creation of neighborhood spirit that would bring people of different nationalities together and foster shared feelings of citizenship.

Clearly, it is important not to take the settlement residents' interpretations of their work entirely at face value or to canonize them because they had a broader approach than the men of the research bureaus. A number of recent scholars have pointed to evidence of settlement racial, ethnic, and class prejudices. For example, Gwendolyn Mink sees women reformers as interested in Americanizing immigrants by educating them about American habits and values; their gender-based policies, Mink argues, left race- and class-based discrimination in place. Elizabeth

Lasch-Quinn interprets the settlement movement in terms of a "tragic failure . . . to redirect its energies toward its black neighbors." Ruth Hutchinson Crocker's study of second-tier settlements seeks to correct what she calls the "heroic account" by pointing to the settlements' failure to alter existing structures of economic and political power. Like Mink and others, she sees settlement workers as "missionaries for the American way. . . . The goal was 'adjusting their life to ours.' "[76]

Although settlement residents harbored racial and ethnic prejudices and may have been too sanguine about their ability to transcend class differences, there is no question that part of their sense of the public interest was based on what they perceived to be concerns of home and family that they hoped would unite women whatever their material circumstances.

SETTLEMENT WORK AND MUNICIPAL RESEARCH

Both the men and women of the settlement movement and the men (and occasional women) of the research bureaus believed that they were reforming urban society generally and municipal government in particular. Both groups gradually became disillusioned with electoral politics after a series of contests in which the reform candidates they backed were either defeated outright or ousted after only one term in office, and either turned to or persisted in alternative strategies. "I never go into a tenement without longing for a better city government," settlement worker Jane Robbins once remarked.[77] Both settlement workers and municipal reformers espoused general goals having to do with improving the quality of urban life.[78] And members of the two movements knew one another, interacted regularly, belonged to many of the same organizations, read the same newsletters and journals. Many settlement workers joined reform organizations led by business and professional men, formed to encourage honest and efficient city government. Settlement workers in New York, Boston, and Chicago worked with businessmen to revise antiquated city charters. They also served as resources and advisers in various municipal reform efforts, including electoral campaigns.[79] Thus female and male social reformers shared the municipal arena with male structural and administrative reformers. The two approaches went on side by side, sometimes even intertwined.

For example, some of the men who later became prominent in the research bureau movement and other aspects of municipal reform studied social work. In 1901, William Allen, soon to become a leader of the New York Bureau of Municipal Research, attended the New York School of Philanthropy, a pioneering effort to educate people for social work, where he heard lectures by Lillian Wald and Mary Simkhovitch, as well as group discussions by settlement house residents about their experiences.[80] Other men who went on to prominent places in the research bureaus or other aspects of the growing enterprise of "public administration" were associated with settlement houses. Frank Goodnow, whose theory about the separation between politics and administration more directly inspired research bureau men than did Woodrow Wilson's now better known essay, served on the council of University Settlement in New York and was "strongly influenced by the settlement idea of neighborhood reconstruction." Charles Beard, associated with the New York Bureau of Municipal Research and its director for a short time, was profoundly influenced by his association with the settlement movement: "I was introduced to a new world at meetings in the Hull-House in the summer of 1896," he later recalled.[81] Rufus Miles, who headed the Cincinnati bureau, spent two years at Boston's South End House after graduating from college and then became head resident of Cleveland's Goodrich House. John Gaus, who became a prominent researcher and theorist in public administration after the Progressive Era, was also a settlement resident as a young man.[82] Charles Merriam, member of President Franklin D. Roosevelt's Committee on Administrative Management and a major figure in the development of public administration education, taught a course at John Elliott House in Chicago.[83]

Most strikingly, Henry Bruere, founding director of the New York Bureau, the municipal research movement's model, had been a resident of Denison House in Boston, where he was director of boys' clubs. Bruere had made frequent visits to New York settlements and was profoundly influenced by Robert Hunter of New York's University Settlement. Through Hunter's good offices, he met Stanley McCormick, who persuaded him to come to Chicago to apply settlement approaches to the McCormick Works. In Chicago, Bruere associated with settlement leaders such as Jane Addams and Graham Taylor and often visited Hull House. He studied their investigative methods, which he applied to his work at the Bureau of City Betterment and the New York Bureau of Municipal Research (see chapter 4).

Settlement leaders and residents also worked closely with men who were prominent in the research bureau movement or other aspects of municipal reform. For example, James B. Reynolds of New York's University Settlement was one of the founders of the Citizens' Union headed by R. Fulton Cutting, president of the New York Bureau. The two worked together with others to elect reform candidate Seth Low as mayor of New York. After Low was finally elected in 1901, Reynolds headed an informal brain trust of social workers who spurred Low toward expansion of the social welfare functions of the city government. Raymond Fosdick, who had been a resident at the Henry Street Settlement, became John Purroy Mitchel's assistant when Mitchel was commissioner of accounts, at the time of the founding of the New York Bureau. Fosdick went on to hold this position himself under Mayor William Gaynor. When Mitchel became mayor in 1914, he appointed as commissioner of correction Katherine B. Davis, who had been head resident of College Settlement in Philadelphia.[84]

In Chicago, Jane Addams, Julia Lathrop, and Graham Taylor worked with a group of business and professional men to establish the Civic Federation. One of the principal aims of this organization was to drive the "boodlers" out of the city council. Its failure led to the founding of the Municipal Voters' League, where settlement leaders continued to play important roles. They led in the effort to ferret

out the records of candidates for city offices and in the fight for municipal ownership of the street railway system. Hull House became the headquarters for a citywide campaign.[85]

Bruere referred to the trained staff of the New York Bureau of Municipal
Research as "social workers, expert accountants and investigators."[86] William Allen
called the bureau "an outpost for social workers . . . a unifying force to make effective the interest of those who wish 'good government.' "[87] Thus the connections
between settlement work and the municipal research bureaus were many. Despite
these close connections, however, men of the New York Bureau from time to time
displayed notable ignorance and stereotypical thinking about women's civic and
reform activities. Allen urged women to get involved in improving city life as if
they were still sitting at home, even though *The Survey* and its predecessor, *Charities and the Commons,* had been filled since the beginning of the century with
reports about women's many and varied civic activities. For example, Allen commented: "There is a tradition that women and pins are congenial. I hope it is true,
because one of the best next steps for women, whether they vote or not, is to make
'pin maps' to describe graphically the social work in which they are most interested."[88] A review of Allen's book *Women's Part in Government* commented sarcastically: "If one did not know who wrote [it,] the most sympathetic friend
possible as well as the not-yet-voter would say, it is a book evidently written with
all the prejudices of ages gone by, from a distinctly masculine point of view for
the masculine reader. . . . Dr. Allen gives his positive assurance that women will
have the vote, whether they want it or not; it is one of the inevitable things he does
not seem able to prevent."[89] Like Allen, Frederick Cleveland argued that "the social-
ized natural instinct and social convention" made women better fit than men in
such areas as public health, care of the defective, and education. "Likewise the
nature of woman fits her especially for the administration of charity . . . while the
man has business qualifications superior to those of women."[90]

As subsequent chapters suggest, it is likely that several ideas that became central to the research bureau movement had their origins in settlement houses. These
close ties between the two movements show that they did not grow up in isolation
from each other; rather, they began in close connection and later diverged, for reasons that will become clear as the story proceeds.

During the first decade of the twentieth century, clubwomen and settlement residents shared with municipal government reformers a vision of the close link
between good government and social welfare and other philanthropic work. And
in many cases, they shared organs of information and exchange. Yet, as this chapter suggested, the two groups developed distinctive interpretations of the most
promising approach to improving city life. Although men's and women's reform
clubs came into existence ostensibly for the same purposes, they interpreted these
broad purposes quite differently—men's clubs emphasizing structural reforms and

making city government more like a business, and women's clubs emphasizing the improvement of living conditions and making the city more like a home. Settlement residents and other social welfare advocates attacked what they took to be basic causes of poverty and pressed governments to start new programs and offer expanded services, while municipal researchers operated on the principle that government would continue to be ineffective if better administrative methods were not found and instituted.

Reformers who viewed the city as a business claimed that the ultimate aim of government reform was the improvement of city life, while those who viewed the city as a home accepted the importance of efficiency and effective administrative methods. For a few years, substance and procedure were intertwined in reform work, just as male and female members of reform clubs and settlement houses interacted with one another in what, despite variations, they viewed as a common cause. One can imagine that men's and women's approaches to reform might have grown closer as the years passed, and that an applied field might have developed in which expertise in and dedication to amelioration of social ills marched shoulder to shoulder with expertise in and dedication to better administrative methods. Over time, however, the interconnection of procedure and substance weakened, particularly among the research bureau members and other structural reformers. The previous chapter suggested that a split between purpose and procedure began to be evident in research bureau work almost immediately; this was a gulf that widened over time, for a number of reasons, but finally became institutionalized by the dynamics of professionalization that established public administration and social work as separate fields. As it happened, in these dynamics there turned out to be no place in either profession for policy advocacy or the improvement of living conditions. In order to understand this development, however, we must first take a closer look at contrasts between the woman-oriented social welfare arena and the work of the municipal research bureaus.

4

Two Philosophies

Although at first they may not have been conscious of it, the men of the New York Bureau of Municipal Research and the other bureaus that followed its lead were not just improving government methods, they were framing a new way of thinking about government. Theirs was an understanding of government that for the first time undertook sustained consideration of the role of administration, its place in public life.[1] A central question for the bureau men became the relationship between administrative and political values.[2] A quest for administrative efficiency and effectiveness, which were the bureau men's watchwords and the basis of their attack on existing governments, strongly implied the existence of correct answers to administrative questions, while democratic government appeared to be premised on inclusion and the resolution of competing interests through processes such as voting and lobbying. Democratic processes might sometimes result in least-cost, effective answers to public questions, but this was not their point. In fact, the bureau men's principal charge against city governments of the time was, in effect, that they were too democratic—too bent on including people of questionable intelligence and morality and not concerned enough about whether taxes were being put to the best use.

If there were right answers to questions of administrative effectiveness, then management of public agencies required not party loyalty or patriotic fervor but managerial expertise. The need for expertise became the administrative reformers' justification for their own place in public life. Given the American public's deep skepticism about the power exercised by giant corporations, the rationalization promised by professional management tamed the idea of hierarchical organization and made it fit for democracy.[3] Not arbitrary authority but facts would rule—facts supplied by administrative experts like the men of the research bureaus. The need for expertise, in turn, raised the problem of how to furnish governments with an adequate supply of experts and define the appropriate content of their expertise—

leading to a move toward the professionalization of government administration and establishment of the training that would make it so. The philosophy of administration implicit and explicit in the words and actions of the bureau men formed the basis for the establishment of public administration as a profession and for the university training that evolved to ensure it.

The bureau men's philosophy, however, cannot be understood adequately outside of its context. The political theory at the heart of the bureau movement springs into bolder relief when set next to settlement and clubwomen's philosophy of public life and the role of administration in it. Comparing the two, we see how deliberate the bureau men's choices were and what the rationales behind at least some of them might have been.

THE BUSINESS OF GOVERNMENT

The extent to which business served as the model for government reformers in the Progressive Era has been a matter of controversy among historians and political scientists. Samuel Hays and James Weinstein are notable for stressing a heavy degree of business influence, while Kenneth Fox characterizes the municipal reform movement as bureaucratic but not necessarily businesslike in its orientation.[4] Regardless of the thrust of municipal reform overall, however, the research bureau movement in particular reflects not only consistent interest in making government agencies more like businesses but also a view of *city* government, at least, as little different from a business corporation. Dayton, Ohio, industrialist John H. Patterson declared in 1896 that "a city is a great business enterprise whose stockholders are the people,"[5] and bureau reformers took this viewpoint as their watchword.

The most consistent bureau spokesman for a view of the city as a business was accountant Frederick A. Cleveland: "Considered administratively," he wrote, "the elements of successful management of municipal enterprise are the same as the elements of successful management of private enterprise."[6] The differences between the two, Cleveland maintained, were differences not of principle but of methods. By methods, however, Cleveland meant issues such as how city government was to be controlled and how its benefits were to be distributed—both long-standing topics in political philosophy. He argued that the world of profit-making business was the source of growing public interest in governmental efficiency and good management, as "rules of private thrift were translated into principles of public well-being."[7] The requirements for sound government management were business requirements, that is, the problems were largely administrative rather than political: "The success of public administration depends on ability intelligently to direct and control the millions of details rather than ability to organize and crystallize popular opinion in support of political theories."[8] For Cleveland, "politics" always meant party politics; on this basis, public administration could be considered nonpolitical.

Cleveland's codirectors of the New York Bureau shared his views, although William Allen made the argument in terms of government modeling itself after efficient charitable organizations—which in turn modeled themselves after businesses. Henry Bruere's study of commission government detailed the accomplishments of ten cities that "had discard[ed] the old political makeshifts of public administration to adopt business methods in imitation of private enterprise."[9] The view of city government as more business than politics did not, however, prevent the bureau men from arguing that their approach and their recommendations were consistent with democracy. Cleveland presented the argument as follows: The business of government is public welfare. There are both political and nonpolitical (administrative and technical) sides to public business. Regardless of what part the general public plays in the political aspects, the administrative side must be conducted by authorized agents. These agents are public trustees, whose actions to fulfill their trust are dependent on the effective use of factual evidence, facts that should also be available to the public at large. In Cleveland's eyes, the bureau approach could be seen as democratic, first, because it enabled officials to fulfill their public trust competently, and second, because the same facts that supported the work of officials would also be made available to the public as a matter of principle.[10]

The role of the public in the bureau men's scheme, however, was a carefully circumscribed one, derived from the view of government as a corporation. Again, the chief exponent was Cleveland, whose two books on political theory articulated a notion of government in which citizens were the ultimate source of governmental legitimacy and power but had little actual hand in government operations beyond voting. Cleveland presented the founding of the United States as analogous to the initiation of a business enterprise. "The people" took on "self-government" by "incorporat[ing] themselves for purposes of public business. . . . [T]hey decided what agents they would employ and assumed the right to select their own trustees; they executed to their business agents limited deeds of trust, and made these . . . revokable at will."[11] The idea of the citizen as stockholder in a public corporation appears throughout his work.[12]

But there was a problem, Cleveland maintained, with taking this scheme too literally, for most citizens knew little about government and confined their involvement mainly to casting votes at election time or complaining.[13] Society had become more complex and government more removed from citizens, who had occupied themselves with the pursuit of private gain and lost sight of public needs. "Not until the last few years," Cleveland declared, "when increased burdens of taxation have fixed attention on public administration, have the people stopped to inquire whether multiplied duties and responsibilities of citizenship have been attended to."[14] But citizen complaints by themselves would do little to enforce governmental responsibility and effectiveness, nor would the average citizen's criticism carry much force: "Petitions and remonstrances which are effective are those which come from organizations that represent the opinion of a community or of a class in the community which must be respected in a government by majorities."[15]

In other words, what average citizens needed was an organization, or group of organizations, that could get the attention of government: an organization made up of "public-spirited men of means"[16]—that is, something like a municipal research bureau. Cleveland characterized the bureaus' role vis-à-vis average citizens this way: "Citizens who have acquired wealth have, to a degree before unknown in history, devoted themselves to constructive civic education, to finding out what are the welfare needs of the community or the nation, to founding laboratories of research, to maintaining staffs of trained experts as a means of developing facts about social conditions, for the purpose of enabling citizens to think intelligently about questions of community welfare."[17]

Research bureaus and other reform groups were the result of efforts on the part of "natural leaders of men" who had become aware of the necessity for taking action and of their obligation as citizens to be the ones to act[18]—a noblesse oblige of sorts. Citizen organizations—meaning groups of "public-spirited men"—would "keep in touch with the details of public business . . . [obtain] definite unbiased information . . . [make it] available to citizens at large . . . [and thereby assist] materially in keeping officers in touch with what was being done by employees." To do this required citizen groups like the bureaus to place themselves "in the attitude of cooperation with the official who is trying to do his duty, instead of seeking to use such information as is obtained for the purpose of creating a public opinion . . . which would . . . make it more difficult for those in office to discharge their functions effectively."[19] Research bureaus and other organized reformers would somehow identify key officials who wanted to improve administrative efficiency but were hampered in doing so by outmoded administrative mechanisms and, by cooperating with them to modernize agency processes such as accounting and purchasing, enable these officials to reach the goal of better agency management.

A careful reading of Cleveland's political theory makes it clear that not all citizens, in his scheme, played the same part in government. The mass of citizens would continue to serve in a somewhat theoretical fashion as the fount of government legitimacy. A much smaller group of well-to-do, well-educated citizens would actively participate in government. In fact, Cleveland characterized the municipal research bureaus as a new form of citizen participation in administration, with government officials requesting citizen assistance and the bureaus as the mechanism: a "citizen organization which is equipped with technical staff and which employs a method of research adapted to the purpose."[20]

Out of context, it is possible to read Cleveland and other bureau leaders as more democratic than they actually were. Their talk of "citizen participation" and "citizen cooperation with government" can ring in our ears in a way the bureau men did not intend. Thus, when Cleveland posed the challenge, " As citizens your business is public business. Have you been mindful of it?" we need to hear it in the context of his reliance on "recognized leaders" to shape the substantive content of citizen participation, and to note that Cleveland posed this challenge in a speech to the Real Estate Board of Brokers.[21] It might have had a different flavor if it had been delivered at a political rally or at the meeting of a neighborhood block club. Bruere's writings display understandings of citizenship similar to Cleveland's. When he talks of "citizen organizations," he means municipal research bureaus and not the kinds of grassroots organizations the term might connote today.[22]

The bureau men's understanding of citizenship has to be considered in the context of the Progressive understanding of the term "the public" not as the citizenry at large but as the third member of a troika that also included "business" and "labor." The public consisted of "social workers, journalists, lawyers, educators, and other middle-class opinion makers who were supposed to represent some disinterested general will."[23] Having rejected the Democratic Party because it served working-class immigrants and the Republican Party because it served big business and finance capitalists, Progressives identified themselves and those of similar background and interests as "the public" and their opinions as "the public interest." Such ideas embodied the Progressive vision of a classless society, where differences could be transcended under the rationalizing and harmonizing guidance of expert professionals.

Among the men of the New York Bureau, the only possible exception is William Allen, who was readier than his colleagues to entertain the possibility that working people of limited education might be able to understand governmental processes. Allen saw government as the greatest philanthropic organization and modeled his understanding of it on the kinds of charitable organizations he knew best. After receiving his doctoral degree from the University of Pennsylvania in 1901, Allen joined the State Charity Aid Association of New Jersey. His administration there, *Charities and the Commons* reported, was marked by energetic efforts toward "more efficient administration of public charities."[24] In 1903, Allen was appointed general secretary of the Association for Improving the Conditions of the Poor (AICP), which had been founded in 1843 by Robert M. Hartley, a wealthy Presbyterian merchant. The AICP was the precursor of the "charity organization society" movement that began in 1877 and produced a host of organizations in America's cities formed to exert social control over the urban poor by practicing what became known as "scientific charity."[25] Since its founding, the AICP had been at the center of a quest by intellectuals and businessmen to bring order to urban life by creating institutions and machinery of control. In the 1850s, the AICP had managed to get asylums and orphanages built at county expense; in the 1870s, it had succeeded in persuading New York to terminate municipal outdoor relief.[26]

According to Roy Lubove, "no charity organization leader was more convinced of the moral roots of poverty than Robert M. Hartley." He and his successors saw charity as the city's "surest safeguard against revolution." Scientific charity implied "the efficient organization of the philanthropic resources of the community. Efficiency depended upon the adoption of those techniques of functional specialization and centralized coordination and administration that characterized the business world."[27] Using business techniques, charity workers would reform poor people through the good offices of "friendly visitors" who would "coordinate, investigate and counsel" rather than provide material relief.[28] The visitor's primary duty was to canvass his or her territory (in its early years, AICP visitors, in contrast to those of later charity organization societies, were all males), visit the poor, "probe their habits of life for flaws and weaknesses," make them aware that the roots of their suffering lay in their own feckless behavior, offer encouragement, and, finally, "file a report with the AICP central office to prevent their obtaining charitable relief elsewhere under false pretenses."[29]

Robert Hartley was a hero to William Allen, and his approach was Allen's model for philanthropy. Hartley's career, Allen wrote in *Efficient Democracy,* "epitomises in a helpful degree the motives and methods upon which successful charitable work in our own time must rely."[30] Allen praised Hartley's penchant for fact gathering and his mentor's ability to use facts to persuade, such as when he traced high infant mortality in New York City to the practice of feeding cows distillery slops, which lowered the food value of the milk. But, Allen noted, Hartley's organization had failed to keep pace with the demands of modern city life because Hartley insisted on relying on volunteer visitors instead of a paid staff—hence the advent of the Charity Organization Society, which improved on the AICP's approach by hiring staff, coordinating charitable work throughout the city, keeping better records, and in general applying what Allen called "the efficiency test" to all its efforts.[31] According to Allen, the AICP got on the efficiency bandwagon in 1897, when its general agent at the time, Frank Tucker (who became a founding officer of the New York Bureau of Municipal Research), began to reorganize the AICP staff and administrative practices to make them more businesslike, a process that Allen himself enthusiastically continued when he took over the organization's leadership. Allen concludes his forty-page story of the AICP's evolution with this object lesson: "Efficiency in charitable work requires constant tests of worker, of director, and of work itself. . . . [E]very contributor [should] apply efficiency tests to any society's appeals, to its annual statements, or to its answers to specific questions. When those responsible for the direction of charitable work substitute result for motive, efficiency for goodness, as a test of their own efficiency—then and only then will charitable work have more general and more generous support."[32]

Although he was thoroughly immersed in the idea of making philanthropy businesslike, Allen's commitment to efficiency testing made him, somewhat paradoxically, more of a democrat at heart than his colleagues, especially Cleveland. Efficiency, because it was objective, was something anyone could learn to practice. Devoted to modeling charitable and governmental organizations on private business, Allen still recognized the average citizen's potential to join in efficiency work. He observed: "Given a hundred so-called best citizens in a millionaire's parlour, and a hundred frequenters of a Bowery saloon, and it would be a rash man who would feel sure that the average intelligence as to government, its needs, its justice, its methods is higher in the parlour than in the saloon" (264). The average person's lack of involvement, Allen argued, could be traced to inertia and lack of information rather than innate inability; realistically, however, only an "active minority" would be likely to work to improve government. The problem was how to use the efforts of this small group most efficiently—how to promote "efficient citizenship" (265).

Allen's answer was "to get facts, verify facts, base our conclusions on facts, and then publish them so as to enlighten and convince public opinion" (268). For Allen, educated public opinion was a tremendous resource for positive change, enabling a small cadre of leaders to marshal support for their recommendations by enlightening the citizenry: "To harness a whole community to an idea is infinitely better than to try to carry it alone" (270). The possibility of disagreement about what to do seems never to have occurred to Allen, convinced as he was of the power of what he saw as indisputable information to rouse public support.

The idea of "fact publication" became the basis for the aspect of the New York Bureau's work that its leaders characterized as civic education. As Bruere argued, "Fact publication is unquestionably the most effective means available to citizens for maintaining control over government."[33] The bureau men depended on publicizing government inefficiency and immorality as a major element in their reform strategy, at least in the organization's first decade. Allen argued that the problem with city governments was not so much politics as it was politics "working out of sight." Since one could not get rid of politics, the next best thing was "a public well enough informed to put a premium on politics in the open."[34] For most citizens, then, their civic obligation lay in informing themselves about their governments. Now that it was realized that public business, in large measure, was administrative rather than political, citizenship could be considered a sort of business, too: citizens would "seek to inform themselves concerning the problems of management which public officials are called upon to solve."[35]

The bureau men disagreed not about the need for efficient citizenship but about how extensively it might be applied. Allen had the broadest idea, Cleveland the narrowest. Allen spoke consistently of a variety of approaches to civic work, with some citizens "urging, some protesting, some teaching, some blazing trails."[36] Cleveland's view of citizenship was considerably more constricted. He thought that for all practical purposes, "the people" meant "the business people." It was they who had taken upon themselves the responsibility for improving city governments by investigating administrative practices.[37] In between Allen and Cleveland was Bruere, who thought that "civic intelligence need not depend upon making every public-spirited inhabitant of a city a fact depository regarding city business." Organizations would mainly do the work of securing efficient government, especially the "citizen-supported fact center[s]" like the New York Bureau. The bureau men would perform the investigations out of which reforms would flow, and the rest of the citizenry would show its efficiency by "readiness to understand facts and to cooperate when special problems arise."[38]

The differences between Allen and Cleveland were obscured in the bureau's early days, but they assumed a high profile once John D. Rockefeller laid down his ultimatum (see chapter 2). Part of the reason that Allen, the publicist, had such a free hand prior to 1914 may have been that publicizing the shortcomings of the New York City government played a big part in the bureau's early successes. Although not all the press coverage the bureau received was favorable, much of it was, and glowing newspaper accounts stimulated interest in other cities about municipal research as a reform strategy. In addition, from 1911 to 1913, Cleveland was away from New York, heading up President Taft's Commission on Economy and Efficiency.[39] His absence gave Allen more maneuvering room. But after the bureau bowed to Rockefeller's order to curtail publicity and become more soberly scientific, Cleveland and Allen (the latter having left the bureau to form a rival research organization) sniped back and forth at each other in print about their respective understandings of civic education. Allen's associate, Edward Fitzpatrick, argued that the bureau movement had been based from the beginning on the idea of "civic education for adults" and that publicity had been "the primary method of awakening citizens to a demand for improved public administration." But now that effort was "shipwrecked."[40] Cleveland retorted that although it was true that the "policy of regular rapid fire, 'punch and pepper' publicity had been deliberately abandoned," this did not mean that the bureau had given up on the idea of interesting citizens in the work of their government, only that Allen's idea of publicity was superficial and had not had as many concrete results as hoped. The bureau had abandoned the earlier approach, but it was still informing citizens through its monthly magazine, *Municipal Research,* and other periodic reports. It now believed that civic education should be based on the results of "long, painstaking and expert studies such as certain municipal reformers cannot endure." In fact, Cleveland argued, the shift was the result of the bureau's successes. Ten years ago, "flamboyant announcement" might have been needed because the public was less well informed. "We have made progress. The ordinary city official as well as citizen has come to have a more intimate knowledge of public affairs. No callow youth equipped with a little 'research lingo' can educate the government or help the citizen."[41] Fitzpatrick's rejoinder was that the controversial publicity, particularly the "Efficient Citizenship" postcards, had been "evidence of a spirit to inform the citizenship generally," an aim that was more important than imposing business methods on government agencies. Now bureaus of municipal research were "no longer agencies of citizen inquiry but co-operative agencies with public officials. . . . [T]he larger service was in the original conception."[42]

Clearly, after Rockefeller ordered the bureau to mend its ways or face the loss of his support, there was a shift in the organization's priorities and approach. The question is, how big a shift? Was the bureau a crusading organization aimed at broad-based citizen education and participation that underwent a major sea change in the face of pressure from a wealthy donor? Or was the shift a less fundamental one? How democratic was the philosophy of the bureau men?

SCIENTIFIC KNOWLEDGE

As we have seen, municipal researchers based their approach to reform on the idea that, in generating knowledge about and for public agencies, they were serving the interests of democracy. In their world, there was no tension between science and politics. Henry Bruere said that the bureau "sees in the science of government an opportunity of continuous interest for democracy. . . . It seeks to awaken popular intelligence, not about political principles, but with respect to current acts and omissions of governmental agencies."[43] Frederick Cleveland argued: "The great political campaigns of today are campaigns for facts, for publicity, for light, for the keeping and the preservation of records by which the responsibility of every person connected with the government may be proved, for making these records public records."[44] Systematic investigation of governmental processes furthered democracy because it opened up government to the people's scrutiny.

Elite reformers like the bureau men seized on "science" as a rationale for their criticism of existing governments partly because it supported their argument that the control exerted by political machines, which awarded government jobs and contracts on the basis of favoritism, worked only when it operated out of sight. Science, in contrast, worked on principles of objectivity, visibility, and openness. Investigation, the uncovering of facts about existing practices, would serve democracy by bringing misdeeds and incompetence out in the open. "The modern municipal grafter thrives best in silence and in darkness. He desires no language that may leaven popular ignorance as to his doings."[45] The cure for this lack of public accountability was to end the grafter's ability to "work and trade and plan in secret," Allen argued. The public, once exposed to facts about government, would learn to pay attention to them, "just as it uses trolleys and subways for distances it once used to walk. There is something about facts which opens the public eye and something too about an open public eye which hungers for more facts."[46] Therefore, the bureau men could maintain that by furnishing the public with facts about government, they were strengthening public spirit and fostering active citizenship. Science was the perfect banner under which to lead the march against machine politics, because the objectivity that characterized the scientific approach was a living reproach to the kind of quid pro quo politics that depended on operating out of sight. "Science," declared Cleveland, "is a codification of exactly determined commonsense. . . . The end of science is to establish conclusions that may be accepted without question for purposes of research or instruction."[47] Because politics has no established method of analysis, there is no system by which consensus can be reached, but administration can and must develop such a method. It must become a science.

Besides enabling administration to separate itself from politics, the banner of science turned the bureau men from "man milliners" into muscular crusaders, utterly distinctive in comparison to the usual run of female and feminized male do-gooders. According to Cleveland, the best thing about America's many research bureaus was their "virility."[48] The bureau men insisted that they were not "volunteers" in the normal sense, but expert scientists. Volunteers were people who acted on the basis of emotions rather than reason; by extension, volunteers were amateurs rather than professional experts armed with scientific knowledge.[49] The gender implications of the distinction between the volunteer and the professional would have been clear to reformers of both sexes. "The new city government will not permit public service to remain an avocation, a pastime, a way station," declared Bruere, "but will establish it as a technical, professional pursuit progressively developing increased efficiency. . . . So long as government remains inefficient, volunteer and detached effort to remove social handicaps will continue a hopeless task."[50] The key to effective reform was science.

The net result of unearthing facts about government, in the bureau men's eyes, would be "efficiency." As Samuel Haber has shown, to persuade an early-twentieth-century audience that something was efficient was to win it over. Efficiency was self-evidently good. But what was it? Haber demonstrates that the term had a multitude of connotations, and vagueness about its meaning in a particular instance increased its power by enabling listeners to invest it with their own favorite content.[51] Given how the term impressed people of the time, especially well-to-do people, efficiency frequently had a taken-for-granted quality in the bureau men's writings. But to the extent they defined it, the term typically implied the existence of precise standards by which government performance could be assessed—usually, standards that enabled the public to judge the outcome achieved for tax dollars spent. Reformer John Allder Dunaway, for example, said that "efficiency . . . involves the setting up of definite standards by which progress can be measured."[52] Allen argued in favor of information that would show the public "what we get, what it is worth and what it costs."[53] Anticipating the possibility that such standards could lead simply to more bureaucratic inefficiency, Jesse Burks of the Philadelphia Bureau argued that "formulation of standards is open to the charge of being useless 'red tape' only when the standards are of the expression of arbitrary opinion; not when they are the result of scientific determination."[54] When arrived at through scientific methods—that is, ones that made it possible for the full situation to be known and responsibility for every act to be assigned—efficiency would "necessarily follow."[55] Somewhat more pointedly, Allen defined the kind of knowing in which the bureau men were interested as "*not mere feeling sure. Knowing becomes evidence when it is able to prove the truth to those who do not know and who do not want to know.*"[56]

The bureau men felt that it was the undeniability of scientific truth that gave it its power. Ordinary politics consisted of useless and wasteful wrangling over the meaning of situations and what to do about them. Science, in contrast, would untangle and clarify situations and make their solutions obvious. This approach permitted municipal researchers to maintain that they were not trying to assign blame for inefficiency and waste but simply trying to straighten things out. "Waste and inefficiency in government is [*sic*] the natural result of inability on the part of citizens and on the part of officers serving them to think intelligently about questions which are presented for expression of opinion and for action," Cleveland declared.[57] The problem was simply lack of accurate information. The impersonality of the scientific method, "discovering and publishing facts," demonstrated that the investigators intended to help, not to find fault.[58]

The kind of information they meant included "knowledge about what public officials are doing, what they spend, what they accomplish by their spending, and what they leave undone that could be accomplished. Record of work done and money spent must be made at the time work is done and money spent. The story must be told first, by those who work and spend. Then both record and story must be read, understood, summarized and used by supervising officials."[59] In such minutiae of administrative life, the bureau men argued, lay the key to improving government as a whole. It was this strategy, this belief, that led them to emphasize proper budgeting so strongly (see below). Once the facts and the connections between them were laid out for all to see, enlightenment would ensue. If it did not, it had to be encouraged ("the public must be told and *made* to understand," said Allen[60]), for the sake of the results that would be possible. Allen and the others insisted that the point of publicizing systematic studies of government agencies was not to "keep tabs" on government workers but to "insure favorable conditions and to correct bad conditions. This is done best by giving everybody the facts. The objective test of the efficiency of a method throws emphasis on the method, not on the motive of those operating it."[61] The implication was not only that the bureau men sought to help rather than to blame but also that their own motives were rendered irrelevant by the purity of the scientific method. And of course, they continued to insist, efficiency had a broader meaning that linked it to the conditions of people's lives—to the content of government work. "No city government, no citizen agency, no community can achieve efficiency in any branch of city service merely by bringing about precision, orderliness and economy in the performance of existing tasks" said Bruere. "City government must match its efforts against a background of knowledge regarding opportunities for service."[62]

THE SURVEY METHOD

The backbone of the bureau systematic approach to knowledge acquisition was the survey, a tool that Donald and Alice Stone have called "a new kind of literature about public administration" that enabled bureaus of municipal research to demonstrate "the value of the analytical approach in solving policy and administrative problems." So important was the survey to the bureau method, Stone and Stone argue, that "the establishment of public administration as a field of study and professional practice could not have taken place without this empirical experience."[63]

At this remove from the work of the bureaus, the term "survey" is somewhat misleading and needs to be placed in the context of the times. The method was nothing like contemporary social science techniques that depend on statistical sampling; instead, it was much more like a case study in its in-depth investigation of a particular situation. Taken on natural science terms, the early-twentieth-century survey was only problematically "science," since it employed none of the tools that aim to ensure that the results are not due to chance and may be applied to similar situations. Yet at the time of the bureau men, the survey had the status of a scientific method. In fact, Luther Gulick, who assumed directorship of the New York Bureau when it was reorganized in 1921, said that the bureau had seized upon the term "survey" for its investigative work "because it conveyed the idea of the inclusive, objective, and scientific approach."[64]

The survey—term and technique—was not invented by the bureau men, as the Stones' account implies. It was a well-developed method that had been pioneered much earlier than the advent of municipal research in the United States and had a considerably different subject matter. Its roots lie in nineteenth-century England, in the efforts of well-to-do individuals to understand the causes of poverty. For example, in 1851, Henry Mayhew published a four-volume work entitled *London Labour and the London Poor* that presented descriptive and statistical information on its topic. The real inventor of the survey approach, however, was Charles Booth, whose seventeen-volume *Life and Labour of the People in London,* published between 1889 and 1903, constituted the first great empirical study in the social survey tradition.

Booth's work was groundbreaking in concept and thoroughness. He and his team of investigators drew on the systematic observations of school attendance officers, who performed house-by-house surveillance and could be interviewed about the conditions of the families in each dwelling. He used the data to attempt to introduce an element of precision into the term "poverty." The results included detailed, color-coded maps of East London neighborhoods, delineating levels of poverty on each block. Booth's research supported a number of reforms, including old-age pensions.[65]

Using Booth's work as a model, the residents of Chicago's Hull House conducted the first full-blown social survey in the United States. They adapted the survey to systematic and exhaustive fact gathering in a neighborhood. The leader in the research effort was Florence Kelley, a pioneering child labor reformer who, in 1892, had been appointed a special agent of the Illinois Bureau of Labor Statistics to investigate Chicago sweatshops. From this position, Kelley was able to mobilize resources of the U.S. Department of Labor to support the Hull House study, which was published in 1895. The report included articles on sweatshop labor, charities in Cook County, child labor, women's labor organizations, and living conditions among various ethnic groups in Chicago's Nineteenth Ward. The volume was notable for its large and detailed maps, which conveyed with a vividness unmatched by dry tables and graphs the concentration of ethnic groups in certain blocks, the relationship between ethnicity and income, and the relegation of the very poor to crowded, airless rooms in the rear of tenements while those with more resources clustered at the front. The Hull House maps equaled those of the Booth study in

graphic detail; they surpassed Booth's in providing household-by-household information and in delineating patterns of ethnicity. According to Kathryn Kish Sklar,[66]
Hull House Maps and Papers was the flagship example of social scientific analysis of working-class life in the first decade of the twentieth century. Other settlement houses followed suit in their own neighborhoods, notably South End House
in Boston. In 1909, the Pittsburgh Survey, funded by the Russell Sage Foundation,
expanded the survey idea to encompass an entire city. By 1913, more than a hundred cities in thirty-four states had requested foundation support to conduct their
own surveys.[67]

Paul Kellogg, director of the Pittsburgh Survey, described it as a "blueprint"
that would bring out "the organic truth of the situation."[68] The Pittsburgh study
involved between ten and twenty-five researchers who spent nearly a year at the
task, but it also drew on the work of community representatives. The survey staff
felt that they could not do the study in isolation from people who lived in the community. The team saw their purpose as conducting investigations that would support advocacy for community improvement; this link between fact-finding and
policy advocacy was a hallmark of the survey method. It is significant that pioneers of the method saw themselves as scientific but not as objective, in the sense
of separating themselves from the field of study. On the contrary, they immersed
themselves in it, expressing their aim as follows: "We want to make the town
real—to itself; not in goody goody preachment of what it ought to be; not in sen-
sational discoloration; not merely in a formidable array of rigid facts. There is the
census at one pole; and yellow journalism at the other; and we are on the high
seas between. . . . As one of the collaborators in the work puts it, the standard
ahead of us is 'piled up actuality.' "[69] The "great, grimed question mark" they
hoped their studies would raise was whether conditions in Pittsburgh were the
best that an industrial society was capable of. "What," they asked, "are American
standards anyway?"[70]

In adapting the survey method to investigation of municipal agencies, the
bureau men maintained the link between science and advocacy, but they shifted the
focus markedly, from knowledge gathering about an entire neighborhood or city to
fact-finding concentrated on a single agency (later, a single unit of government).
From available records, it is not clear whether Bruere thought of his investigation
of the Manhattan streets as a "survey"; the word does not appear in his report. But
his experience as a settlement resident (Boston's Denison House) and his interac-
tions with residents of Hull House, Chicago Commons, and New York's University
Settlement might well have given him the term and almost surely inspired the
approach, since the foundation of settlement house knowledge acquisition was getting out in the field to observe firsthand (see below). In his reminiscences, Bruere
recalls: "We called these studies surveys—they were intended to show what the
existing situation was in these cities and to point out where we thought improvements could be made [such as] setting up standard practices . . . with respect to purchasing, accounting, budget making, and health administration. . . . As far as I know

this was in the United States . . . the first development of scientific techniques respecting Municipal Administration."[71] Both Bruere and Gulick credited the Pittsburgh Survey rather than the earlier settlement house efforts with providing the model for bureau surveys. The publication of the Hull House survey predated Bruere's report on Manhattan by eleven years.

Bruere's description was a considerable departure from the thrust of the settlement house surveys, with their "great, grimed question marks," but the term had a certain appeal, and Bruere's field study taught the bureau men the power of information that could be defended as "scientific." Though neither Bruere nor his colleagues ever acknowledged the survey's roots in settlement house advocacy, Murray Gross's 1914 review essay on the survey approach included both settlement house and research bureau approaches. He noted that "surveys may now be regarded as the recognized method of social discovery."[72]

The survey became the heart of the bureau men's research approach. As Gross describes it, the full-blown administrative survey was conducted by a team of "trained and experienced men," grouped in terms of significant administrative functions, such as organization and finance, public safety, health and welfare, and public works. After reviewing charters, statutes, and regulations, the team would gather information about revenues and expenditures, the budget, and the accounting system and details about various operating units. They made "tests" to determine the efficiency of government operations and to discover whether there were ways to cut costs. They specifically investigated whether the agency or government was making full use of efficiency and economy measures found in private enterprise. Their report outlined a "constructive program of improvement" and suggested practical strategies for carrying out the recommendations.[73]

Quoting William Allen's 1913 article in *The American City,* Gross cites a wide variety of projects conducted by research bureaus. They included a study of charities in Syracuse, performed at the behest of the city's Associated Charities; a citywide survey of accounting methods, budget making, and various operations in response to "ten men" in Waterbury, Connecticut, interested in the adequacy of the city's accounting system; a survey of Atlanta's government that grew out of chamber of commerce interest in working with the government to stimulate economic development; a St. Louis survey sparked by the Voters' League; and a Milwaukee survey stimulated by interest on the part of the "Socialistic administration" in making good on its pledges of efficiency. Gross reported that surveys had increased administrative efficiency in Dayton; Dobbs Ferry, New York; Jersey City; Philadelphia; Pittsburgh; Portland, Oregon; Rochester, New York; and Springfield, Massachusetts, among others.[74]

The bureau men hoped that reports outlining survey results would furnish officials with exact knowledge that would enable them to take action to make their agencies and governments more efficient and effective. The idea was that, because the reports would be presented in plain English and would be made available to the public as well, their message would be so compelling that a groundswell of public sentiment would support the efforts of leaders to implement the recommendations. Frederick Cleveland saw the reports as similar to corporate annual reports presented to citizen stockholders.[75] The possibility that the contents or their implications might not be transparently obvious to all, that there might be disagreement or debate about findings and recommendations, seems not to have occurred to bureau leaders, or if it did, they did not discuss it. Their view that the facts would speak for themselves can be traced to their faith in the power of knowledge that could be viewed as scientific. Cleveland said, "Most controversies grow out of the failure of parties contestant to make clear what they are talking about. Words in ordinary use make expression of thought difficult whenever exactness is required. It is for this reason that science has gone entirely outside the common language for its terms."[76] Science, as a systematic body of knowledge, was dependent on a precise language so that scientists could benefit from one another's work and results could be cumulative. Scientific language held the key to rationalizing public decision making.

Cleveland argued that accounting could furnish public agencies with the sort of language that would support making public administration into a science. He held that public administration had gotten so complex that no one person could analyze and classify its transactions. Information had to be organized, and that organizational effort would require an exact nomenclature: "A well-devised system of municipal accounts and statistics when properly coordinated should give a direct and accurate answer to *every* question about which the officer and citizen must think."[77]

One problem with this scheme was that not everyone spoke or would be likely to learn to speak the language of accounting. Another was that not "every" administrative question about which officers and citizens needed to think was a technical one. The bureau men's dream of bringing utter clarity to public life obscured the political dimensions of administrative actions and accorded a central place to experts, since accounting, or any other purportedly scientific argot, belonged to the few who had learned to speak it. As Jonathan Kahn notes, by styling themselves as keepers of the language of public life, the bureau men assumed the role of authoritative interpreters.[78] This authority, hidden in the very terms of the public conversation, gave experts the power to translate government lingo into terms they thought citizens would be able to understand and thus to shape citizen understanding of public life. If experts maintained the prerogative of defining issues and shaping data, citizen involvement would be constricted to the dimensions experts chose.

The bureau men were not unaware that in gaining control of knowledge they and the officials with whom they cooperated gained power at the expense of ordinary citizens. For some, like Frederick Cleveland, this was as it should be. Henry Bruere generally agreed, noting that "whatever intelligence the average citizen will have regarding the details of government will continue to be gained as now, either from personal observation of physical conditions or from newspaper accounts"[79]— not from systematic investigation or even from reading the bureau reports. In a typical rhetorical move, William R. Patterson maintained that skilled investigation was essential to rid municipal research of the "sentimental bias of many social workers."[80] Science would masculinize reform. William Allen, however, worried about displacing the ordinary citizen from public affairs. For him, the big question connected with scientific knowledge was how to gain the advantage of expertise without turning the public into a "helpless, unthinking followership. . . . Efficiency of participation," he argued, "is more important than efficiency of immediate results. . . . [I]t is better to make blunders in presenting facts, urging changes, and opposing reforms than to paralyse a civic body by benumbing its members."[81]

New York City comptroller William Prendergast, a friend to the New York Bureau, wrote in an *Annals* symposium on city government that efficiency was nothing more than "applied common sense." He warned that it should not be permitted to become the "proprietary possession of a group of expert theorists. The word should not be permitted to have a technical meaning."[82] The danger lay in the gulf that would grow up between experts and ordinary citizens. Shortly after Prendergast's cautionary remark, however, expert reformers learned the lesson he had warned them about. Reformer John Purroy Mitchel, elected mayor on a fusion ticket in 1913, filled his administration with experts, including both municipal researchers and social workers; settlement house resident Katherine B. Davis, appointed commissioner of corrections, became the first woman to head a New York City agency. Reformers throughout the city rejoiced. Mitchel's biographer notes that the new mayor believed deeply that efficiency in government would serve the people's needs so well that they would never again have to vote for machine candidates. Efficient government would be its own reward.[83] Despite good intentions, however, the Mitchel administration came to grief because reformers seemed unable to translate their theories into concrete actions that would provide tangible benefits to voters. During the 1917 campaign, in which Mitchel lost to a Tammany candidate, one friendly observer noted the reformers' lack of political savvy. He called them "scientific highbrows . . . [who] got up early in the morning and counted 166 superfluous jobs in the Department of Bridges, and abolished them and made 166 enemies, and put it into a report quite unintelligible to nine out of ten citizens and went home and called it a grand day's political work."[84] Notions of scientific government had turned out to be a more equivocal basis for actual governing than the systemizers had thought.

"THE BEST MEANS YET DEVISED"

In the bureau men's scheme for reforming government, for making both administration and citizens efficient, the centerpiece was the municipal budget. The budget brought together all the ingredients of the research bureau approach. It laid out, for all to see (including ordinary citizens), what the city government was doing or intended to do with tax dollars; it forced government officials to justify their requests for funds and therefore made them more accountable to the citizenry; it gave citizens an opportunity to gain facts and figures about government operations that would enable them to judge whether the city was using their money wisely. William Allen wrote that the budget was "the best means yet devised for making the story understood by the public, and for preventing a recurrence of public ignorance about public affairs."[85]

Henry Bruere's cooperation in 1907 with medical officer Hermann Biggs in preparing the first municipal agency budget had solidified the place of municipal research in the panoply of reform work and put the bureau men on a sound footing with the Board of Estimate and Apportionment. A notice in *Charities and the Commons* at the time of the New York Bureau's incorporation said that the new organization's initial focus would be to replicate the health department budgeting process in all city departments, so that the Board of Estimate would be able to exercise "proper control . . . and make . . . regular and intelligible accounts of their stewardship to the public."[86] The bureau's own report on the fashioning of the health department budget called it a document that could tell in condensed form many significant facts about community needs and referred to "budget making as a method of publicity."[87] Thus, at least initially, the bureau men appeared to think of the budget mainly as a fact-clarifying accountability mechanism that supported the desire to bring government operations into the light of public scrutiny. Frederick Cleveland said that the "growing hostility to doing business in the dark, to 'boss rule,' to 'invisible government,' became the soil in which the 'budget idea' took root and grew."[88]

The next step in the bureau campaign was to sponsor a budget exhibit in New York City in October 1908, intended to bring to life the otherwise dry details hidden in the city's budget document. The exhibit was becoming a favorite tool of reformers. A pioneering exemplar was the Charity Organization Society's tenement house exhibit in 1900. Arranged by Lawrence Veiller, a leader in tenement house reform, the exhibit included more than a hundred photographs, detailed maps of slum districts, statistical tables and charts, and papier-mâché models of tenement blocks. As Robert Bremner comments, "The lesson of the tenement house investigation seemed to be that the path to reform lay through research."[89]

The men of the New York Bureau set out on the path with gusto. *Charities and the Commons* commented: "New Yorkers are now given an opportunity to see in graphic form that their tax budget of $143,500,000 is not only the largest of any city in the world, but that extravagance and inefficiency play a large part in its disposition." The exhibit presented charts, graphs, and other tangible evidence of how the city was misusing public funds. For example, there was an exhibit of hat hooks, telling the public that the city had paid sixty-five cents apiece for hooks that could be bought anywhere for six cents. When labor costs were added in, the hooks had cost $2.21 each. The Tenement House Commission presented photographs and charts to justify its budget request of $184,966; other agencies that participated included the Department of Taxes and Assessments and the borough presidents' offices.[90] After two weeks, the exhibit closed on November 2, the day before the fall election. Some 70,000 New Yorkers had visited it. The bureau repeated the exhibit the next year; in 1910 and 1911, the city assumed sponsorship.[91] The bureau also sponsored "budget days" in city churches, characterized in *The Survey* as efforts on the part of clergymen to support "social service measures advocated by the Bureau of Municipal Research."[92]

In 1909, the bureau convened a budget conference that brought together reformers to consider the upcoming city budget. William Gaynor had just been elected mayor; control of the Board of Estimate and Apportionment was in fusion hands, and at its first meeting the board passed nine resolutions for budget control—all conditions favoring a bureau effort to strengthen its influence on the conduct of city business.[93] But, as Veiller noted, not all those interested in proper budgeting had the same motivations. Social workers were interested in freeing wasted resources to meet additional needs; taxpayer associations wanted to reduce taxes even if it meant cutting back on certain activities; agency heads hoped that the budget process would enable them to justify increased allocations for their departments. The budget conference was billed as a clearinghouse that would bring these conflicts out in the open and, as Veiller hoped, allow social workers to educate others on the potential that lay in budget reform.

Veiller commented that the previous year the Bureau of Municipal Research had been allied with "selfish" interests—taxpayers, boards of trade, and property owners associations—in opposing all budget increases. By the time bureau men called the conference, however, they had apparently changed their position somewhat, realizing "that there are other things to be considered besides the elimination of waste and modern methods of accounting."[94] Attendees at the conference debated the respective merits of cutting costs versus helping those in need: " 'Sooner or later . . .' said one speaker[,] 'we cannot go on appropriating money without cutting out useless expenditures. . . . ' 'Granted that money is wasted now,' [said another,] 'should the business men and voters . . . bear the cost, or shall it be thrown on the children of the poor through failure to make needed expenditures?' "[95]

The bureau might have created its image as a selfish or penny-pinching organization through its initial approach to budgeting, which was essentially to create separate line items for each agency expenditure, a method called "segregation." This approach directed everyone's attention to the minutiae of governmental activity, but, as Veiller noted, it did not provide a clear basis for weighing the conflicting demands made by different agencies, each of which seemed important to some interest group. Which was more vital, education or tuberculosis prevention? Competent hospital workers or street cleaning? Policing or tenement supervision?[96] In general, social workers saw the budget as an opportunity to squeeze more resources for social needs out of the city, if they could show that extra dollars could save extra lives. They hoped that the Board of Estimate would find this an undeniable position: "[The] plea that money efficiently spent on child saving is a good investment cannot be rebutted with the contention that the funds, however much the authorities might desire to spend them, cannot be found."[97]

The city's annual budget hearings were another important part of the bureau men's budget-making strategy. Despite their claim that the hearings would be a chance for citizens to make their views known directly to government officials and for officials to make good on their accountability requirements, in actuality, the hearings were dominated by lobbying on the part of organized groups and were limited in the kind of citizen input they permitted. Citizens were not allowed to vote on budget items and had no control over the agenda for discussion. The board imposed a rule that "citizens must discuss specific budget items and not . . . dilate on the State of the Union." In other words, citizen participation in budget hearings was carefully structured by experts (the bureau men) and officials.[98]

As budgeting became a routine element in city government, bureau men began to reflect on their approach and to grow more sophisticated about it. They began to realize that simply "segregating" individual budget line items went too far in one respect and not far enough in another. Segregation tied the hands of agency officials, making it difficult for them to have any flexibility at all in the way they spent money, and it did not make possible the kind of strategic thinking on the part of government leaders that the bureau men came more and more to advocate. Undoubtedly an element in the evolution of the bureau's budgeting theories was Frederick Cleveland's involvement in President Taft's Commission on Economy and Efficiency from 1911 to 1913. During his work in Washington, Cleveland more openly emphasized the budget as a mechanism to oversee and discipline government, likening budgeting to a conning tower that would lift government executives out of day-to-day complexity and allow them to see the big picture. He saw a federal budget as a device through which Congress would supervise the executive branch but still leave it the necessary discretion.[99] Upon Cleveland's return to New York, and particularly after William Allen left the bureau, increasing stress was placed in the bureau men's thinking of the budget as an instrument of executive control. Discussions of budgeting shifted from its power to impose accountability on government to its potential to strengthen the executive's ability to manage government operations rationally and efficiently. The New York Bureau's work put greater focus on matters of public budgeting and finance.[100]

Both Henry Bruere and Frederick Cleveland published important articles on budgeting in 1915. Bruere was by this time speaking as city chamberlain in Mayor Mitchel's administration. From this vantage point, which undoubtedly gave his views added weight, at least in some quarters, Bruere noted that budget segregation as an instrument of control over administrative discretion had not worked as well as reformers had hoped, so further rules had been piled on. These included restrictions on the rate of expenditures for salaries, specifications governing the purchase of supplies, and prohibitions on transferring funds between accounts. The cumulative effect, Bruere said, was "a degree of regimentation which restricts and in a measure paralyzes the freedom" of administrators. But since the advent of budget reform efforts, the attitudes of government officials had altered dramatically. Now, instead of "mere opportunism, evasion and compromise, . . . department heads are . . . seeking to increase . . . the quality of service . . . and to exercise increasingly effective discretion." Henceforth, argued Bruere, budgeting should not concentrate simply on systematizing funding requests and expenditures; rather, it should be the "summation with respect to the scope of municipal activities and the methods of their administration."[101]

Cleveland's article, "Evolution of the Budget Idea in the United States," set forth a full-blown concept of public budgeting. He argued that the budget was "a plan for financing an enterprise or government during a definite period, which is prepared and submitted by a responsible executive to a representative body (or other duly constituted agent) whose approval and authorization are necessary before the plan may be executed."[102] The budget was an instrument for making the executive responsible to the people through their elected representatives. It was appropriate that the executive develop the plan, because he was answerable not to a single district but to the people as a whole; as such, he was responsible for managing the affairs of the entire government. The legislature's role was to consider the executive's budget and either approve or disapprove it, as well as to review the executive's past performance through independent audit and by requiring the executive to appear before legislators, answer questions, and fill in details. Cleveland emphasized that the budget idea was not merely a mechanism for holding government officials accountable but a constitutional principle that was both democratic and in harmony with representative government.

Cleveland's argument makes it clear that the bureau philosophy came to entail not merely marginal adjustments in agency practices to make them more businesslike but also a theory of government that centralized power in the chief executive at the expense of the legislature. In Cleveland's scheme, legislatures retained the authority to say yea or nay to the executive budget, but they had virtually no say in the development of the budget's contents. Since only those policies for which funds have been approved can be implemented, his theory turned the chief executive into the principal policy architect, with relatively little legislative check and balance possible, since the legislature's entire power was reactive. The bureau's 1916 publication "The Elements of State Budget Making" reinforced this idea, calling "a scientific budget . . . both an instrument and a process of government . . . a means of getting before the representative body . . . a well-considered plan, with all the information needed to determine whether the plan should be approved before funds are made available for its execution . . . [and] a procedure . . . for requiring those whose future acts are to be controlled to assume full responsibility for preparing, explaining and defending their plans and proposals for future grants."[103]

A year later, another bureau publication emphasized that the budget was not just an appropriations bill but a plan and a way of publicizing government operations. It argued that earlier efforts had not been real budgeting but rather an attempt to "functionalize to death" the appropriations bill by segregating requests in ever greater detail. This attempt had "forced every officer of the city to become a lawbreaker," because no one could get all the minute requirements right. The bureau's initial goal had been to use budgeting as a weapon against patronage by limiting the freedom of officials; that battle had now been won, and emphasis could shift to "improving administration."[104] As the bureau constructed the story, then, the evolution in its budget thinking was a natural one, driven by the diminishing need to impose control on irresponsible government agencies and the growing potential to strengthen the hand of the executive. It was a shift from a negative to a positive strategy. But given the intimacy, by this time, of the bureau men's cooperative relationships with government officials, and given the reform orientation of Mayor Mitchel, it is likely that the shift occurred partly because the bureau men were no longer dealing with adversaries but with friends.[105] When Mitchel was swept out of office in 1917 and a Tammany-backed government installed, the bureau's cozy relationships with city government ceased. Minutes of the bureau's board of directors at the time spoke optimistically of how "this doesn't necessarily mean that corruption will break out again or that the Bureau's relationship with city agencies will be truncated" and pointed to continuing cooperation with the president of the Board of Aldermen and comptroller.[106] In actuality, the new mayor, John Hylan, viewed the bureau men as a bunch of elitist troublemakers and took measures to cut off bureau access to city agencies.[107]

Perhaps the clearest evidence of the bureau men's interest in strengthening executive power is its study of the New York state government conducted in preparation for the state's constitutional convention in 1915. Researchers studied 169 departments, bureaus, boards, institutions, and commissions. The resulting report called the study "the first complete description of a state government that has ever been prepared."[108] The report called for an executive budget, the consolidation of administrative agencies, and a short ballot. Heads of all state departments would submit itemized budget requests to the governor, who would hold public hearings, make revisions, and submit the result to the legislature.[109]

In the May 1915 issue of *Municipal Research,* the New York Bureau's own publication, bureau men set forth the assumptions on which they had based their assessment and recommendations for the new constitution. Proper accountability to the people required adequate mechanisms for achieving it, and the only real way to ensure accountability was to provide for responsible leadership, that is, require the executive to formulate and present a plan, and give the legislature a chance to turn it down. This scheme took explicit aim at the principle of separation of powers, calling it "the chief source of the wastefulness, irresponsibility, and inefficiency which characterize the present system of government." Checks and balances, said the bureau men, simply added to the burden of government and failed to cut down waste and confusion. Similarly, the merit-system approach had not worked, and the principle of geographic representation had failed to give adequate weight to "important groups of people in a highly complex society." The result was unproductive localism, gerrymandering, and logrolling. The bicameral legislature, originally intended to represent differing class interests, now simply blocked effective leadership and blurred responsibility. Relations between the executive and the legislature were fraught with unproductive conflicts. The governor's power was inadequate to the tasks assigned to him, and a tangle of boards and commissions stripped him of further control. It was clear, the bureau concluded, "that the problem . . . involves more than a mere readjustment of parts. . . . In fact it goes to the very root of the whole system of government. Responsiveness and responsibility for economy and efficiency cannot be secured by administrative alterations alone." They required constitutional changes to strengthen the executive and "concentrate" public opinion at election time.[110]

The report raised a storm of controversy. Despite the bureau's intent after the Rockefeller ultimatum to conduct itself in a soberly scientific manner, the implications of the report's supposedly objective findings went to the heart of American political arrangements and as such drew fire from those whose power stood to diminish if the bureau's recommendations were implemented.[111] The newspapers were filled with stories detailing the accusations and defenses that flew back and forth. One account sarcastically commented that the bureau men were "incapable of error" and suggested that the state constitution should read, "The State of New York shall be governed by the Bureau of Municipal Research."[112] Frederick Cleveland, however, was "undismayed in his research effort,"[113] issuing a leaflet entitled "Samples from a Pork Barrel" and attacking "bargain counter government run by seven men in the dark,"[114] a rhetorical flourish worthy of his ousted colleague William Allen.

Although New York's voters rejected the new constitution in 1916, the bureau men's ideas had profound effects elsewhere. Between 1911 and 1919, forty-four states passed budget laws, and by 1929, every state except Arkansas had an executive budget. Many of the ideas recommended by the bureau were finally adopted in New York in 1925, after Governor Al Smith appointed his own constitutional commission headed by Robert Moses and staffed by A. E. Buck and John Gaus, all New York Bureau graduates. The philosophy is also discernible in the Brownlow Report on administrative management issued during the Roosevelt administration, authored by bureau man Luther Gulick, among others (see chapter 6).

THE BUREAU PHILOSOPHY AND AN ALTERNATIVE

What the bureau men thought about government and the place of administration in it varied from man to man. William Allen had a more democratic vision than did Frederick Cleveland. Clearly, though, there were assumptions and beliefs that municipal researchers shared that varied more in degree than in kind. Considered as a body of thought (while making allowances for individual variations), the bureau philosophy—and Dwight Waldo was right, it *was* a political philosophy and not merely a set of technical nostrums—reveals consistent themes.

1. Municipal government was more business than politics, or at least society would be better off if this were the case. Management of public agencies could be safely and usefully modeled on business management. Politics was largely an electoral matter, in which the general public registered its opinion on the merits of particular candidates. Administrative questions lay outside its purview.

2. The attempt to oust corrupt officials and their minions through the electoral process was a failure; therefore, concerned citizens should develop a strategy to work with officials, offering objective methods for improving administrative processes instead of trying to "throw the rascals out."

3. The grounding for citizen cooperation with government was scientific investigation that would produce factual knowledge about the best—most efficient— way to manage the public's business. Science was the ideal basis for the identification of efficiency because it was a precise, impersonal language of inquiry, producing truths that everyone would accede to because of the method by which they were arrived at.

4. Scientific inquiry to increase the efficiency of public management was democratic because it opened up government to citizen scrutiny, forced officials to practice accountability, and gave them the means to do so. If trained public administrators executed legislated mandates in an effective and efficient manner based on science, democracy would be well served.

5. The quest for efficiency required systematizing governmental processes, such as through proper budgeting and accounting, and centralizing and concentrating power in the hands of the executive. Although the legislative branch continued to represent diverse interests among the people and retained final say over policies, efficient government required a central point of accountability— the executive—who could plan, lead, and coordinate on behalf of the people as a whole.

6. Because government processes would now be based on science, which would reveal the best way to manage, administration should be in the hands of trained people rather than loyalists. The science of administration was a complex body of knowledge whose implementation was best assigned to experts. The role of the people, both directly and through their representatives, was to exercise oversight and call administrative experts to account, rather than to participate in shaping the content of government policies or programs. "Efficient citizens" would rally around agencies if they had the information necessary to understand administrative action.

These ideas are not obsolete antiques; indeed, with only modest variations, they still form the core of American public administration (see chapter 6). Ever since the days of the bureau men, people in the field have argued over such issues as whether private business and public administration are fundamentally alike or different, the proper balance between bureaucratic and democratic values, the appropriate role for ordinary citizens in administrative governance, and the extent to which the practice of public administration can be made susceptible to the dictates of science. And they have pretty much conducted these debates on ground staked out by the bureau men. Although public administrationists disagree about the answers to these and similar questions, they have rarely argued in terms that would be unfamiliar to the municipal researchers, were they around to join in. With occasional exceptions, then, the terrain of public administration theory has a rather taken-for-granted quality. Tracing the field's origins to the activities and ideas of the bureau men, public administrationists have often quarreled with various ingredients of their vision but have rarely if ever stopped to wonder whether there might have been a different way to define the field, one that would have admitted to the canon another set of questions and concerns.

The work of settlement residents and clubwomen, going on side by side—even mingling—with municipal research (see chapter 3), suggests that the construction of public administration was selective, based on the values, semiconscious assumptions, and priorities of its makers; other approaches can not only be imagined, they can be examined. What were the ideas that women's club members, settlement workers, and other social welfare reformers contributed that, together with municipal research, might have shaped a field whose broad purpose was helping governments better serve their people?

"POLITICS AIN'T BEANBAG"

Even though many settlement house residents and social welfare reformers were men, the arena in which they acted had been defined by politicians—indeed, by society as a whole—as women's territory. Both male and female reformers chafed under this sharp division: politics was a defining feature of masculinity, and benevolent work (indeed, any other public activity, including municipal reform) was emblematic of the female propensity for virtue. But few escaped the strictures of this dichotomy. "Politics ain't beanbag," commented political satirist Finley Peter Dunne's creation, Mr. Dooley: " 'Tis a man's game; an' women, childer, an' prohybitionists'd do well to keep out iv it."[115] In reaction to being characterized as "man milliners" and "the third sex of politics," male reformers defended the virility of their work; meanwhile, women asserted their capacity to function effectively in the public sector and lamented the stereotypes that made such defenses necessary. In a review of Mary Ritter Beard's catalogue of women's municipal activities, Grace Abbott commented that "women who have been active in civic work will be relieved when they will not be asked to stop and prove that because they are women they are not devoid of a sense of responsibility for community conditions and are not without the ability to help in determining along what lines the community life should develop."[116] Settlement leader Helen Campbell declared: "We face again the sharp division of thought which sets men and women apart and devitalizes all the machinery of work among working men and women. In Mothers'

Clubs, Working Girls' Clubs, and the like, even at their best, the woman is held to what is counted her 'proper sphere,' this meaning actually a series of limitations. It is the lack of [male-female comradeship] that sends men to the saloon and leaves women to the grind of daily petty tasks"—or, it could be added, that sets men to budgeting and women to starting up playgrounds and kindergartens.[117] Campbell argued that settlement work deserved its place side by side with other types of municipal reform.

Because of the strength of these unwritten regulations about the proper sphere of men's and women's activities, women seized on the terms of their feminine role to define and justify their civic work. In general, they shared societywide notions about what women could and could not appropriately do. But even if they had not, the strong link between masculinity and politics would have driven them, if they were to have any active public role, into ostensibly nonpolitical (meaning nonelectoral) activity and into a different sensibility than that of either party politicians or male reformers. For women, civic reform and femininity became easily congruent, making it possible for them to generate an alternative vision of public life and government reform based on feminine notions that male reformers could adopt only equivocally. And, as Kathryn Kish Sklar has argued, women's organizations, clubs, and settlement houses created a civic space where women's understandings of urban problems could coalesce and become the basis for spurring governments to act.[118] These institutions constituted an alternative public sphere, one that made it possible for women to spearhead reforms based on a distinctive set of purposes.

From this institutional base, women generated not only recommended policies, model programs, and services attacking a host of urban ills (see chapter 3) but also a view of government administration as similar to housework. Clubwoman Mrs. Frederick P. Bagley commented: "Institutional management is merely housekeeping made large, and if hereditary instinct as well as daily experience count, women should be good judges as to the administrative skills of a superintendent."[119] Women's reform activities extended domestic values into the public sector, thus blurring the divide between them. Settlement leader Jane Addams argued that the family grounded social relations, and the state took on social concerns. Thus "family" became a metaphor for the wider society. This slippage between the literal and the symbolic family became the gateway to women's practice of citizenship.[120] "The very multifariousness and complexity of a city government demand the help of minds accustomed to detail and variety of work, to a sense of obligation for the health and welfare of young children, and to a responsibility for the cleanliness and comfort of other people," Addams wrote.[121] From women's perspective, their typical homely duties had qualities that prepared them for governmental work. As the civilizing force in society, moreover, they were "natural enemies of dirt" and therefore well suited to working effectively to clean up government.[122] A suffrage cartoon at the time trumpeted: "Male-administration of government is maladministration of government."[123]

Although feminine values led reform women in the direction of blurring the divide between public and private, they always intended that women's benevolence and nurturance should be extended into public life, not that public service should model itself after private enterprise. Addams, for example, saw little difference in substance between what was called "philanthropy" and public service.[124] *The Settlement Horizon* characterized the settlers' motive as reducing statesmanship to neighborhood terms, minimizing the distinction between formal government operations and other types of public service, so that settlement projects could be taken over by governments at the appropriate time.[125] But settlement residents and other social reformers generally agreed that there was a big difference between public service and private business, and they looked askance at municipal reform efforts to model government on the private profit-making corporation. The Reverend John Haynes Holmes, for example, argued:

> There is . . . a basic fallacy involved in the conception of the city as a mere business corporation. . . . [Instead] the city is regarded as a great family to be guarded, guided, controlled and uplifted. . . . The municipality, in other words, is a community. . . . The ideal thing today is not a business administration, but a social administration. The ideal city official is not the business man, but the man whose whole life is aflame with the spirit of brotherhood. . . . Economy is all right as a method of government, but all wrong as an ideal.[126]

Along similar lines, settlement residents had a different understanding of politics from that of the bureau men. Although they shared the desire to oust corrupt machine politicians, they realized that in many cases aldermen were elected because they were viewed by their constituents as friends and neighbors. Addams contrasted the settlement view of politicians with that of "the well-to-do men of the community," who thought of politics as "something off by itself. . . . As a result of this detachment, reform movements started by business men and the better element, are almost wholly occupied in the correction of political machinery and with a concern for the better method of administration, rather than with the ultimate purpose of securing the welfare of the people. They fix their attention so exclusively on methods that they fail to consider the final aims of government."[127]

For social welfare reformers like the settlement women, final aims were always more important than methods, though they gave considerable attention to the latter. In the ward politician, they saw not only a rascal but also a neighbor. But settlers were neighbors, too. They were not that different from the ward politician; by going among the people of their districts, they sought, as he did, to know their "needs and yearnings. . . . Neighborliness is at the basis of even bad politics, and sound government can be built upon no other foundation."[128] In their neighborhood networking, they had in mind the vision of a commonwealth "in which every effort was to be as truly political . . . as were the endless operations of the ward machine."[129] "Political" here meant not corrupt but focused on fostering a government better able to cope with the human problems of its constituents. Aldermen were admirable in the attention they paid to the daily survival and development needs of the people of their districts; their standards, said Addams, suited those of their constituents.[130] In contrast, most municipal reformers were never able to cultivate the common touch. Mary Simkhovitch, commenting in retrospect about the reform administration of John Purroy Mitchel, said that although it was a "brilliant group" that made city government fresh and interesting, "it never took pains to interpret itself to the people at large." The people never ceased to regard the reformers as outsiders, because the reformers never found a way to bridge the gulf between themselves and the people.[131]

Unsurprisingly, since they lived in the urban neighborhoods to whose problems they were devoted, settlement residents gave the idea of community a tangible quality. A biographer of Chicago's Mary McDowell observed that McDowell's life became interwoven into the life of the "behind the yards" community: "In developing a neighborhood consciousness, she does not *stay*, but she *lives*, in the stockyard region and is learning to say 'we' unconsciously."[132] Settlement women saw what united them with their neighbors rather than the elements that divided them, such as class. They stressed the creation of a neighborhood spirit linking them to men, women, and children of different nationalities, enabling them to serve as catalysts for bringing together the diverse residents of their communities to "learn the meaning of citizenship. Out of the neighborhood feeling will grow the social consciousness," commented English visitor Percy Alden after touring American settlements, "and slowly but surely the settlement will become the voice through which the civic conscience makes itself heard."[133]

Clubwomen shared the settlers' vision of a unity of interests among people of different classes and the possibility of forming common cause based on shared needs that bring human beings together. This, they believed, was particularly true of women, whose feminine values somehow surmounted the property interests that divided men. Mrs. T. J. Bowlker said that women of different classes could "converge" around "the health and the happiness of those they hold dear," realizing that these were "unattainable for any one of us unless they are attained by all."[134] Civic work would even educate well-to-do women, raising their consciousness so that they were able to see the factors that linked them with the lives of poor families. Addams commented: "The daintily clad charitable visitor who steps into the little house made untidy by the vigorous efforts of her hostess, the washerwoman, is no longer sure of her superiority to the latter; she recognizes that her hostess after all represents social value and industrial use, as over against her own parasitic cleanliness and a social standing attained only through status."[135] Mrs. Bowlker echoed Addams's sentiments, suggesting that uneducated women felt even more sharply than their educated sisters "their own personal responsibility for making of their city a home. . . . This," she said, was the "spirit of a true democracy."[136]

Clubwomen and settlers interpreted social ills as a mandate to each individual to do something; the good of one and the good of all were intertwined. They contrasted their approach to that of male politicians and reformers: "We have no old scores to settle, no axes to grind. We do not want a penny or an office. All we ask is the privilege of working for the children of the state to see that they get what President Roosevelt calls a 'square deal.' "[137]

Women reformers recognized that private philanthropy was ill equipped to cope with the scale and seriousness of urban problems; charities had neither the public authority nor the necessary financial resources. Struck with the immense difficulties of poor—especially immigrant—families crowded into fetid tenements and working at what were called the "dangerous trades," settlement residents and clubwomen argued that conditions such as these required state action, otherwise citizenship could not develop. Settlement women saw their own work, in fact, not as philanthropy but as fulfilling the duties of good citizenship.[138] They were often sharply critical of organized charity. Addams observed: "Even those of us who feel most sorely the need of more order in altruistic effort and see the end to be desired, find something distasteful in the juxtaposition of the words 'organized' and 'charity.' . . . [W]e distrust a little a scheme which substitutes a theory of social conduct for the natural promptings of the heart."[139] Such a statement is in stark contrast to the bureau men's reliance on systematization as the cure for municipal ills. Even the relatively democratic William Allen took his cues from what he saw as the accomplishments of scientific charity. The women defined citizenship as active involvement in solving the problems of their cities.[140] By first taking on public problems and then arguing for governmental expansion, reform women exercised the kind of authoritative judgment on public questions that has long been a hallmark of active versions of citizenship in Western societies.[141] In calling for new governmental services and policies, they invoked the public interest. They saw themselves as acting for the greater good and as qualified to enter the public realm as effective actors, armed with what Addams, describing Julia Lathrop, called "that sort of disinterested virtue which has been designated as 'the refusal to nurse a private destiny.' "[142]

Clearly, statements of reform women that emphasized similarities between themselves and poor immigrants must be assessed in context. In many ways, their desire to wipe out the differences between themselves and the poor was unrealistic, given the enormous disparities in economic resources and life opportunities that divided them. As Riva Shpak Lissak's study suggests, settlement workers tended to interpret economic differences as cultural and therefore to see their task as some form of Americanization, whether it was assimilation or the achievement of a more flexible form of cultural pluralism.[143] Yet the idea that the settlements and the women's clubs with which they formed alliances to push for social welfare policies constituted a class-bridging phenomenon is not entirely implausible. Theda Skocpol, for example, demonstrates how much a network of settlements and women's clubs was able to accomplish in contrast to an analogous network of men's organizations, arguing that the women could use maternalist rhetoric to unite women of all classes to win approval of policies to benefit mothers and children.[144] Without glorifying female reformers, then, it seems justifiable to point to real differences between them and their male counterparts and to suggest that the obliteration of their perspective from public administration constitutes a real loss.

"SOMETHING MAJESTIC ABOUT A FACT"

Virtually everyone interested in improving city life, men and women alike, had a burgeoning faith in the power of knowledge to transform society. But science and "facts" meant something rather different to women reformers than to their male counterparts in the municipal research movement. Women of the period had a more equivocal view of the possibility and desirability of objectivity than did the bureau men.

In the early part of the twentieth century, many social researchers regarded settlement houses as windows on the world, serving as laboratories where city life could be studied. Mary Jo Deegan traces this idea to Robert A. Woods of South End House in Boston. He envisioned poor city neighborhoods as microcosms of all social problems and settlement residents as experts who would colonize them in order to study and experiment. Deegan argues that this view was characteristic of male settlers, but the women rejected it.[145] Addams commented: "I have always objected to the phrase 'sociological laboratory' applied to us, because Settlements should be something much more human and spontaneous than such a phrase connotes, and yet it is inevitable that the residents should know their own neighborhoods more thoroughly than any other, and that their experiences there should affect their convictions."[146] Despite Hull House's leadership in conducting early systematic studies of social conditions in poor neighborhoods, such as *Hull House Maps and Papers,* for Jane Addams, the needs of the people came before the needs of urban researchers. She turned down a proposal that Hull House serve as a base for research by the new Rockefeller-funded University of Chicago, because settlement residents, she said, were "not students but citizens, and their methods of work must differ from that of an institution established elsewhere and following well defined lines."[147] Addams once pointed out that the settlement houses predated by three years the first university sociology departments and by ten the first foundations for social research.[148] As we have seen, they predated municipal research bureaus by more than a decade and gave the latter their model methodology.

For settlement residents, physical location in the neighborhoods they served made possible their brand of science. They operated on the premise that "only that which is lived can be understood and translated to others."[149] Trustworthy, accurate knowledge came from "minute familiarity"; science, in fact, "demanded" not only alertness but also the kind of sympathy that came only from intimate knowledge of neighborhood life and thought. "Scientific disinterestedness [called] for, not the separateness of the observer, but suspended judgment in the midst of action."[150]

One had to start at the micro level, "block by block—learning the location of all the public buildings, the charitable agencies, the schools, the saloons, the disorderly houses"—until settlers knew, "in some instances better than the police, what each house represented."[151]

According to Herman F. Hegner, a resident of Chicago Commons, science meant viewing things from inside them, not picturing them from the outside. The settlement method of knowledge acquisition was scientific because it was empirical, because it tried to understand society by studying "real facts of the lives of the people," because it tried to improve the social environment, and because it tried to "test economic and social laws by actual experiments."[152] Settlers took this approach to the neighborhood itself and extended it to investigations of problems that affected neighborhood people in their workplaces and poor people in public institutions. Alice Hamilton, for example, investigated the prevalence and effect of white lead paint on factory workers by talking her way into factories she had no authority to enter and visiting workers in homes and saloons, a process she referred to as "shoe-leather epidemiology." She was able to show a statistical correlation between employment in a paint factory and diagnoses of workers' illnesses. Her report, published by the Bureau of Labor in 1911, was written in dry, technical language to avoid charges of sentimentality, but it nevertheless dispelled the notion that American industrial conditions were better than those in Europe.[153] After Julia Lathrop was appointed to the Illinois Board of Charities in 1892, she visited every one of 102 county farms and almshouses, discussing conditions with superintendents. She once gathered her skirts around her and slid down a new fire escape to see if it really worked. In her chapter on Cook County charities in *Hull House Maps and Papers,* Lathrop wrote: "There is constant criticism of the county relief office from the recipient's point of view. He says the coal is delivered slowly and in scant measure, that favoritism is shown by visitors, that burials are tardy and cruel; and the facts justify him. There is a certain satisfaction in the philanthropist and sociologist alike in having touched bottom, reached ultimate facts, and this in a sense we have done when we have reached the county institution . . . the infirmary, the insane asylum, the hospital."[154]

Mary Simkhovitch of New York's Greenwich House once commented: "There is something majestic about a fact. What is, is. This monumental character of facts cannot but make the deepest kind of impression."[155] But for settlement residents, facts were a different phenomenon than the facts the bureau men sought to pile up, because they were arrived at by means of connection with the field of study rather than an investigative posture of objectivity. Simkhovitch argued that the settlements "let life, not theory, lead the way."[156] She saw the reformer and the settlement worker as distinct: the reformer was a sort of missionary, a dogmatist out to convert; the settlement worker tried by constant association with the people to get "the slant of the neighbors."[157] It was the difference between trying to impose one's views on those who were conducting themselves incorrectly (inefficiently) and letting understanding emerge from contact with situations. Chicago's Mary McDowell agreed: "The settlement work is not the presentation of an ism or theory, but of life. It is carried on on the principle that what men want primarily in the struggle for life is life itself and not theories about life."[158]

Simkhovitch outlined the settlement approach to knowledge acquisition in three stages: (1) "social impressionism," which was a process of "constant listening, feeling, learning"; (2) "interpretation," that is, "understanding, appreciating, and sympathizing with the surrounding life"; and (3) "action" on the basis of the knowledge thus acquired.[159] By letting life, not theory, lead the way, settlement residents opened themselves up to their neighborhoods, letting the facts well up and attempting to see them the way neighborhood people did, then translating the results into advocacy. They spoke consistently of submitting or surrendering themselves to the situations they studied. Addams, for example, said that the true "scientist exhibits his skill not only in assembling his data but in . . . surrendering himself to it with no wish but to understand."[160] Robert Woods and Albert Kennedy characterized settlement work as a process in which residents submitted themselves "to be tested mercilessly by local standards, that there might be free trade between them and their neighbors in the costly products of experience."[161]

In this process, settlers knew, they learned as much as or more than anyone they sought to teach, whether it was neighborhood people or government officials. Simkhovitch called settlement work "a new kind of university with the lessons hot from the griddle."[162] Katherine B. Davis, who went from settlement work to the reform administration of John Purroy Mitchel, said that the training received in settlement houses was one "no university could give. It was human; it was practical; it was universal. We learned through our own blunders how to arouse public concern and how to approach public officials in a way that would secure their cooperation."[163] Like the bureau men, then, settlement residents linked science with advocacy. They aimed at knowledge not just for its own sake but for what it would enable them to accomplish. Bureau researchers and settlers had different goals, however. The settlement workers wanted to improve the conditions of poor people's lives by getting governments to put in place new services and programs. They sought to present facts, statistics, and practical suggestions in a manner that would rouse public opinion and generate demand for improvements in the lives of city residents. For example, Chicago's Mary McDowell, armed with stories of actual living conditions in Packingtown, stereopticon slides, and factual analysis, appeared before clubs and church groups, organized mass meetings, and tirelessly laid before her audiences what it was like to live near—virtually in—a city dump. The city council became interested, but foot-dragging ensued. Then, in 1913, after women secured the municipal franchise, the city finally approved and built an improved system of garbage disposal.[164] By such means, settlement folk sought to transform neighborhood knowledge about living conditions into the basis for practical solutions to the problems at hand.[165]

ADMINISTRATION

Although settlement residents took a different tack than bureau reformers when it came to applying science to the solution of city problems, they shared the municipal researchers' awareness of the importance of sound administration and the impact that reliable knowledge might have. In her early investigation of Cook County's outdoor relief office, included in *Hull House Maps and Papers,* Julia Lathrop reported: "The methods of this office, with its records kept as each changing administration chooses, its dole subject to every sort of small political influence, and its failure to co-operate with private charities, are not such as science can approve. . . . We are shocked by the crudeness of the management which huddles men, women and children, the victims of misfortune and the relics of dissipation, the idle, the ineffective criminal, the penniless convalescent, under one roof and one discipline."[166] According to Jane Addams, the county agency responsible for charities and corrections was so fearful that "outdoor relief" would expand endlessly that when needy couples were placed in the poorhouse, they were separated into men's and women's units and allowed to talk to each other only once a week, and then with heavy screening between them. "Such a state of mind," Addams commented, "affords one more example of the danger of administering any human situation upon theory uncorrected by constant experience."[167] Faced with such bloodlessness, Addams's friend Lathrop constantly worked to bring state and county officials into closer touch with real life, at least through the experiences and attitudes of settlement workers, in order to push them toward better—that is, more humane—administration of existing laws.

Lathrop was quite effective in getting the attention and the cooperation of institutional officials. Alice Hamilton recounted the experience of accompanying Lathrop on a visit to an insane asylum. The superintendent was suspicious but, according to Hamilton, gradually thawed under the influence of Lathrop's charm and finally poured out his troubles. After the tour, Lathrop "gently but with devastating thoroughness" told the man that he was the one with the authority and he should shoulder it. As Lathrop and Hamilton left, the superintendent was promising to do his best. Hamilton reflected: "Often since then . . . I have felt myself tempted to rest content with the achievement of a pleasant relation in the place of an initial hostility, to look upon harmony as an end in itself. . . . [T]hen the memory of Julia Lathrop's example has pulled me up and made me say the disagreeable things which it is so much easier to leave unsaid."[168] Settlement residents were particularly sensitive to the human impact of public institutional practices because they tried to function in their communities as clearinghouses of information on public services and resources. In this capacity, they encountered almost daily situations in which men and women were being treated as cases instead of human beings because of administrative methods that had become frozen into standard procedures. They saw how lack of economic power made people vulnerable to administrators.

This attitude toward agency procedures was a product of their sensitivity to the place of administration in the overall scheme of governance. This is most clearly set forth in Jane Addams's 1905 essay "Problems of Municipal Administration."[169] Rather than lamenting the inefficiency of city agencies, Addams argues that the difficulties faced by city governments are rooted in an outmoded understanding of government, one that treats it as an instrument of control and not as a mechanism for strengthening community life as a whole. When administration consists largely of restrictive measures, Addams says, the only people who come in contact with government are the vicious, the poor, and disgruntled taxpayers who resent "the fact that they should be made to support that which, from the nature of the case, is too barren to excite their real enthusiasm" (428). Meanwhile, city governments ignore the people's "primary needs and experiences" and the potential to ignite a "passion for self-government" among them (438). The problem, then, is not efficiency or control but seeing city government in a new way, as a vehicle for ministering to its population's basic needs and for enabling people to take part in the process of deciding what to do. Administrative mechanisms become instruments for achieving much larger and more basic public purposes than simple efficiency.

In 1910, Julia Lathrop became the first woman to head a federal agency, the Children's Bureau. She went to her new assignment filled with the knowledge that the efforts of settlement house residents had brought the new bureau into being. Through their direct experiences with the lives of neighborhood residents, they had learned "certain aspects of dumb misery" that they had translated into effective policy advocacy. The need for reliable knowledge was a centerpiece of Lathrop's understanding of her job. She argued that her bureau needed "the sternest statistical accuracy" to guard against the charges of sentimentality that would inevitably dog an agency headed by a woman.[170] Yet she meant to avoid allowing her "distant office in Washington" to become abstract, so that gathering and classifying facts about the nation's children would actually help them.[171]

Lathrop's approach to managing the new bureau took advantage of the considerable network of contacts, both professional and volunteer, she had built up in the course of her previous work. These organizations, which included members of women's clubs, philanthropists, scholars, physicians, lawyers, and politicians, constituted an "informal administrative constituency" that she consulted with regularly before making decisions and used to gauge the level of political support for various strategies. She filled two key posts with young men from the Bureau of the Census, one of whom, Lewis Meriam, later became a leading figure in public administration.[172] According to Robyn Muncy, the new bureau chief manipulated the civil service regulations in order to populate the rest of the bureau's professional ranks with college-educated women.[173]

Lathrop used the settlement house survey method to good effect. Her bureau had been charged with investigating and reporting on matters pertaining to the welfare of children. With this as her mandate, Lathrop characterized her agency as "purely a statistical bureau," intending to assuage the fears of the medical community that the bureau might be a clinical rival. The bureau conducted a door-to-door investigation of infant mortality rates that showed their correlation with poor housing, low family wages, unsanitary conditions, and bottle feedings. The infant mortality studies, although "statistical," conveyed a radical message about the impact of poverty on the infant death rate. Lathrop went on to launch a national campaign for birth registration, in which she drew on networks of clubs and other women's groups to assist with house-to-house surveys to identify babies born in the preceding year and compare findings with official birth records. A third important project consisted of individual child health "conferences" in which doctors and nurses were able to assess the health status of children against national norms. This effort became part of a national campaign to popularize child health, including "National Baby Weeks" in 1916 and 1917. As Jacqueline Parker and Edward Carpenter note, "the Children's Bureau became in fact as well as name a 'popular bureau.'"[174] Thousands of women wrote to Lathrop to ask her questions about how to care for their children; the bureau staff answered every letter. Bureau pamphlets became best-sellers among federal government publications.

Lathrop's approach to public administration was notable in several respects. She made strategic use of discretionary authority to define an area of operation for the bureau; took advantage of gaps in governmental responsibility; avoided areas of extreme controversy, such as child labor; and developed grassroots as well as elite constituencies, based on her previous contacts. This approach contrasts with the bureau men's scientific management recommendations, which put heavy emphasis on systematizing functions such as budgeting, accounting, and record keeping and paid little attention to the political dimensions of administration. Lathrop realized from the outset that a bureau chief was not just a scientific manager but a political animal as well. Undoubtedly she leaned in this direction because, unlike the bureau men, she developed her administrative ideas on the basis of her practical experience rather than out of abstract theory.

Grace Abbott, a Hull House resident who succeeded Lathrop as head of the Children's Bureau, is another good example of the settlement attitude toward public administration. Early in her career, she had studied immigrant men's lodging houses; according to her sister Edith's reminiscences, Grace's sense of how the men were being exploited awoke "an interest in the writing of better social legislation and in finding better methods of administration."[175] Grace Abbott saw her work at Hull House as "a new opportunity of studying public administration in . . . social welfare by living and working with the people for whom the laws were passed" (356) and getting direct evidence of whether existing administrative procedures were adequate to the implementation of new policies. When Lathrop asked her to come to the Children's Bureau to take on enforcement of a new child labor law, Abbott again saw "new and challenging problems in public administration" (380). She faced the challenge of coordinating federal, state, and local government activities and relationships and working out the administrative machinery necessary to make the law effective. Abbott's career embodies an approach to public administration in which the need and desire to solve human problems are what make administrative mechanisms important and interesting. In contrast to many of the municipal researchers, Abbott saw administration as a means to make life better for people affected by social legislation, rather than an end in itself. Edith Abbott referred to Grace and to Julia Lathrop as "statesmen," staunch in their principles but aware that "administrative work often involved a kind of very subtle strategy and a quick and unerring ability to distinguish between important questions of principle and minor questions of policy." The capacity to tell the difference between the "essential and the nonessential," Edith Abbott said, was an "important factor in successful public welfare administration" (383–84).

Looking back on the settlement movement and its place in public life, Mary Simkhovitch observed that it was possible to balance efficiency and democracy, but society had not yet figured out how to do it.[176] As a group, settlement residents and members of women's clubs understood the importance of sound administration, but they consistently placed this goal within the broader context of the substantive improvements that they hoped government activity would make in people's lives.

In summary, women's reform work reflects distinctive perspectives and insights that might have been integrated with the structural and procedural interests of their male counterparts in the municipal research bureaus to create a vision of public administration that joined substance with procedure:

1. The city was a home for its people; therefore, city government should be thought of not as a business but as a kind of homemaking, devoted to creating the conditions under which residents could live safely and in relative comfort. Politics was not a contaminant of city governance; rather, it entailed the broad questions of public purpose that ought to be the central concern of anyone in government. Public service was a distinctive calling, not a form of business management.
2. If government was a means of achieving larger public purposes, politics and administration could not be separated. Methods were at the service of final ends. Decisions about proper administrative methods should be based not solely on their efficiency but on their humanity as well, with the latter taking precedence if there was an apparent conflict—for example, when efficiency measures would have inhumane consequences.
3. City officials should develop policies rooted in the lived experience of city residents, collaborating with those closest to problems to develop and implement solutions. The neighborhood spirit, which weaves residents together in a network of mutual knowledge and aid, should be the model for public spirit, for relationships between the government and its people.
4. Public administration should be scientific, but not in the objectified sense. Science was a means of gaining intimate knowledge about the conditions of people's lives through connection rather than separation. Life, not theory, would

lead the way. The goal of science was piled-up actuality that would make the city real to all its people and, with its great, grimed question marks, spur them to concerted action on behalf of the worst-off residents. The administrative standards science would produce would be "American" standards, that is, ones that joined considerations of efficiency and democracy.

5. Administrative practice consisted not merely of learning and applying a set of rules for scientific management but of judiciously exercising discretionary authority to take advantage of opportunities for strategic action based on a sense of the public good. Effective administration required political as well as managerial acumen: building constituencies, developing strategic alliances, understanding the difference between the marginal and the fundamental, being able to negotiate and compromise.

Although there are obvious conflicts between this philosophy of public administration and the one promulgated by the bureau men, one can still imagine a field in which the two philosophies were, if not integrated, at least in creative tension with each other—a profession in which ideas of public service encompassed managerial considerations and substantive aims for the improvement of human life. Although the ideas of settlement women and women's club members have emerged here and there since the reform era, they have had to struggle to maintain a foothold in the face of more business-oriented and efficiency-minded perspectives. The proposition that the knowledge needed to guide public decisions might sometimes best be arrived at through connection rather than objectification is still controversial, as is the image of a politically astute, public-interested administrator. The norms of administrative practice today remain much closer to business management than to housekeeping or motherhood.

Taken as a whole, the work of settlement residents and clubwomen created an alternative public space and an alternative understanding of the role of administration in governance. Immersed in domesticity, women developed a standpoint that enabled them to reshape public life. Given room in civil society and a value-based analysis of society's problems, women's organizations served as vehicles for political action and made their exclusion from existing public institutions a surmountable barrier. Settlement houses and women's clubs were a way around women's political disadvantages, as well as a strong institutional framework in which they could encounter like-minded people and engage in collaborative practices "in public." They saw their work as a form of citizenship, and they were unwilling to settle for the citizen-as-onlooker role that the bureau men had in mind for those who were not elite men like themselves. Yet women's distinctive vision of public life was unable to sustain itself. As the Progressive period gave way to the 1920s, women finally got the vote, the reform impulse waned, and a new set of factors came into play. These elements shaped two emerging professional disciplines, but in ways that made little room for the kinds of substantive concerns to which settlement women and other social welfare reformers had given center stage. As public practices became bifurcated into two disciplines by traditional definitions of appropriate public activity for men and women, a substantive idea of public service could not find an institutional home.

Women may have viewed housekeeping and motherhood as natural instincts that legitimated their institution building and their social policy proposals, but over time, women's distinctiveness began to work against them rather than in their favor. To accomplish its purposes, the female public sphere had to permeate and be permeated by the public world of men. As this happened, the politics of difference and indirection became more handicap than workable strategy. Julia Lathrop's Children's Bureau, for example, lost power once it became clear that newly enfranchised women would not vote as a bloc. Male politicians who had approved the Sheppard-Towner Act of 1921, which authorized state maternal and child health programs, now began to ridicule women reformers. They pointed to the "celibates" at the Children's Bureau who were interfering with the lives of women and children, conjuring up visions of a "bespectacled lady, nose sharpened by curiosity, official chin pointed and keen," authoritatively demanding admission to private homes in the name of the law. Sheppard-Towner was repealed in 1929, and the bureau lost the fight to control programs authorized by the Social Security Act of 1935.[177]

Outside the bureaucracy in civil society, a similar struggle occurred, one that women's "special nature" also lost. As women's groups moved from charitylike services to broader municipal reform issues, their ideals shifted from sisterhood and alternative politics to a more professionalized form of action within or in concert with the structure of municipal government. As nonpartisan reform efforts weakened the neighborhood base of city politics, settlements like Boston's Denison House were forced to build citywide political bases and to learn the language of municipal efficiency. The more involved in city politics they became, the more their own sense of an alternative civic space and vision of the city was dispelled. The more activities of this sort they took on, the greater their need for money, therefore the greater their dependence on male allies who could raise funds on the necessary scale. The greater this dependence, the more their radicalism was watered down by businessmen's fears about their propensity to organize factory workers, and the less unique their contributions seemed.[178]

Exclusion from ordinary politics had promoted a limited form of women's citizenship, one that depended on stereotypically feminine virtue and a strategy of indirection and persuasion. But acceptance, even grudging acceptance, into the political mainstream with the passage of the Nineteenth Amendment was a mixed blessing. Granted formal equality, women could no longer sell their concerns as special or justify their participation based on unique characteristics that the polity otherwise lacked. The risks of formal equality were dilution, marginalization, even effacement. Katherine B. Davis, the first woman to head a New York City department, declared upon her appointment that she would run her agency "exactly as a man would."[179] The question facing women as they began to move toward the mainstream of public life was whether this was the best they could hope for.

5
Professionalizing Public Service

In 1911, the New York Bureau of Municipal Research opened its Training School for Public Service. The school was the brainchild of William Allen and Mrs. E. H. Harriman, widow of the railroad executive who had been an early benefactor of the bureau. While traveling in Europe, Mrs. Harriman had been seized with the idea that government service in the United States ought to be professionalized along the lines of the civil services in Great Britain and France. Upon her return, she wrote to a number of prominent businessmen, educators, and civic leaders to ask whether they thought a training school for public service would be a useful idea.[1] Ironically, according to Allen's reminiscences, the only one to question the notion was Woodrow Wilson, whose essay "The Study of Administration" later assumed iconic status in public administration.[2]

While supporting the need for public service training in principle, representatives of leading universities such as Yale and Columbia declined to act as sponsors, apparently on the grounds that such training was not academic enough. Mrs. Harriman and Allen developed a plan and raised the initial funds to open the school under bureau auspices. Mrs. Harriman herself put up $80,000, and she and Allen raised an additional $120,000 to make possible a five-year test.[3] She was elected to a seat on the board of directors of the New York Bureau, the only woman to serve in that capacity.[4] The list of the training school's founding directors includes such legendary names as August Belmont, Andrew Carnegie, Samuel Insull, J. P. Morgan, John D. Rockefeller, Jacob Schiff, Cornelius Vanderbilt, and Felix Warburg, a lineup that suggests the extent to which a professionalized civil service was of interest to men of wealth.

According to its inaugural announcement, the school aimed "to train men for the study and administration of public business . . . [and] to furnish wherever practicable a connecting link between schools and colleges and municipal or other public departments for practical field work."[5] The initial thrust of the training was eminently practical, essentially imparting to students the how-tos of efficiency measures the bureau men were trying to get established in city agencies. Allen wrote that students would be trained in "the analysis of budget estimates, charter drafting and exposition, management of school problems, standardization of salaries, contracts and specifications, methods of assessing and collecting taxes, the preparation of handbooks of administrative practices, the investigation of proceedings of public bodies, and the preparation of public statements."[6] With typical pungency, Allen declared: "Lectures about Aristotle don't help a man understand the business aspect of government."[7] He emphasized that learning would take place by doing, not by standing by and observing. Students would engage in fieldwork supervised by bureau men or by agency officials cooperating with the bureau.

The *New York Tribune* announced the formation of the school as "an experiment in training men till they become experts in municipal government."[8] Allen insisted that the point of the school was rather "an experiment in training men in the interests of efficient municipal government." There had been a "nation wide awakening to the need for efficient methods and efficient agents," he wrote. In other words, citizens had recognized the importance of efficiency in the struggle to improve city governments; all the bureau was doing was "accelerating the supply" of men who knew how to manage efficiently.[9]

The initial announcement of the school prompted a flood of applications. The first class was made up of thirteen men, eight on stipends and five "volunteers." They included two school superintendents, an army officer and engineer, a sanitary engineer, a physician, a teacher, and a Columbia University doctoral candidate. According to minutes of the board of directors, the leaders of the school decided that it would be "inadvisable" to admit women, although several had applied. Subsequent classes contained a scattering of women, though the minutes made no further reference to the advisability of their presence.[10]

At first, the theory behind the school seems not to have been the development of a separate profession of public service. Instead, the rationale was that the ranks of government administrators included men trained in different specialties, all of whom would need, in addition to their technical education, specialized training in scientific management. "Public service is not a single profession," commented Charles A. Beard, who left Columbia University under fire and became director of the training school in 1915. "It calls for persons trained in all professions. . . . There can be no common education for all divisions of the service although there is undoubtedly a highly desirable type of training in administrative science which should be superimposed upon each of the various disciplines."[11]

On a parallel track to that of the New York Bureau, the American Political Science Association formed a Committee on Practical Training for Public Service in 1912. This committee was charged with making a list of institutions offering laboratory work for political science graduate students; recommending that credit be given for such work; obtaining scholarships; mobilizing an endowment; and coming up with assessment standards so that fieldwork would have scientific significance. This committee persuaded Mayor John Purroy Mitchel to call the first national conference on universities and public service training, which was held in New York City in 1914. The conference took up such topics as relationships between cities and universities and between universities and bureaus of municipal research.[12]

Tension between the academic interest in theory and the bureaus' emphasis on practicality was evident from the beginning. The New York Bureau's training school curriculum consisted almost entirely of fieldwork at first. The only required course was elements of accounting; students also attended a regular dinner symposium on efficient municipal government. Assignments put students to work on real governmental tasks, many of which agencies had contracted with the bureau to perform. For example, in January 1914, S. G. Lindstrom was assigned to a study of tuberculosis clinics. Allen's instructions read:

> We have undertaken to make a study of the tuberculosis clinics at Gouverneur Hospital at the request of Dr. Huddleston, director of the clinic. . . . We are to outline a plan for adoption next Monday morning, January 19th, which will go into the whole question of clinic efficiency, including the routing of work by field nurses, checks on attendance and results, . . . relations with the department of health, school inspectors and the women's auxiliary. . . . Outline a plan which will clearly distinguish the following parts of this study: that which can be done by the employees working to a plan outlined by us, that which can be done in cooperation between us and them, that which will require your personal attention; that which can be done by other members of the Training School. In addition, plan the work by periods showing what can be done the first week and what can be done the second week, so that when we come before them Monday morning there will be a clearly comprehensive program. Assume that we must finish the field work within two weeks. Use in your study the report of the board of estimate committee on dispensaries. . . . Speak to me daily regarding the progress of the study.[13]

Other fieldwork assignments were equally practical and immediate:

- Study and prepare a report upon the supervision, procedure, records, expenditures and physical condition of the 43 pumping stations operated by the water department.
- Study and criticize the form of comptroller's reports, New York and Pittsburgh.
- Make a study of the whole election machinery of New York with a view to showing the attitude of prosecuting officers, judges and jurors toward violations of the election laws.
- Continue at police headquarters your analysis of complaints against disorderly and gambling houses. . . . Prepare on the 9th day after receipt of your

assignment, and on every 9th day thereafter, a comprehensive memorandum of steps taken and results obtained up to the date of your report.[14]

Implicit in these assignments is the clear idea that public administration is learned through hands-on experience rather than by means of lectures and theoretical reading. In 1916, Charles Beard argued: "Why should we give a student academic credit for writing a thesis based on the reports of probation officers and deny him credit for doing the work of a probation officer? This is in effect saying—'If you know how somebody else did a thing you are entitled to a degree, but if you can only do it yourself you are a barbarian.' "[15] Despite the emphasis on practicality, students were required to read a number of books, including works by Allen, Henry Bruere, and Frederick Cleveland, and Frederick Taylor's *Principles of Scientific Management*. According to Jane Dahlberg, the training emphasized Taylor's approach, which centered around detailed analysis of work activities in order to find the most efficient way of accomplishing tasks. Cleveland and Taylor became friends, and Cleveland emerged as a major exponent of scientific management applied to government agencies.[16]

The possibility that public administration itself might become a profession began to insinuate itself into the thinking of the bureau men, bringing with it notions of a specific body of expertise peculiar to the new field. At the same time that Beard was calling for cooperation among an array of existing disciplines in the preparation of people for public service, he introduced the idea that "a new field of public service" was evolving, one that might have its own curriculum. A "science of public administration distinct from any technical specialty" was emerging, he said. Its content would include administrative law, budgeting and finance, scientific management, public works, personnel, city planning, departmental organization, report preparation, and statistics—a list not too different from today's master's-level curriculum.[17]

In this movement toward a science of public administration lay a fateful narrowing of the new field's purview, one that crowded out questions of purpose in favor of proper techniques. The seeds of the shift had been planted earlier, in the bureau men's insistence on scientific methods as the basis for reform of municipal agencies. Unlike methods, issues of purpose entail nontechnical questions about whose needs should be served, what kinds of services should be offered, and who should participate in deciding, questions that cannot be resolved by means of scientific techniques but must be debated. The Rockefeller ultimatum of 1914, with its preference for science over "publicity," must have helped push the New York Bureau in this direction. The groundwork, however, had been laid in the bureau's earliest self-definitions and projects. Might the bureau men have developed the substantive idea of public service that is visible in their early writings (though not as clear in tangible activities)? The existence of such an idea in the writings and activities of social reformers puts the growing emphasis on scientific management among municipal researchers into a broader context.

"A NEW PROFESSION"

The early twentieth century was a time when educated people sought to establish a place for themselves in American society, one that would legitimate the application of their knowledge to social problems. Industrialization, urbanization, and immigration had generated new and growing dilemmas; the educated middle and upper-middle classes believed that systematic knowledge, perceptively applied, held the keys to their solution. Groups of educated people staked out new conceptual and practical terrain for themselves. They hoped to institutionalize and perpetuate what had started as relatively informal and experimental approaches and thereby instantiate society's need for what they claimed as their particular knowledge and technical skills, even though in some cases the knowledge base was still embryonic. As Magali Sarfatti Larsen notes, would-be professionals appealed to science to justify their claims to authority, but it was science as method and worldview rather than as clearly defined body of knowledge.[18]

In the early twentieth century, "public service" was a term that encompassed widely varied bodies of knowledge and activities. Its conceptual boundaries were relatively fluid, able to accommodate projects as diverse as the bureau men's improvement of an agency's voucher system, settlement residents' lobbying to limit the working hours of children, and charitable workers' efforts to improve the lot of individual poor families. At this critical moment in American history, reformers as different as Frederick Cleveland and Jane Addams could share a commitment to the notion of public service precisely because the tensions among the various definitions of it had not become apparent, and the question of professionalization was still incipient.

In 1906, settlement leader Robert Archey Woods set forth his vision of a profession of public service, one that integrated government reform, settlement work, and charitable activities. Woods was a leading figure in urban reform. A founder in 1889 of South End House in Boston, Woods organized one of the first social surveys of a city neighborhood. He also played a central role in the Pittsburgh Survey. South End House residents were ardent advocates of many needed improvements in urban life. For example, they appealed to the Boston City Council in 1892 for funds to establish a public bathhouse, and the mayor appointed Woods to chair a committee whose lobbying efforts led to the necessary appropriations. With other settlement houses, South End House spurred local businessmen's interest in city problems and played leading roles in the Good Government Association and the City Club of Boston. Their political analysis of the Boston machines led to a change in the method of electing aldermen, although the settlers were frustrated in most of their attempts to elect reform mayors. With Albert Kennedy, Woods published *The Settlement Horizon,* a landmark review of the accomplishments of the settlement movement.[19] Throughout his life, Woods was an ardent proponent of the importance of reviving neighborhoods to the overall success of municipal reform.

Woods's essay "Social Work: A New Profession" was an early statement of the meaning of the term "social work" and of its potential as the basis for a lifetime career. It is particularly interesting for the way it weaves social work together with ideas of public service and statesmanship. In this respect, it shows how an expansive understanding of social work could mingle with themes from public administration to offer a form of public professionalism that joined systematic study with practical application and advocacy. The essay appeared in *Charities and the Commons*, the leading reform publication, in the same year the fledgling New York Bureau of Municipal Research performed its first investigations of the New York City government.[20] Although we have no way of knowing, it is possible, even likely, that municipal researchers such as William Allen and Henry Bruere read Woods's essay. Both Allen and Bruere considered themselves social workers, and their names appeared regularly in the journal, which was—to judge from its contents— widely read by reformers of all stripes.

The essay is organized around the question of how an educated man is to spend his life. Woods's use of the term "man" equivocates throughout the article. Sometimes it clearly seems to apply to educated people of both sexes, sometimes to men alone—an ambiguity that increases its relevance today. Certainly the question of how to make meaningful use of one's education was one that concerned both men and women, the latter because of sharp restrictions on appropriate occupations for well-to-do women. Woods points out that social work brings men and women together in "common work" that reflects "real equality between the sexes" (474).

Woods argues that the times make a particular demand on the educated not to rely on the accepted wisdom of the past but to understand and act on contemporary conditions by direct contact with them. "The new type of effort called social work," he writes, "gets its distinctive quality in seeking first to understand, and secondly, to affect the problems of the community by means of direct contact with all sorts and conditions of men." Like the bureau reformers, Woods specifically connects the activities of understanding and affecting to government. By government, he means not a body of traditional institutions but a "science" based on principles derived not only from the past but also from "wrestling with many new situations." But Woods separates himself from the kind of government reform that confines itself to "mere technical efficiency of administration" and is therefore ill prepared to deal with emerging problems. In contrast, "the new social work profession has for its object to restore to its true place in the field of politics, industry and culture this end and aim of all things in the life we are now living" (470). For Woods, the crux of social work is serving human needs; it is activity on the part of the privileged to study and experiment in order to improve people's lives and to "bring people together belonging to separate classes" (471).

Woods is convinced that systematic knowledge is a resource for solving the life problems of the poor. Social work's aim, then, is "to train the people to trust the expert"—again, a goal similar to the one espoused by the bureau men. But, Woods argues, the reason ordinary people do not trust experts is because experts do not understand their lives. Social work's mandate, then, is immersion in the life of poor neighborhoods in order to understand life as neighborhood residents do and then take steps to improve it. While this approach to social change contains a considerable degree of elitism, it is a more democratic impulse than the bureau men's, which was heavily dependent on detached scientific investigation aimed at bringing to light administrative misdeeds and shortcomings. (Imagine, for example, that the bureau men had simply gone to work in public agencies in order to understand the details of administrative problems as they were understood by those who were confronted with them every day, and on that basis decide collaboratively with agency personnel what changes to make.) Woods's elitism is tempered by his belief that people from various countries and backgrounds all have something to contribute to American life; it is the social worker's job to facilitate those contributions: "Social work has to do with the building up of a natural federation among all our different racial groups, which will in reasonable degree preserve all that is valuable in the heredity and tradition of each type, but will link all types together in a universal yet incoherent and distinctively American nationality" (472). It accomplishes this aim by establishing "bits of neutral territory" where members of various ethnic groups can establish "friendly relations" and consider their common interests with regard to particular steps in political development, industrial progress, or the "betterment of family life and neighborly intercourse." Social work, then, is far more than "sporadic labors of compassion" aimed at isolated individuals or families; its eye is always on the big picture, the "great forces of society" that produce the evils that afflict poor immigrants. Although Woods's essay lacks a theory of how social work is supposed to change capitalism so that it need not inevitably produce poverty, he advocates that social workers be involved in improving working conditions, schooling, and other social systems that limit the lives of the poor.

Social work is, therefore, in Woods's view, a kind of "unofficial statesmanship." He takes aim at the idea, common among the well-to-do, that no man of means could possibly be attracted to a political career, since politics was so thoroughly driven by party loyalty rather than by merit. He calls upon young men to enter "public service at those points where the public need is greatest, . . . not only correcting the technique of government in our cities, but . . . humanizing them" by ensuring that they "meet great collective human needs." Statesmanship entails not only direct contact with government but also activity that builds up, "first in local units, and then in larger federations, a kind of moral municipality and commonwealth. The social work profession thus provides a distinct and inviting opportunity for those university men who feel the moral attraction of public service, but have thought that conditions being as they are, the door of such opportunity is closed" (473). Woods presents social work and public service—the essay virtually equates the two—as a career that conceivably encompasses a range of activities, including holding public office ("so long as political and ethical conditions allow"); making administrative improvements; conducting the kinds of experimental programs in which settlement houses specialized, which could then be taken over by governments; starting up new organizations and strengthening existing ones; and in general, improving citizenship. Social work, in Woods's eyes, is *"the work of public administration of the community."* His mode of public administration, however, clearly entails not just making agencies run more efficiently and effectively but also the opportunity to "create new agencies, new institutions, new laws, which will in large ways actually shut off at their source the influences which produce great social miseries and inequities" (473; emphasis added). His vision is based on an understanding that government has a responsibility to attack the societal conditions of human want; his is an activist intepretation of the uses of government, one in which what government does is as important as how. Social work–public administration–public service addresses both the what and the how.

Woods concludes his argument with the observation that social work is a particularly pragmatic activity, one focused on next steps rather than on preserving ancient wisdom or on "distant Utopias." The first step is to try to permeate existing institutions with a new spirit; only if this proves inadequate should one create new organizations. Social work is a kind of "practical university" that applies knowledge to "new fields of life." Social workers as a group represent "a community of practical scholars" in which, through activity, each member finds fellowship and intellectual exchange, new ideas and suggestions that enrich and strengthen the profession as a whole (475). Social work itself is an experiment that will help determine the broader dimensions of professionalism in society. The doors it opens to the well educated will help remedy the lack of a tradition of public service in American life. By spurring college graduates to lives of public service, the universities where they received their education will at the same time fulfill their own sort of public service mission.

In sum, Woods's vision of public service had four principal aspects: a focus on the ends and aims of life, on human need and how organized effort can address it; an emphasis on community, on interests and beliefs that tie people together, and on how to facilitate collaborative work; a view of government, statesmanship, and citizenship as positive forces in society; and a pragmatic and practical approach. Together, these elements might have formed the basis for a profession of public service. Such a profession would have been based on the application of a varied body of systematic knowledge acquired in intimate contact with lived experience both inside and outside the walls of the government institution. It would have been one in which theory and practice were intertwined to attack actual human problems through experimentation with new programs, development and implementation of new public policies, and the improvement of administrative methods.

Although Woods's essay presents a more fully developed idea of public service than most and is particularly interesting for the way it weaves together social work and public administration to produce public service, its ingredients are not entirely idiosyncratic to its author. A number of social reformers articulated a vision of their work that emphasized what Edward T. Devine, general secretary of New York's Charity Organization Society, called "conscious social action" that "makes of Charity a type of anticipatory justice." Every social worker, said Devine, speaking at the National Conference of Charities and Corrections in 1906, should "seek out and . . . strike effectively at those organized forces of evil, at those particular causes of dependency and intolerable living conditions which are beyond the control of the individuals whom they injure and whom they too often destroy."[21] Sophonisba Breckinridge, founder with Edith Abbott of the first graduate program in social work, also emphasized "revolt against injustice and a love of equality," along with "reasonable knowledge of the causes." She combined these values with an insistence on building what she thought of as a science of public welfare administration: "a very adequate preparation in the field of government, in the field of social case work, and in . . . various other special professional bodies of knowledge." She saw the professional curriculum as a combination of the historical ("This was tried with this result"), the analytical ("Those factors were lacking"), the interpretive, and the suggestive.[22]

Many of Woods's themes were also sounded here and there by municipal researchers in the early days of their movement. Leaders of the New York Bureau, for example, insisted that their reason for striving to make government agencies more efficient was so that more could be accomplished with a given amount of money to help people in need. Henry Bruere wrote that "death, disease, distress, ignorance and crime" were the "direct . . . consequence of . . . waste."[23] Bruere also emphasized the link between experts and the community, envisioning a city where "the thousands" were developing a "consciousness of kind, a solidarity of interest" that would support the application of expertise to government, while the municipal research aim became a "citywide, community-planned and community-executed program of citizen well-being."[24]

On the role of government, William Allen was the activist among the bureau men, calling it the most important agency for benevolence, the greatest philanthropist. He insisted that only government had the resources to understand and remedy the causes of poverty rather than simply to treat its effects. Allen also stressed the importance of practical knowledge, arguing that virtuous indignation about conditions in city governments was a weak substitute for intelligent demands based on factual analysis.[25] Bruere shared the interest in applying knowledge and insisted that fact-finding would bring to light the gap between needs and existing services, thus making resources go further.[26]

Thus, in the early twentieth century, "social work," "public administration," and "public service" were not the sharply differentiated terms they were by century's end. No one in the reform community would have been surprised to hear municipal researchers refer to themselves as social workers, nor to find that settlement residents were in favor of administrative efficiency. As a group, reformers were unified by a commonly held commitment to public service, albeit one they translated into different kinds of actions. As they began to differentiate themselves into separate professions, the bureau men took a decided tack toward scientific management, an emphasis on correct procedures to the neglect of substantive purpose.

"Service" began to be displaced in favor of "administration." But if municipal researchers were not to produce a profession of public service, could their compatriots in reform, the social workers, do the trick?

PROFESSIONALIZING BENEVOLENCE

Of the two nascent professions, social work was the first to raise the issue of how to ensure that people practicing under its banner possessed the proper qualifications and had mastered the requisite body of knowledge and technical skills. This was a particularly acute issue for social workers, in that many of them were women volunteering as "friendly visitors" of the poor. Women who engaged in charitable work had struggled since the mid-nineteenth century to balance their need to engage in businesslike activities such as fund-raising, lobbying, and managing charitable activities with a rhetoric that justified their involvement in terms of female benevolence. Even though careers in benevolence, whether paid or volunteer, entailed decidedly unsentimental approaches, women's rhetoric masked business aspects of the work behind a veil of sentimentality. After the Civil War, male values of efficiency, order, and punctuality became increasingly evident in charitable work. Calls for professionalism competed with older notions of women's moral superiority.[27] Ideas of "scientific charity" began to replace the rhetoric of female benevolence.

The first charity organization society, formed to put scientific charity into practice, was established in Buffalo, New York, in 1877, but its principal antecedent was the Association for Improving the Conditions of the Poor, where the New York Bureau's William Allen had worked before plunging into municipal research. The AICP had practiced scientific charity prior to the term's invention. The approach was premised on the need to organize society's philanthropic resources efficiently through the adoption of business techniques such as functional specialization and administrative centralization. As Roy Lubove notes, the rationale for scientific charity was that efficiency enabled society to help those in need, a precursor of the municipal research argument that efficiency was democratic.[28]

Scientific charity used female friendly visitors to visit, educate, and advise the poor. According to Robert Bremner, friendly visitors were expected to be "combination detectives and moral influences,"[29] a role not unlike that of the municipal researchers who came after them. Given Allen's previous involvement in scientific charity, it is not implausible that the municipal research approach, perhaps unconsciously, took some of its cues from friendly visiting. Both friendly visitors and municipal researchers worked to get the facts of each case through painstaking investigation and hoped to inspire those under investigation to better behavior. Increasingly, though, an emphasis on science eroded the earlier stress on "simple friendliness" in social work, which now seemed to smack of a class-based paternalism—or maternalism—that turn-of-the-century Progressives aimed to reject.

Devine argued that "good motives" were not always consistent with the "interests of humanity. . . . A picked band of a hundred devoted, trained and capable workers, especially adapted to the task in hand, will not only accomplish more than a thousand untrained, unassorted volunteers, but they may actually do more to develop the genuinely spontaneous charitable tendencies of the whole population"[30]—an argument that parallels the bureau men's rejection of the civil service reform movement's reliance on good men in favor of a scientific approach rooted in good methods. In both cases, the claim of scientific expertise served as the purported antidote to class bias and feminine do-goodism. Yet some social work leaders worried that professionalization would transform the social worker from "the embodiment of sentiment" into the "symbol of technique."[31]

Social work, then, embarked on its quest for professional status permeated with tension between the older feminine ideas of care for others and emerging notions of scientific, businesslike charity that had a decidedly masculine tinge. The Progressive determination to deny the importance of class divisions and to assert that their values united people of all classes made an emphasis on expertise acceptable and the old-style patronizing benevolence of the volunteer increasingly suspect. "The only valid form of superiority in a democracy was the superior knowledge of the expert."[32]

In 1897, Mary Richmond, director of the Baltimore Charity Organization Society, delivered a paper at the national conference of charity workers calling for organized training in social work.[33] The next year, Devine initiated a summer training program, which soon blossomed into the New York School of Philanthropy. Allen attended the summer training program in 1901. In Chicago, settlement leaders Graham Taylor and Julia Lathrop launched the Chicago Institute of Social Science; similar efforts got under way in Boston (1904), St. Louis (1908), and Philadelphia (1908). As the fledgling programs developed, a lively debate ensued over two versions of social work education.[34] In this debate are visible not only the tension between benevolence and efficiency but also a parallel struggle between a casework-oriented emphasis on helping individuals and the need to prepare people to craft and advocate social welfare policies.

One side in the debate recommended an academic curriculum with a social reform orientation and heavy doses of social theory. This was the approach favored by Samuel McCune Lindsay, a professor on leave from Columbia University to head the New York training school, and Simon Patten, economist at the Wharton School and mentor of both Allen and Cleveland. Patten argued that social work should focus on social policy issues rather than casework. This social theory approach captured the emphasis of Robert Woods's seminal article on the ends of government as well as his faith in government as a positive force, but it neglected Woods's reliance on interaction with community residents as the way toward practical solutions to social problems.

The competing vision of social work education, advocated by Mary Richmond, was a curriculum based on practice wisdom and including a great deal of fieldwork experience, with the objective of preparing people to be caseworkers.[35] Richmond's model, a modernization of the old "friendly visitor," was consistent with Woods's stress on practical knowledge but lacked his community-level focus and his emphasis on the need for statesmanship. Richmond did maintain that social workers should have an interest in reform: "The champions of casework are the champions of social reform also." But she saw good casework as the necessary prerequisite to broader change.[36]

Richmond and Patten clashed openly on the issue of whether social work entailed personal service or a more systemic approach. Richmond criticized Patten for deprecating altruism. In a tart reply entitled "Who Is the Good Neighbor?" Patten commented that Richmond "would have us go out and be friendly with this great mass of citizens differing from ourselves. . . . In my opinion the need of the poor is not for advice but for a better environment, and the duty of the rich is not to spend an occasional half day in moralizing to the poor, but to give a definite part of their income to improve the conditions under which the poor live." Duplicating arguments being advanced at the same time by bureau men, Patten concluded: "Mere goodness must be replaced by efficiency and the trained paid agent must replace the voluntary visitor who satisfies her curiosity at the expense of those she meets, and in the end loses her faith in humanity or turns socialist."[37]

Thus, early on a split developed in social work between a macrolevel emphasis on societywide strategies and a microlevel focus on addressing the problems of individuals and families. The former captured the settlement house awareness of the social and economic roots of poverty, and the latter preserved the older idea prevalent in scientific charity that the causes of poverty lay in individual pathology. Woods's vision of a social work that kept its eye both on the larger dynamics of urban problems and on the potential in the knowledge of ordinary people never became the basis for a profession. No professional group, neither social work nor public administration, claimed practical approaches to societal problems as its particular turf.[38] The respect Woods and other settlement workers had for the knowledge of ordinary people was fundamentally inconsistent with the drive to assert specialized expertise grounded in a recognizable science. When Edith Abbott and Sophonisba Breckinridge founded the first graduate program in social work (see below), they emphasized social welfare policy, but the practical orientation of settlement leaders toward dealing with problems by collaborating with those affected by them failed to find a place at the center of the social work identity.

As social work developed, the social policy emphasis embodied in the activities of settlement residents and other social welfare reformers grew increasingly weak, while the search for a unique set of technical skills and a unique body of scientific knowledge took pride of place. In part, this trend was the outgrowth of a famous speech delivered at the social workers' convention in 1915 by Abraham Flexner, assistant secretary of the General Education Board, an organization set up by John D. Rockefeller to coordinate his donations to educational interests. As a result of his earlier report on medical training, Flexner had become perhaps the most influential person in the United States on the topic of professional education. His report had recommended a shift from medical apprenticeship to a laboratory-based form of training that emphasized medicine's scientific dimensions. Flexner told the social workers that in his view, social work was not and never would be a profession, because it essentially involved mobilizing and coordinating the expertise of others, such as lawyers and physicians, to help people in need, rather than any expertise of its own. Flexner disparaged the social work emphasis on practice wisdom for its lack of the theoretical coherence characteristic of a science like physics or chemistry. His pronouncement set social work on a quest to develop the kind of scientific basis Flexner insisted was the hallmark of a profession. Freudian theory ultimately became the chosen dogma, even though in practice, social workers made little or no use of psychoanalytic techniques.[39]

As Clarke Chambers observes, over time, what had been in many respects a culturally feminine pursuit emphasizing service, helping, and the fostering of community became increasingly oriented toward scientific objectivity, formal bureaucratic structures, and careerism. Chambers attributes this trend to a number of factors: the rise of community chests, which coordinated efforts among charitable groups to secure donations from business elites and therefore required benevolent organizations to appear efficient; the decline of residency in settlement houses, which led to a loss of community feeling and respect for neighborhood knowledge; and the rise of welfare bureaucracies during the New Deal, which opened up careers in public administration that favored men. The stress on businesslike efficiency, the rejection of collaboration and community in favor of expertise, and the increasing importance of management in social welfare agencies all had their roots in traditionally masculine values and activities.[40] Certainly the shift from social reform to casework as the centerpiece of social work had a drastic narrowing effect that attenuated the wider public service vision of Woods and others. The problem seems to have been that no one was able to articulate social reform in terms of a scientific skill. The conflict between the advocacy needed for successful reform and the objectivity characteristic of science was just too deep. No clearly defined body of expert knowledge coalesced on which to base a public profession whose aim was tied to questions of purpose, to testing and refining practical solutions to societal problems, rather than simply to proper techniques.

As in the case of social work, among municipal researchers, what started as a concern for balancing technical skill with a broader vision of public service became, over time, an increasing focus on the technical and scientific. In part, this trend was a function of the emphasis in municipal reform on reclaiming the public service from the clutches of the machine boss, a project that required public administration to find a distinctive definition for itself, one that not only separated it from party politics but also raised its prestige above the reach of machine criticisms. The more scientific public administration seemed, the higher its societal standing and the stronger its claim to public authority. Because of the ancient equation between science and masculinity, a grounding in scientific expertise also helped remove the taint of femininity with which all antiparty reform efforts appeared to be infected. Bureau men were quick to point to the "virility" of their activities and to promote businesslike management over volunteerism, which was looked on as feminine.[41] Charles Beard defined public administration in terms of a "deep thrusting" effort "by which modern mankind is striving with all its resources to emancipate itself from the tyranny of rules of thumb and the blind regimen of nature, becoming conscious of its destiny as an all-conquering power."[42] Both public administration and social work, then, came to define professionalization in terms of rejecting feminine sentimentality and embracing masculine objectivity and efficient business practices. At least in part, this is a reflection of the lure science holds for any group seeking professional status.

Public administration's professional development parallels the process in social work in another interesting respect. The year before his speech to the social work convention, Flexner reported to the Rockefellers on the work of the New York Bureau of Municipal Research. His report had an even more profound effect on the subsequent development of public administration than his broadside against social work had in that field. The central role of the New York Bureau in municipal research generally and in the inauguration of professional training in public administration meant that the impact of the Flexner report reached far beyond one organization to the dynamics in an entire field.

Flexner was called in by John D. Rockefeller, Jr., to assess the bureau's research on public schooling. The bureau had taken a highly visible and partisan stance in this area, one that generally favored public involvement and accountability over a model that centralized power in the person of the school superintendent. Prominent men raised the question of why Rockefeller money was supporting so controversial a stance and, in particular, an advocate as fiery as Allen, who was leading the bureau's school reform efforts.[43] Flexner's report exposed the bureau's "scientific" approach as more rhetoric than reality. He accused the bureau of shoddy and superficial investigative methods, calling its approach too crude and one-sided to be worthy of the term "research." A "real" research bureau, Flexner maintained, "would study a situation thoroughly and dispassionately and present its results fairly and objectively." Flexner also criticized the training school for inadequate "direction, oversight, and control" due to lack of "necessary training, experience, ability, [and] time."[44]

Flexner's report moved Rockefeller, as we have seen (chapter 2), to issue an ultimatum to the bureau. Either it pulled back from its more controversial activities and ended the practice of involving trainees in poorly supervised hands-on activity in public agencies, or Rockefeller would end his support. The bureau's surrender turned it in a markedly more conservative direction. It pulled in its horns, suspended its more colorful and partisan activities and publications, and styled itself as a more scientific and objective investigative body. Its new publication, the monthly periodical *Municipal Research,* which replaced the brash "Efficient Citizenship" postcards, took as its motto: "To promote the application of scientific principles to government." As in social work, Flexner—in concert with Rockefeller—had managed to tip the balance away from advocacy toward a more detached approach to knowledge, one whose objective grounding was less threatening to established arrangements. In each case, the power of the scientific mandate lay at least partially in its ability to dilute the femininity with which the practice would otherwise have been associated, and thus to strengthen its legitimacy.

INSTITUTIONALIZATION

As the professionalization of social work and public administration proceeded, both fields sought to institutionalize their claims by lodging their training within higher education. In both cases, the price of the university imprimatur was an increasing emphasis on the theory base, which held out the promise of full-fledged disciplinary status. Tension grew between the academic development of theory and the inevitable need to redeem it in the world of practice. Impulses toward caring and service struggled to survive within frameworks of dispassionate study.

As the twentieth century rounded out its second decade, the fate of public administration as an identifiable field of study grounded in practical activity was still tied to the fortunes of its host institution, the New York Bureau of Municipal Research.[45] Despite its apparent reinvention in response to the Rockefeller dictate, the bureau continued to find itself embroiled in controversies of various kinds and having to struggle to maintain an adequate funding base. Its involvement in the debate over the New York State constitution generated the same charges of elitism and power hunger that the bureau had faced in its early days. The press regularly referred to the bureau in terms calculated to appeal to popular disdain for pointy-headed experts. In 1916, the *Brooklyn Standard* editorialized that "even professional reformers . . . are rarely practical. That is one of the reasons why Tammany so often comes back into power after indignant expulsion at the polls by the people." Reformers installed inexperienced men in important city jobs, the paper charged, while the "moneyed businessmen" who financed the reformers went back to their private affairs and let the government drift. "Professors of efficiency [were] quite as impractical in many respects as the crude fusionists of a decade or more ago."[46] "Investigate Them!" cried the *Brooklyn Eagle*. "Everybody is investigated nowadays except the Bureau of Municipal Research. It should no longer be exempt." The *Eagle* called for an appropriation of $100,000 to "research municipal research, with the proviso that none of the money be spent in visiting fairs, buying theater tickets, hiring expensive hotel rooms, or in eating beyond the actual requirements of appetite."[47]

The bureau's investigative work continued to be met with countercharges by public officials. Dr. Hermann Biggs, once a friend of the bureau, attacked it from his new position as state health director, accusing the bureau's assistant director, W. B. Holton, Jr., of ignorance about public health matters after Holton questioned the establishment of an enlarged public health laboratory at Albany.[48] Frederick Cleveland's investigations of state government led "men at Albany" to ban bureau researchers, calling Cleveland's efforts "the hand of insinuation which dares to reach after the reputation of men not dead."[49]

While these charges and countercharges flew back and forth, Charles Beard, director of the training school, reminded the bureau's board of directors that the school's five years' worth of funding was about to run out; students were inquiring whether the training would continue. The board appointed a committee to raise money to keep the school open.[50] In April 1917, Cleveland tendered his resignation as bureau director, perhaps weary of the unavoidably political struggle to systematize state government. The minutes noted: "Mr. E. P. Goodrich was elected Director with the proviso that he can continue private consulting in city planning,"[51] a bland statement that may have masked the difficulty of finding someone willing to make a full commitment to the organization.

Charles Beard became director of the bureau in February 1918. Later that year, he recommended that the training school be made national, with a broader base of support, to recruit and train men and women for governmental research, administrative positions, and other kinds of civic activities. Beard advocated training as the principal thrust of the bureau, with research and fieldwork seen as contributions to the educational purpose. The probable subtext of this proposal was that reorientation in this direction would make the bureau more fundable; as it was, the bureau had difficulty maintaining its funding base. Beard himself may have been a liability in this regard. As Charles T. Goodsell notes, Beard's reputation was that of a "wild-eyed and even unpatriotic iconoclast, an image that can be traced to his critique of the [framers of the U.S. Constitution]."[52] Goodsell suggests that Beard was forced to resign the directorship of the bureau in 1920 because he had become a "fund-raising liability among businessmen in the New York area."[53] Although Mrs. Harriman remained loyal, in early 1921, the Carnegie Corporation turned down a request for $100,000, and the handwriting on the wall seemed clear. Some sort of major restructuring was necessary.

The bureau adopted Beard's plan, creating the National Institute of Public Administration (NIPA), incorporated in April 1921, for the purposes of sponsoring "a school of public administration dedicated to the training of men and women for the public service, for research in government, for intelligent citizenship, and for the teaching of civics; to study and report on principles and practices of public administration; and to maintain and develop a library of public administration." The Carnegie Corporation and John D. Rockefeller, Jr., pledged support for the new organization.[54] Thus Beard, despite being forced out of the bureau, left his stamp on it. He had initiated the process of shifting the training program's emphasis away from fieldwork and toward organized courses that included classroom lectures and discussions. By 1918, Columbia University, New York University, and the University of Chicago recognized the training school's program as worthy of academic credit and agreed to exchanges of students.[55] By 1920, the school's bulletin listed a full year's offering of such courses. The training program was now styled as "scientific and educational," distinct from the "survey work" that continued under the bureau name, which was, in most cases, paid for by the governments that requested it.[56] Beard's former student at Columbia, Luther Gulick, became president of the NIPA; a year later, the bureau board was dissolved, and the bureau for all practical purposes merged with the NIPA. Practical studies conducted for governments continued under the bureau aegis, but this was a paper designation aimed at keeping potentially controversial real-world activities from contaminating the "scientific" training. Barry Karl observes that the selection of Gulick symbolized an unresolved conflict within the organization, between the "accountants" interested in systematizing government agencies and an increasingly academic interpretation of the term "research," the one Beard represented.[57] In any case, even the government surveys had moved quite a long way from the combative posture the bureau had maintained in its early days, when publicity about the results of investigations was its principal weapon in the fight to systematize city government.

Despite skepticism among bureau leaders about the wisdom of formal linkages with academic institutions, Gulick attempted to resolve the conflict between science and practical research as well as reduce the fund-raising burden by forming an alliance with Syracuse University.[58] George Maxwell, a Syracuse alumnus and Boston shoe manufacturer, had offered to contribute $500,000 to establish a school of citizenship at the university. Through the influence of Frederick Davenport, New York state senator, U.S. representative, and professor of political science at Hamilton College, Maxwell's original vision of an undergraduate program dedicated to "intelligent patriotism" was broadened to include graduate training, to address what Davenport perceived as the need for trained specialists in government. Davenport turned for advice to the NIPA and Gulick. According to Peter Johnson, "The input from NIPA/BMR [Bureau of Municipal Research] provided the single most important influence on the development of the Maxwell School."[59]

For Gulick, the overture from Syracuse was a godsend, an opportunity to offload some of the cost of maintaining the training school and institutionalize it within a university. The agreement specified that William E. Mosher, then director of the training school, would assume the duties of managing director of the Maxwell School. The NIPA would conduct at its New York City offices an annual three-month course in public administration, which would be a required part of the school's one-year graduate program. NIPA staff would provide up to twelve days of lecturing in Syracuse. The school would set aside $10,000 a year for NIPA research, the content to be jointly decided by the school's advisory council and Mosher. Syracuse would pay the NIPA $5,600 annually, plus incidental expenses, to cover the three-month course and $2,500 for the additional lectures, and it would defray the students' living expenses in New York City.[60]

Mosher was one of two men in public administration whom Dwight Waldo called major advocates of scientific management; Waldo also cited Mosher as the leading exponent of "new management," an approach to public administration that stressed "finding ways and means of managing the public's business efficiently."[61] A student at the training school before he became its director, Mosher told Waldo that "from the beginning" he had seen his " 'mission' as the extension of scientific management to the public's business; his special contribution in personnel administration was conceived as such an extension."[62]

The selection of Mosher to head the new Maxwell School ensured that a university-based graduate program there would have a strong thrust toward science. A twenty-year retrospective in Mosher's files notes, "The basic concept of the curriculum throughout the years has been the belief that there is such a thing as the science of administration and that men may be trained in this technique just as they are in other well established technical callings." But the public administrator was not himself to be a technician. "It is his business not to know how to run the fire department but to ascertain how well it is being run." The public administrator was a scientific generalist, a leader, planner, and coordinator of technical work.[63] Mosher became an advocate for a professional corps in public administration that was scientific in spirit, the product of organized training.[64] Interestingly, in 1933, Mosher couched his vision of the modern government in terms of a shift from "policing" to "housekeeping," that is, "seeking in an affirmative way to promote the welfare of its citizens," but by this time, women's municipal housekeeping and public motherhood had faded into obscurity.[65]

The germ of Mosher's vision lay in Beard's insight that beyond the addition of administrative training to other disciplines, there was a core body of knowledge that might constitute the basis for an autonomous profession. Maxwell's original idea had been a school that would promote good citizenship at least as widely as the population of students who could afford to attend, but Davenport's interest in a cadre of governmental experts was more in line with Mosher's thinking and that of the other bureau men. "Government and political action are complicated and increasingly difficult to understand," wrote Davenport shortly after the school opened. "The executive, legislative, and judicial processes are intricate—comparatively few intelligently master them; the business is technical, the processes involved, the machinery complex." Although the American people needed to become better informed about their government, they also needed well-trained leaders and specialists in technical administrative knowledge.[66] Johnson notes that Maxwell "viewed moral education as the key to reform," but Davenport, Gulick, and Mosher, practitioners all, believed that "a democratic society could only be protected from the divisive forces of the modern world by a system of careful administrative management and control." Professional bureaucrats would provide this guidance.[67] Syracuse University set about the task of ensuring an adequate supply of leaders and specialists; other universities followed suit.

Meanwhile, parallel efforts took place in social work. Edith Abbott and Sophonisba Breckinridge, both of whom had been associated with Hull House, joined the faculty of the Chicago School of Civics. Both held doctoral degrees but found that there were no academic career possibilities for them outside departments of home economics. As a result of their affiliation with the Chicago program, they became interested in transforming social work into an academic discipline and thereby turning it into a profession.[68]

The issue of university-based social work training was controversial among academics and social workers alike. While sociology departments eyed the social welfare arena with interest, viewing settlement house neighborhoods as sociological laboratories, academics questioned the appropriateness of "charities" content in their curricula, regarding it as unscientific and difficult to study statistically. Charity workers, for their part, saw social science theory as too remote from the day-to-day problems they tackled. Mary Richmond and others "believed universities had been slow to comprehend the significant service offered by the emerging profession. . . . James H. Tufts, a professor of philosophy at the University of Chicago, characterized this indifference as due to the fact that social work appeared to be a profession mainly for women."[69] Although this may have been true in the case of social work, academics were initially no more amenable to the idea of university-based public administration training. Both fields suffered from the charge of being too applied.

The Chicago School of Civics, always short of funds, reached a crisis when the Russell Sage Foundation announced that it was phasing out support for social work training. Abbott and Breckinridge were in fundamental disagreement with the school's founder, Graham Taylor, who wanted to continue relatively informal training heavy on fieldwork, while they had a vision of rigorous university education. While Taylor was away on leave in 1920, the two women moved to affiliate the school with the University of Chicago. Thus was born the Graduate School of Social Service Administration, the first graduate program in social work.[70]

Abbott and Breckinridge were determined that the school should have a policy emphasis grounded in social science; they rejected "emotional generalizations" that they felt characterized social work in practice.[71] In this respect, they reflected the struggle to cast off the image of female benevolence that compromised social work's quest for professionalism. As Regina Kunzel notes, women in social work "hoped to de-gender the act of helping, to transform it from a religious, feminine calling into a profession worthy of broad respect, legitimacy, and remuneration."[72] In a typical statement, Stuart Alfred Queen urged social work to purge itself of the "sob sisters" and become a true profession, that is, "not an interesting diversion for spare time, but . . . a 'man's job.' "[73]

Abbott and Breckinridge organized a curriculum that included social policy design, the study of governmental structures and processes, public welfare administration and its history, basic economics, and social research. Like the municipal researchers who sought to professionalize public administration, Abbott was convinced that the key to reform lay in research: "How else," she demanded, " can social workers intelligently initiate, support, or reject programs of social reform?"[74] Once inside the university, however, the two found their program under threat of takeover by the sociologists. They fought back with typical institutionalizing moves, including publishing social work textbooks and launching a journal. In doing so, they reappropriated the casework emphasis, which had already achieved status as the field's only identifiable core knowledge. But Abbott and Breckinridge continued to argue that casework was instrumental to the systemic change that ought to be social work's primary emphasis. The thrust of their curriculum is reflected in the policy-level positions many of their early graduates commanded, such as county commissioner of public welfare, head of a state bureau of home relief, staffer to the presidential commission on social trends, and assistant commissioner of a state department of charities and corrections. Many graduates joined the staff of the U.S. Children's Bureau, headed by Julia Lathrop.

Abbott and Breckinridge argued that private, voluntary agencies could not by themselves solve the problem of poverty; government involvement was necessary. The social worker's calling ought to be public service, that is, creating and staffing public agencies. But their vision did not prevail throughout the profession.[75] Outside the Chicago school, casework in private agencies became increasingly important. Casework leaders came to view social work education as at least as much a matter of molding the personality of the budding social worker as of imparting a core body of knowledge. Abbott consistently battled against this tendency: "Are we building on the foundation [our first social workers] so wisely laid or have social workers become so concerned about casework methods and such phenomena as the ego libido and various psychiatric diagnoses and such exigencies as community chest financial campaigns that they have lost their sense of responsibility for this great division of social welfare that should be their professional concern?"[76] She continued to insist on "knowledge courses." Social workers had to know the client's objective environment, not just probe into the client's subconscious.

But the overall trend in the field was not in the direction she favored. Within twenty years, Frank Bruno could say to social workers assembled at their annual convention, "The function of social work is of such exceptional importance to the operation of contemporary society that the sheer bulk of knowledge its practitioners need to possess is staggering in its scope."[77] Few in the audience would have had any inclination to disagree with him. Social work had, at least in its own eyes, reached disciplinary maturity; it had done so based neither on the pioneering advocacy of the settlement houses nor on the systemic theoretical purview of Abbott and Breckinridge, but on Richmond's casework approach and the Freudian theory that appeared to render it scientific.

In both public administration and social work, the quest for a scientific base rendered advocacy suspect. It appeared that professionals could not be simultaneously rigorous and critical. Knowledge required detachment. Commitment to improving the lives of the poor and to ameliorating the worst effects of capitalism was labeled as feminine and therefore soft, sentimental, and unrealistic, but also as class oriented and therefore divisive and potentially destabilizing. Progressives, as a rule, had sought improvements rather than fundamental changes, but the Bolshevist coup in Russia in 1917 and post–World War I unrest at home made even modest reforms look risky in the eyes of established interests and leaders. The Red Scare of 1919–1920 produced widespread arrests in immigrant neighborhoods, strikebreaking campaigns in steel and other industries, and race riots toward which governments turned a passive eye. The Supreme Court upheld contracts that prohibited workers from joining unions and struck down child labor laws. Many Progressives, shaken by the violence, turned toward Americanization as a safer mode of reform.[78] Against such a background, the lure of scientific objectivity and professional legitimacy seemed undeniable to public administrationists and social workers alike.

6

Constructing Public Administration

In 1948, in the first study of public administration's origins, Dwight Waldo made the iconoclastic argument that despite the field's claim to be "a science with principles of universal validity," it operated on the basis of "political theories unmistakably related to unique economic, social, governmental, and ideological facts." Rejecting the image of themselves that municipal researchers had proclaimed, Waldo argued that the questions with which reformers had wrestled and to which they claimed to have the right answers, far from being technical issues, were the same fundamentally contestable questions Western political philosophers had debated since ancient Greece: the nature of the good life, the bases for public decisions, the question of who should rule, and the appropriate way to organize governments. Waldo saw the field of public administration as grounded in fundamental tension between scientific, efficient, businesslike management of public agencies and the political implications that permeate the substance of agency work. In Waldo's eyes, these two forces, efficiency and democracy, defined public administration as an intellectual enterprise. He saw the tension between them as irresolvable. At least he believed that it would have to remain so if public administration were to survive as a distinct body of thought. Without a concern for efficiency and effectiveness, the unique contribution of administration to governance would be lost. But absent normative questions, the public dimensions of administration would be obscured.[1]

Of the two potential threats, the latter worried Waldo more. By emphasizing public administration's political significance, he hoped to maintain the tension between science and democratic politics—the one striving for right answers, the other grounding itself in the argument and ambiguity that mark public life. His examination of municipal research pointed out that beneath its emphasis on a science of public management lay a clear public philosophy—a positive view of government based on the promotion of a planned, managed society in which educated

124

citizens would support the informed decisions of experts. By bringing to light the value implications of seemingly neutral, procedural recommendations, Waldo hoped to raise awareness among public administrationists that although it might be possible to rid government agencies of partisanship, there was no avoiding politics per se. By pinning so many of their hopes on business methods as the key to better public administration, municipal researchers and those who followed in their footsteps committed themselves, whether consciously or not, to the political values that a business orientation entails: executive over legislative power, economy and efficiency, hierarchy as an organizational principle, and the bottom line as the sine qua non if not the only criterion of administrative performance.[2]

This study has sought to follow Waldo's lead. It has told the story of the New York Bureau of Municipal Research and the fateful events and choices that shaped the subsequent construction of public administration, but it added a new contextual and comparative element. As Waldo noted in 1948 and is still largely the case today, though criticism of public administration's business orientation has been heard from time to time, the field has "hardly a suggestion as to what might replace business spirit, organization, and methods in government—except the *ancien regime*."[3] But by examining the work of women's clubs, settlement houses, and other social welfare reformers alongside the work of the bureau men, I hoped to articulate the alternative Waldo found lacking: a different way of thinking about public life and the place of administration in it. This alternative vision is based on the notion of public service not conducted in procedural isolation from the conditions of citizens' lives but premised on the impossibility of separating methods from their substantive implications. My argument is that at least part of the reason for public administration's preference for scientific administration over the values that animated municipal housekeeping—for efficiency over caring—was the threat to municipal reformers posed by the gender accusations of party politicians: specifically, the risk to their masculinity that lay in associating themselves with women's benevolent activities. In America as in other Western societies, the public sector has traditionally been the province of men, a space where males debated with one another, struggled for dominance, sought fame and honor, and made tough-minded decisions untainted by sentimentality. The image of neutrality that the municipal researchers conveyed, even though it masked a political effort to wrest control of city governments away from party machines, laid the bureau men open to charges of femininity. If they were not party men, they were the third sex of politics, man milliners fatally under the influence of a monstrous regiment of women bent on injecting inappropriate emotionalism into public life. My thesis is that, by adopting a rhetoric of science—a pursuit that has been constitutively masculine since the early Christian era—the bureau men were able to counter and deflect the castigations of machine politicians about their deficient masculinity. Waving the banner of science, they could also justify a "businesslike" approach to public administration, even in the face of mixed feelings, at best, among the public about the role of *big* business in American life. The idea of scientific management joined two notions that were theoretically at war: objectivity and self-interest, both of them masculine by long-established convention.

As we have seen, an interest in science also influenced the development of the profession of social work. Both social work and public administration found in science irresistible support for their claims to professionalism. Over time, both downplayed the concern for improving the lives of immigrants and other poor people in favor of applying purportedly objective techniques to relatively circumscribed questions. But the profession of social work emerged from a battle between caseworkers and social policy advocates for the soul of the discipline, a struggle in which impersonal analysis eventually defeated social change. In public administration, there was no such protracted contest. The choice of science over caring was made in practice by the bureau men before the question of professional identity began to be posed. In addition, since virtually all early public administrationists were men, they had an easier time convincing the world that they could operate in an objective, unsentimental way than did social workers, most of whom were women. But for both, the struggle to professionalize was a struggle to cast off femininity by claiming the status of science.

In order to conclude my argument, this final chapter points to features of contemporary public administration that underscore how long lasting the formative influence of the bureau men has been in American public administration. A comprehensive review of the literature since the early 1920s would document how pervasive this influence has been, but such a review lies beyond the boundaries of this project. My goal is to offer enough evidence to encourage readers to ponder the argument and explore its implications. The positive side of public administration's still rather tenuous claim to disciplinary status—a problem with which all applied fields wrestle—is the room it makes for a diversity of perspectives. This very diversity has been the source of both hand-wringing and celebration, the former because it signals how far the field is from "true" science, the latter welcoming the evidence on that very basis. Like Dwight Waldo, I reject the notion that there is any final answer to the question of how to approach the study of public administration and seek only to give plausible reasons for my position.

THE SCIENCE OF ADMINISTRATION

The most fundamental and long-lasting idea public administration inherited from the bureau men is the possibility and desirability of a science of administration. During the 1920s and 1930s, pursuing the direction taken by the municipal researchers, the quest for science took the form of articulating principles of administration, such as chain of command, span of control, and Luther Gulick's POSDCORB, an acronym that captures what Gulick believed were the basic functions of management: planning, organizing, staffing, directing, coordinating, reporting, and budgeting. All these maxims are still known to virtually every student striving for a master's degree in public administration, albeit not uncritically, and they all still occupy the status of conventional wisdom in public agencies across the country. The idea behind the "principles" approach was that there were certain universal verities that, if clearly stated, could guide managers regardless of the particular agency contexts in which they found themselves. Much of the actual research in the field during this period took the form of studies modeled consciously or not on the municipal researchers' surveys. Most were done for client governments and were deliberately practical. The approach was to describe particular contexts faithfully and meticulously, and then show how application of principles of administration to each situation would result in improved performance. Principles were scientific because their applicability to every possible situation could be demonstrated in practice. This early deductive method perpetuated Woodrow Wilson's idea that it was safe for American administrators to adopt techniques from less democratic countries (Germany was the favorite of the municipal researchers) and from business corporations because techniques—principles of administration—were neutral.

This deductive approach was swept away following World War II by the so-called behavioral revolution, which sought to impose natural science methodologies on the study of social phenomena. Adopting a demanding form of empiricism, behavioralists maintained that knowledge came only from controlled experimentation on that which could be observed and measured—in the case of social processes, the "behavior" of individuals rather than feelings, subjective meaning, or intersubjective phenomena. In public administration, Herbert Simon led the behavioralist charge. He accused the field of being too descriptive and insufficiently explanatory or predictive. He dismissed the case study as a research approach because, without being grounded in protective devices such as randomized sampling and the quantification of variables, the results could not be generalized to other administrative settings and could not be used to predict and control future organizational events.

Simon was particularly scornful of administrative principles, which he characterized as "proverbs of administration." He pointed out that proverbs almost always occur in mutually contradictory pairs: "look before you leap," but "he who hesitates is lost." Simon argued that although such sayings may help justify actions that have already been taken, they are not scientific because they can be used to prove virtually anything. The same was true for principles of administration. By articulating principles and then using them to interpret particular administrative problems, public administrationists were putting the cart before the horse. The correct approach was inductive rather than deductive: study administration experimentally, carefully testing hypotheses about causal relationships among variables, so that findings could be generalized from one situation to others.[4]

Like Woodrow Wilson and the bureau men, however, Simon wanted the study of administration to be scientific; he simply meant something different by the term. Simon's argument with traditionalists was not over whether there were universal principles but how they should be arrived at. He too believed that there were administrative truths, but they had to be demonstrated experimentally rather than articulated up front. Where bureau men had sought to be systematic in their investigations, following a methodology of careful enumeration and description, Simon upped the ante in the direction of natural science. Under Simon's behavioralist influence, in the study of administration and in the training of administrators, the emphasis gradually shifted. Less weight was given to grounding knowledge production in the world of practice, to involving students in the work of actual agencies, and to careful study of an entire agency in its context. Increasing attention was devoted to building and imparting to students a body of social scientific knowledge developed on the basis of "empirical" research, meaning research that followed the behavioralist paradigm, and applicable to virtually any agency.

In his review essay five years after Simon's opening salvo and some forty-five years after the founding of the New York Bureau, George Graham cited several beliefs that guided academics in the teaching of public administration. They included the power of reason, the rationality and factual correctness of Western cultural values, the essentially administrative nature of the application of reason, and the possibility of finding equitable solutions to public problems—all tenets that the bureau men had endorsed explicitly or implicitly. Simon, as a behavioralist, rejected the rationality of values but otherwise stood for the application of reason, particularly technical rationality, to administrative questions. Although by this time the idea of a politics-administration dichotomy ostensibly had been discarded, Graham fully subscribed to the bureau men's faith in strong and competent administrative leadership and echoed their skepticism about the doctrine of separated powers, which he suggested might usefully be left to "rest uninterrupted in antiquarian splendor" in order not to form an impediment to expert determination of scientific solutions to managerial problems.[5]

Public administration's apparent failure during its early years to meet scientific standards promulgated by Simon and other behavioralists led a number of people who agreed with the behavioral assessment to initiate what they referred to as a public policy emphasis. The new focus was "analysis," meaning the application of linear rationality and quantification to public questions.[6] Several schools were established as sites for policy analysis and the training of analysts. The term "public management" was adopted to describe the administrative training offered by the policy schools and to connote a more rigorous form of research distinct from old-fashioned reliance on anecdotal evidence and unproven nostrums.[7] Over the last several decades, "public administration" and "public management," which to the uninitiated undoubtedly sound identical, have proceeded along parallel but separate developmental tracks, vying for pride of place as the preeminent locus of professionalism and disciplinary orthodoxy in the study of the workings of public agencies.

Public management adherents have conceptualized the activities of public agencies as susceptible to exacting scientific study and rejected, much as Simon did, what they refer to as "traditional" public administration. The latter is viewed as "overly descriptive, atheoretical, too problem-oriented, nothing but how-to proverbs, narrowly focused, boring, pompous, turgidly writen [sic], and so on."[8] Intellectually interesting work in public administration is held to be the exception rather than the rule.[9]

By striving for the scientific, however, public management not so much distinguishes itself from traditional public administration as follows in the footsteps of the bureau men. As was the case with Simon, public management's quarrel with what it calls traditional public administration is over the definition of science and not over whether administrative practice can or should be scientific. According to public management scholars, the work of public administrationists has simply failed to achieve scientific status. Yet a case can be made, I believe, that public management is wrestling with the same paradox that has plagued mainstream public administration: the ongoing contradiction between science and managerial practice, between rigor and relevance. One prominent public management scholar has expressed the dilemma this way: "Positive public management research is hard to do. Human beings make choices that confound our analytic designs. We can rarely show a straightforward unambiguous cause and effect relationship. . . . [The best] research in public management . . . is methodologically sound, and explains . . . important [phenomena]. But so far it isn't very useful. . . . What public management research can do is describe what managers do and try to explain it, using practical reason, which is hermeneutic."[10]

One can see reflected here, as in many parts of the public management literature, the equivocal nature of a commitment to science in the study of public agencies. The quest for rigor, which requires strict control of the knowledge-seeking enterprise, is accompanied by assertions of the need for more managerial discretion ("letting managers manage"), for freeing managers from the shackles of "bureau-pathology," that is, regulations that constrain managers' freedom to do as they think best. The contradiction between being scientific and being strategic is seldom explored. Instead, the public management literature continues to operate, even in the face of evidence to the contrary, on the same assumption as the municipal researchers did: that if the right methodology can just be found, the correct answers science provides will be unproblematically applicable to practice situations and useful to practicing managers. Reflection on the story of the municipal research bureaus suggests that the rigor versus relevance dilemma is a product of taking too literally the bureau men's exhortation to science. For the bureau men, with the exception of accountant Frederick Cleveland, "science" was at least as much a rallying cry as an orthodoxy of method. Not until the profession sought to institutionalize itself within the academy did a yawning chasm open up between practice (relevance) and theory (rigor), as applied academics struggled to conform to standards derived from laboratory experimentation.

In mainstream public administration, a debate erupted in the early 1980s over the quality of research in the field, especially dissertation research. Howard McCurdy and Robert Cleary fired the opening salvo with a *Public Administration*

Review article arguing that public administration dissertations generally failed to meet minimal standards of scholarly respectability. The standards they enumerated were by and large those of natural science–oriented social science: Did the writer set out to conduct basic research? Could findings be generalized to other situations? Did the research test or make possible the development of a theory? Did it test a causal relationship? Was the subject important to the field, or did it invent new questions? Of 142 dissertations examined, only nine, according to the authors, dealt with an "important" topic, tested a causal relationship, and had a valid design. (The authors specifically rejected the case study as a valid design.) McCurdy and Cleary concluded that public administrationists were spending too much time working on issues that could not be resolved and were therefore unlikely to contribute to knowledge development. Unless public administration followed accepted social science standards, they argued, it would never reach disciplinary maturity.[11]

A number of scholars responded to McCurdy and Cleary's challenge, some echoing their indictment, others declaring the need for a more diverse range of social science methodologies, including those that are more appropriate to inter-subjective and practice-based subject matter.[12] Jay D. White and Guy B. Adams extended McCurdy and Cleary's research with their own multistaged examination of public administration dissertations, including a comparison with what White and Adams argued were closely related fields such as business, social work, and planning. White and Adams attempted to assess public administration research using a broader, more generic set of standards than those used by McCurdy and Cleary, but their findings were scarcely more sanguine. In contrast, however, they argued that striving to conform to natural science–based principles was unlikely to produce better-quality research in the field. Instead, White and Adams suggested, public administration should be aiming to define workable standards for practice research and to reach a more perceptive understanding of the nature of knowledge and theory development in an applied field.[13]

Between the criticisms of public management adherents and those of main-stream public administrationists, the field has been buffeted from all sides in recent years. Not all the critics want to make public administration more scientific, but the question of what standards, besides those of natural science, might guide the field toward stronger and more compelling research is vigorously debated.

Although public management and public administration remain distinct perspectives, public management's challenge has had a visible impact on scholarly dialogue in "traditional" public administration. A 1998 symposium in *Public Administration Review* presented the New Public Management (a recent variant that stresses market models) as an opportunity for public administration to move beyond "narrow" disciplinary considerations toward more comprehensive under-standing and "theoretically grounded empirical work."[14] The symposium editor, Larry D. Terry, a public administrationist, represented the goal as the promotion of "constructive and meaningful dialogue between scholars in the public policy and so-called 'traditional public administration' communities."[15] One looks in vain, however, for a similar outreach effort on the part of public management adherents. Public administration remains vulnerable to charges of insufficient scientific rigor.

Consider, for example, the 1998 report of the Committee on the Advancement of Public Administration, cosponsored by the American Political Science Association (APSA) and the National Association of Schools of Public Affairs and Administration (NASPAA). The committee's primary recommendation is for research and teaching that "simultaneously reflects the need for scientific advancement of the field" (that is, rigor) and "addresses questions that concern practitioners" (in other words, relevance). In order to banish the "stigma" under which public administration labors, the committee concluded, it should develop a "more robust scientific base leavened by informed respect for the art of administration." It should "develop understanding that facilitates prediction." At the same time, the field should acknowledge the important "unanalyzable" dimensions of administrative practice, which defy "codification and rigorous assessment" but make possible creativity. The report has little to say, however, about where the boundary between predictable bureaucratic behavior and administrative artistry lies, or how the field should attempt either to resolve or to live with the fundamental differences between the two.[16]

The committee's position, like previous critiques, reflects the dilemma that has plagued the effort to transform the bureau men's research-based strategy for reforming municipal governments into an academic enterprise. Like all "applied" fields, public administration suffers from a too-close—in fact, constitutive—association with real-world practices that only with difficulty can be subjected to the kind of controlled study that results in non-context-dependent generalizations.[17] Even if, as the report suggests, public administration broadens its jurisdictional claim beyond public bureaucracies to the network of public, private, and nonprofit agents involved in shaping and implementing government policies, there remains the insoluble problem of the field's subject matter and its apparent refusal to yield, other than on relatively marginal topics, the scientific form of knowledge that brings to scholars academic prestige rather than stigma. The more "academic" public administration becomes, the greater the tension between academic knowledge standards and the kind of practical knowledge that, for all their pretensions to science, the bureau men sought. What for municipal research was a rallying cry and a weapon against the aspersions of machine politicians has hardened, for academic public administration, into an ill-fitting but apparently indispensable ideology. The continuing dialogue revolves around how—sometimes whether—public administration can achieve scientific status. The appropriateness of science as a goal for the field is seldom questioned.

THE BUSINESS OF GOVERNMENT

Another fundamental theme public administration inherited from the municipal research movement is the idea that business practices are an appropriate model for government agency administration. Although scholars have disagreed about the extent to which public administrators can or should act in a businesslike way, there is little sense that there might be another way of thinking about public administration than debating the similarities and differences between the two.

Following the bureau men's lead, the field's first textbook, Leonard D. White's *Introduction to the Study of Public Administration,* published in 1926, referred to public administration as "the business side of government." Its objective was "the most efficient utilization of the resources at the disposal of officials and employees." The word "business" rings over and over in White's account of government administration: "Business commences at nine o'clock. . . . A steady stream of business develops. . . . [S]ome business is transacted by a clerk, other business is referred to the assistant bureau chief. . . . Thus proceeds in an orderly fashion all the complicated business of the office."[18] White credits Frederick Taylor's theories of scientific management with sparking fresh interest in the improvement of government administration, along with efforts by businessmen who, through such organs as the U.S. Chamber of Commerce, had taken an interest in promoting governmental efficiency. Like Woodrow Wilson, whom he cites, White believes that administration will play an increasingly important part in governance; the need for efficiency and businesslike methods is therefore all the more vital.

The close affinity between business practices and government administration remained little questioned until after World War II, when Paul Appleby's *Big Democracy* asserted unequivocally that "government is different." Appleby argued, "Even possessed of patriotism and zeal, the most capable business executive in the country might be a dismal failure in government. . . . Governments exist precisely for the reason that there is a need to have special persons in society charged with the function of promoting and protecting the public interest."[19] Appleby's position was adopted by many who had recognized, during the crisis atmosphere of the war, that the old politics-administration dichotomy was an inadequate framework for understanding the nature of public administration. Writers such as Herbert Kaufman, Dwight Waldo, and Norton Long began to conduct studies and craft new theories that accepted the political dimensions of managerial practice in public agencies. Yet it was also during this period that the competing framework of public management developed, a framework that reasserted the relevance of business even as it sought ways to free public managers from the strictures of bureau-pathology. In 1980, Graham Allison, dean of Harvard University's Kennedy School of Government, a bastion of the public management perspective, asserted that public and private management were "alike in all unimportant respects." Meanwhile, his colleagues at Harvard, Princeton, Berkeley, and other policy-oriented schools pushed for the adoption by government managers of attitudes and practices derived from the business world.[20] A succession of management reforms made their way into the practice of public administration from profit-making business. Management by objectives, PPBS (planning, programming, budgeting system), zero-based budgeting, and a "passion for excellence" came and went, all hailed as the key to more effective public administration, all failing to make any significant alteration in administrative practices.[21]

In 1992, David Osborne and Ted Gaebler fired a salvo whose echoes have yet to die away. *Reinventing Government* was taken up with enthusiasm as a fresh approach to public administration, but it soon became clear, at least to some scholars, that "reinventing" was anything but new. Nevertheless, with no less a champion than Vice President Al Gore, Osborne and Gaebler's advice became the marching orders for federal bureaucrats everywhere. Mouthing the nostrums of reinvention, the Gore report argued that "the central issue we face is not *what* government does, but *how* it works." The main problem is "good people trapped in bad systems."[22] Both these ideas echo the words of the bureau reformers. The first accepts the notion that how government does its work can be separated from what it does (that administration can be separated from politics) and that the one can therefore be addressed without creating implications for the other. In other words, as of old, means can be separated from ends. The second adopts the bureau men's reform strategy, which was to seek to implement good methods rather than to expect to recruit good men, that is, to rely on administrative rather than political solutions (again, assuming the two can be separated). Reinventing government resurrects the politics-administration dichotomy on which bureau reformers relied but public administrationists claim to have banished several decades ago, and it relies on it for the same reason: to strengthen executive branch power at the expense of the legislature. The Gore report's indictment of red tape is a reflection of the administrative expert's dislike for politically imposed controls. The charge is leveled on much the same ideological basis as the early-twentieth-century reformers called for "scientific" approaches to public management: that is, politics as usual is ineffective and inefficient; it doesn't ensure results, and it wastes the public's money.

The Hamiltonian idea that what people want is not participation in government but results—that is, services that work well and do not cost very much—is reflected as strongly in arguments for reinvention as it was in the bureau perspective. Both strengthen the administrator's hand. Today, this is done in the interests of fostering managerial "creativity" and "entrepreneurialism." Formerly, it was for the sake of being "businesslike." Again, just as the bureau men argued for "efficient citizens" armed with facts to rally around expert administration, advocates of reinventing government suggest that "customer service" will win the hearts and minds of a disenchanted public. The "National Performance Review" and similar reinvention efforts at the state and local levels are advanced on the assumption that democratic accountability will best be served by getting government to work efficiently. In sum, the difficulty Waldo saw in the reformers' approach to early public administration exists today: reform is based on an unacknowledged theory of governance masquerading as a set of management techniques.

In a similar way, the public management perspective has also failed to come to terms with the contradiction between scientific management and democratic decision making. Its unquestioning acceptance of a tie between science and business heightens this tension. Its scholarly literature is explicitly normative, urging public managers to be "entrepreneurial" and advocating that they be granted more authority. Little examination is made, however, of the tension between, on the one hand, commitments to managerial power and a free-market understanding of administrative government and, on the other, democratic values such as inclusion, equality, and accountability. Although public management scholars accept the political dimensions of their subject matter, they do so descriptively and instrumentally. The essentially contestable nature of questions such as whether managers should be "engineers" or "entrepreneurs" is rarely acknowledged. The appropriate role of management in the American political system is addressed in terms of its utility (which understanding of public management will enhance managerial effectiveness?) rather than philosophically (who should rule?). The connection between empirical science and business values is taken for granted rather than questioned.

In these respects, like reinventing government, the public management perspective is consistent with that of the Progressive Era municipal researchers, who operated on the premise that science was businesslike because it revealed the most efficient and effective way to manage, and it was democratic because maximum administrative efficiency and effectiveness were in the public interest. Both municipal research and public management tend to view legislative oversight, which results in constraining regulation of managerial prerogatives, as an inefficient and unnecessary handicap to good management; both see executive power and managerial expertise as important aids to effective governance.

As Waldo observed, the most basic postulate among public administration's founders was "that true democracy and true efficiency are synonymous, or at least reconcilable."[23] Contemporary public administration is excessively concerned, just as the bureau men were, with finding the right management technique and insufficiently sensitive to the political implications that inhabit every public administrative procedure, even the apparently innocuous. Business-oriented approaches are imported into public administration on the assumption either that government and business are alike in all fundamental respects or that business techniques are neutral. The history of the field and of the practice of public administration since the days of the bureau men strongly suggests that neither assumption can be taken for granted.

Reminding ourselves of public administration's roots in the bureaus of municipal research and the extent to which today's ideas have been shaped by long-ago reform ideologies should present us with an opportunity to become more sensitive to the intertwining of facts with values, of policies with implementation methods, of politics with administration. A question Waldo posed in 1948 is still relevant: "Are students of administration [including its theorists and its practitioners] trying to solve the problems of human cooperation on too low a plane?"[24]

PUBLIC SERVICE FOR THE NEW MILLENNIUM

Reflection on the early history of public administration suggests that the answer to Waldo's question is yes. Absorbed by the quest for scientific status and the effort to attain businesslike efficiency, the dialogue in the field largely revolves around questions of technique: What methodological instrument will finally enable us to make unarguable generalizations? What are the seven (or five, or three) secrets of highly effective business managers that can be imported into public agencies to make them work better for less money? But, as Waldo noted, the issues that public administration practitioners and scholars wrestle with are issues of "human cooperation"—questions that are inherently value-laden and difficult, if not impossible, to resolve. There are few, if any, questions in public administration that are simply technical, nor will there ever be as long as public administrators have at their discretion the exercise of public power. Certainly the issue of the extent to which government agencies should operate like businesses is not one that is resolvable on technical grounds, nor, I want to argue, resolvable at all. The business perspective is hardly free from political implications. It is permeated with values such as competition, individual liberty, and property, and it is hostile or indifferent to values such as democracy and equality.

If virtually all administrative questions have political dimensions, then we are fated never to know for sure whether we are practicing or studying in the "right way." Yet administrators must make judgments and act. What the field ought to aim for is a perspective that acknowledges the contradictory yet invigorating dynamics that mark our terrain and work with them instead of trying to mask or eliminate them. We need to accept the inseparability of politics and administration, facts and values, policies and procedures, theory and practice, instead of struggling fruitlessly toward a nonexistent conceptual or methodological holy grail that will finally make it possible for us to reach ultimate truth. As Hannah Arendt argued, if truth becomes the grounding for politics, public action is turned into an instrument for implementing the correct decisions made by powerful experts who are the only ones with access to real knowledge. Truth wipes out politics, because there is no point in having a debate about something that is unarguable.[25]

The field owes Woodrow Wilson a great deal for raising and articulating, with a richness that still reverberates, the question of the role of administration in government. Despite the common view, Wilson knew that techniques have political implications. His argument was not simply that one can borrow the murderer's way of sharpening a knife without adopting the intention to murder. The protection against murderous intentions, he argued, was to "study administration as a means of putting our own politics into convenient practice. . . . The principles on which to base a science of administration for America must be principles which have democratic policy very much at heart. . . . In a word, practical statesmanship must come first, closet doctrine second."[26] Wilson's message for public administration seems to be that it must find a way of making science and democracy work together *in practice.* This is the same question posed by the Pittsburgh Survey team: what are American standards anyway? The challenge for American public administration as it moves into the new millennium is to reorient itself to focus on this question.

Can administrative agencies and the scholars who study them find their way toward reliable, practical, democratic knowledge that supports public service? Settlement reformers and other social welfare advocates of the Progressive Era thought so. For them, the way to practical knowledge lay on the "high seas" between the dry statistics of the census and the biased indictments of yellow journalism. They rejected both rigid objectivity and unfettered prejudice. Science was not a pursuit divorced from life but one immersed in it. Social reformers sought not to be experts raised above the people, setting the terms by which public life would be defined and understood, but to be neighbors. Only that which was lived could be understood; therefore, science demanded both alertness and empathy. Like Woodrow Wilson, they sought ways of judging knowledge that were consistent with the best aspirations of American democracy. Did the knowledge process include as collaborators those whose lived experience made them experts on problematic situations? Did it address great, grimed question marks—that is, social problems that, on their face, gave the lie to American values? Did it let life rather than theory lead the way? Did it work within, rather than struggling to eliminate, the tension between systematic knowledge and advocacy? It did not make sense to social reformers that undemocratic knowledge processes could arrive at knowledge that would serve democracy. The processes themselves had to be democratic, which meant that knowledge would be a constantly evolving thing, adjusted and developed in application.

Progressive Era social reformers would tell today's public administrationists to recapture the emphasis of a century ago on mobilizing knowledge to tackle the important problems of the day and to consider the appropriate role of government in that effort. They would caution that improving the conditions of people's lives ought to be the first concern of those who care about what government should do and how it should be done well. As long as scientific legitimacy, defined in terms derived from the laboratory and the controlled experiment, is the first goal of a professional field, adherents will exhaust themselves trying vainly to make life conform to the standards of science, rather than working to put science to the service of life.

As it moves into the new millennium, public administration could do worse than revive Robert Archey Woods's vision of a profession of public service. Public administration could become a "community of practical scholars" dedicated to the application of pragmatic knowledge to the great issues of the day, a science that wrestles with situations instead of observing them from afar, working to humanize the processes of government so that they meet human needs, and collaborating with citizens in the effort to develop workable knowledge.

As it moves in this direction, public administration will have to look at its relationship to business management in a new light. A century ago, the bureau men's commitment to business approaches must have been at least partly driven by their dependence on financial support from such men as John D. Rockefeller, Andrew Carnegie, and J. P. Morgan. Some 80 percent of the trustees of the research bureaus were manufacturers, bankers, merchants, real estate brokers, and financiers. Large contributions made up three-quarters of the bureaus' budgets. As Norman Gill noted, reliance on large donors, together with the dominance of their boards by business interests, must have led researchers to stress the businesslike quality of their recommended approaches.[27] Although most of the bureau men were probably inclined toward these approaches anyway, organizational survival lent their commitment an urgency that may not be necessary today. Given their relatively secure institutionalization in universities, tenured public administrationists have somewhat greater freedom than they might have had a hundred years ago to question, if not to reject entirely, the notion that government and business management are fundamentally alike. By reconsidering the birth of public administration and the alternative vision of government reform in contrast to which public administration came to define itself, this study suggests that, at the very least, public administrationists need not content themselves with simply aping business management any more than they need limit the quest for knowledge to the terms of objective science. There is an alternative to scientific management besides the ancien régime. The settlement workers and other social reformers have shown us so. Will we be wise enough to heed their call to a profession of public service? Constructing such a profession and field of study is, in my judgment, a worthy aim for public administration's future.

Notes

1. FINDING A USABLE PAST

1. Guy B. Adams, "Enthralled with Modernity: The Historical Context of Knowledge and Theory Development in Public Administration," *Public Administration Review* 52 (July–August 1992): 365. Woodrow Wilson argued that all the big constitutional questions had now been settled (despite the fact that women still could not vote) and that the main problem was "running the Constitution." He suggested that attention be given to administrative issues, which, he argued, were neutral in the sense of being outside the purview of partisan politics. See Woodrow Wilson, "The Study of Administration," *Political Science Quarterly* 2 (June 1887): 197–222.

2. Frederick C. Mosher, "Research in Public Administration: Some Notes and Suggestions," *Public Administration Review* 16 (summer 1956): 169.

3. Two recent exceptions are Hindy Lauer Schachter, *Reinventing Government or Reinventing Ourselves: The Role of Citizen Owners in Making a Better Government* (Albany: State University of New York Press, 1997), and Jonathan Kahn, *Budgeting Democracy* (Ithaca, N.Y.: Cornell University Press, 1997), both published as I was writing. My account has benefited substantially from their work, even where we disagree. I take the appearance of these two books as a sign that the historical neglect to which I refer is in the process of being remedied. The generalizations I make about public administration's absence of historical awareness and sophistication still seem in order, however.

4. Donald C. Stone and Alice B. Stone, "Early Development of Education in Public Administration," in *American Public Administration: Past, Present, Future*, ed. Frederick C. Mosher (University: University of Alabama Press, 1975), 17–20.

5. Barry D. Karl, "Public Administration and American History: A Century of Professionalism," *Public Administration Review* 36 (September–October 1976): 490.

6. John Gaus, *A Study of Research in Public Administration* (New York: Social Science Research Council, 1930), 138. Gaus's account, which has fallen into undeserved neglect, credits settlement houses and social workers with early leadership in the study of administration.

7. Stephen Toulmin, *Cosmopolis* (New York: Free Press, 1990), 1.

8. Nell Irvin Painter, *Standing at Armageddon: The United States, 1877–1919* (New York: W. W. Norton, 1987), 268.

9. Richard Hofstadter, *The Age of Reform: From Bryan to FDR* (New York: Vintage Books, 1955), 231–32.

10. Jacob Riis, *How the Other Half Lives: Studies among the Tenements of New York* (1901 [1890]; reprint, New York: Dover Publications, 1971), 6.

11. Richard Hofstadter, *Anti-Intellectualism in American Life* (New York: Alfred A. Knopf, 1963), 197–229; Robert H. Wiebe, *The Search for Order, 1877–1920* (New York: Hill and Wang, 1967), 111–32.

12. Otis A. Pease, "Urban Reformers in the Progressive Era: A Reassessment," *Pacific Northwest Quarterly* 62 (April 1971): 49–58; David B. Danbom, *"The World of Hope": Progressives and the Struggle for an Ethical Public Life* (Philadelphia: Temple University Press, 1987), 62–144.

13. Karl argues that Progressive reformers have been distorted in historiography by their own "vision of themselves as the true reformers, their opponents as the corrupt enemy. . . . Reform interests of the period were never quite what the defending and attacking rhetoric so clearly sought to imply" (Barry Dean Karl, *Executive Reorganization and Reform in the New Deal: The Genesis of Administrative Management, 1900–1939* [Cambridge: Harvard University Press, 1963], 67).

14. Stone and Stone, "Early Development of Education in Public Administration," 21.

15. Samuel P. Hays, "The Politics of Reform in Municipal Government in the Progressive Era," *Pacific Northwest Quarterly* 55 (October 1964): 157–69.

16. Kenneth Finegold, *Experts and Politicians: Reform Challenges to Machine Politics in New York, Cleveland, and Chicago* (Princeton, N.J.: Princeton University Press, 1995), 26–27.

17. Joan Wallach Scott, *Gender and the Politics of History* (New York: Columbia University Press, 1988), 25, 47.

18. Robert H. Wiebe, *Self-Rule: A Cultural History of American Democracy* (Chicago and London: University of Chicago Press, 1995), 61–85.

19. Michael McGerr, *The Decline of Popular Politics: The American North, 1865–1928* (New York and Oxford: Oxford University Press, 1986), 37.

20. Rebecca Edwards, *Angels in the Machinery: Gender in American Party Politics from the Civil War to the Progressive Era* (New York: Oxford University Press, 1997), 15–16.

21. Linda K. Kerber, "A Constitutional Right to Be Treated Like American Ladies: Women and the Obligations of Citizenship," in *U.S. History as Women's History: New Feminist Essays,* ed. Linda K. Kerber, Alice Kessler-Harris, and Kathryn Kish Sklar (Chapel Hill and London: University of North Carolina Press, 1995), 17–35; see also Linda K. Kerber, *Women of the Republic: Intellect and Ideology in Revolutionary America* (New York: W. W. Norton, 1980).

22. Edwards, *Angels in the Machinery,* 4; Scott, *Gender and the Politics of History,* 45.

23. Edwards, *Angels in the Machinery,* 141.

24. Lisa D. Brush, "Love, Toil, and Trouble: Motherhood and Feminist Politics," *Signs* 21 (Winter 1996): 431.

25. Hofstadter, *Anti-Intellectualism in American Life,* 188–90.

26. "Women in Municipal Research," *National Municipal Review* 8 (March 1919): 199–200. Dr. Deardorff was assistant director of the Philadelphia Bureau until she departed

to head the city's Bureau of Vital Statistics. Records of the New York Bureau indicate a scattering of women in lower-level professional positions. Mrs. E. H. Harriman became a trustee in 1910, the only woman trustee during its initial decades, albeit an important one. The apparent rarity of women in the ranks of bureau professionals and trustees seems to justify the practice of referring to bureau researchers as "men." See also Norman N. Gill, *Municipal Research Bureaus* (Washington, D.C.: American Council on Public Affairs, 1944).

27. For an extended argument on the cultural masculinity of notions of professional expertise and administrative leadership in public administration, see Camilla Stivers, *Gender Images in Public Administration: Legitimacy and the Administrative State* (Newbury Park, Calif.: Sage Publications, 1993).

28. Virginia Woolf, *Three Guineas* (1938), quoted in Sandra Harding and Jean F. O'Barr, eds., *Sex and Scientific Inquiry* (Chicago and London: University of Chicago Press, 1987), 1.

29. Carolyn Merchant, *The Death of Nature: Women, Ecology and the Scientific Revolution* (New York: Harper and Row, 1980), 1–41.

30. Evelyn Fox Keller, *Reflections on Gender and Science* (New Haven, Conn., and London: Yale University Press, 1985), 1, 10 (emphasis added).

31. Sandra Harding, *The Science Question in Feminism* (Ithaca, N.Y., and London: Cornell University Press, 1986), 119–20.

32. David F. Noble, *A World without Women: The Christian Clerical Culture of Western Science* (New York and Oxford: Oxford University Press, 1992), xiii–xiv.

33. Ibid., 276.

34. Sharon Hartman Strom, *Beyond the Typewriter: Gender, Class, and the Origins of Modern American Office Work, 1900–1930* (Urbana and Chicago: University of Illinois Press, 1992), 68.

35. Barry Dean Karl, *Charles E. Merriam and the Study of Politics* (Chicago: University of Chicago Press, 1974), 53.

36. Samuel Haber, *Efficiency and Uplift: Scientific Management in the Progressive Era, 1890–1920* (Chicago: University of Chicago Press, 1964), ix.

37. Stivers, *Gender Images in Public Administration*, 37–43.

38. George B. Hopkins, "The New York Bureau of Municipal Research," *Annals of the Academy of Political and Social Science* 41 (May 1912): 235–44.

39. Mark E. Kann, "Individualism, Civic Virtue, and Gender in America," in *Studies in American Political Development*, vol. 4, ed. Karen Orren and Stephen C. Skowronek (New Haven, Conn.: Yale University Press, 1990), 51.

40. Guy B. Adams, Priscilla Bowerman, Kenneth M. Dolbeare, and Camilla Stivers, "Joining Purpose to Practice," in *Images and Identities in Public Administration*, ed. Henry B. Kass and Bayard L. Catron (Newbury Park, Calif.: Sage Publications, 1990), 219–40.

41. Dwight Waldo, *The Administrative State: A Study of the Political Theory of American Public Administration* (New York: Ronald Press, 1948), 202.

2. THE NEW YORK BUREAU OF MUNICIPAL RESEARCH

1. Quoted in David Montgomery, *Citizen Worker: The Experience of Workers in the United States with Democracy and the Free Market during the Nineteenth Century* (Cambridge: Cambridge University Press, 1993), 137.

2. Quoted in Elizabeth Ewen, *Immigrant Women in the Land of Dollars: Life and Culture on the Lower East Side 1890–1925* (New York: Monthly Review Press, 1985), 21.

3. Jacob Riis, *How the Other Half Lives: Studies among the Tenements of New York* (1901 [1890]; reprint, New York: Dover Publications, 1971), 41, 56.

4. Ewen, *Immigrant Women in the Land of Dollars*, 152, 246; Thomas Lee Philpott, *The Slum and the Ghetto: Immigrants, Blacks and Reformers in Chicago, 1880–1930* (Belmont, Calif.: Wadsworth, 1991), 65.

5. Robert F. Peccorella, *Community Power in a Post-Reform City: Politics in New York City* (Armonk, N.Y.: M. E. Sharpe, 1994), 43.

6. This account makes a practice of referring to bureau researchers as "men." Exact data on the number of women among municipal researchers are elusive. We know that there were a few. The Philadelphia Bureau pointed with pride to several women professional staffers, including Dr. Neva Deardorff, who was assistant director for several years and went on to head the city's Bureau of Vital Statistics ("Women in Municipal Research," *National Municipal Review* 8 [March 1919]: 199–200). But, as the *Review* notes, most bureaus employed women only in clerical capacities, and women trustees were rare. See also Norman Gill, *Municipal Research Bureaus* (Washington, D.C.: American Council on Public Affairs, 1944). Mrs. E. H. Harriman became a trustee of the New York Bureau in 1910—the only woman trustee during its initial decades, albeit a significant one (see chapter 5). Records of the New York Bureau indicate a scattering of women in lower-level professional positions, in addition to clerical workers. The apparent rarity of women in the ranks of bureau professionals and board members seems to justify the generalization "men." As chapter 3 suggests, there was a significant percentage of men among settlement residents and other social welfare advocates.

7. According to the reminiscences of Henry Bruere, a founding director of the New York Bureau, "It was Richard Watson Gilder, editor of *Century Magazine*, who suggested the term municipal research so as to sharpen the idea that it was dispassionate, scientific, and removed from partisan intentions, and non-political" (*Reminiscences* [1950; reprint, New York: Columbia University Oral History Project, 1972], 36).

8. James G. Bryce, *The American Commonwealth*, vol. 1. (1893; reprint, New York: Macmillan, 1931), 642.

9. Melvin G. Holli, *Reform in Detroit: Hazen S. Pingree and Urban Politics* (New York: Oxford University Press, 1969), xii; David C. Hammack, *Power and Society: Greater New York at the Turn of the Century* (New York: Russell Sage, 1982), 7–11.

10. Stephen Skowronek, *Building a New American State: The Expansion of National Administrative Capacities 1877–1920* (Cambridge: Cambridge University Press, 1982), 25.

11. Richard L. McCormick, *The Party Period and Public Policy: American Politics from the Age of Jackson to the Progressive Era* (New York and Oxford: Oxford University Press, 1986), 204–5.

12. Montgomery, *Citizen Worker*, 132.

13. Oliver E. Allen, *The Tiger: The Rise and Fall of Tammany Hall* (Reading, Mass.: Addison-Wesley, 1993), 5, 56.

14. Peccorella, *Community Power*, 34–35; Hammack, *Power and Society*, 89.

15. Samuel P. Hays, "The Politics of Reform in Municipal Government in the Progressive Era," *Pacific Northwest Quarterly* 55 (October 1964): 157–69.

16. Joseph McGoldrick, "The Board of Estimate and Apportionment of New York City," *National Municipal Review Supplement* (February 1929): 125–52; John Purroy

Mitchel, "The Office of Mayor," *Proceedings of the Academy of Political Science* 5 (April 1915): 479–94; Hammack, *Power and Society;* Jon C. Teaford, *The Unheralded Triumph: City Government in America, 1870–1900* (Baltimore: Johns Hopkins University Press, 1984), 15–41. A majority member of the Board of Aldermen said in 1918 that nowhere else in the world was there a legislature representing 5 million people with so little power over the purse or "so little disposition to use the limited power which it has." A member during the tenure of reform mayor John Purroy Mitchel (1913–1917) said that the board was mostly fat men whose greatest product was cigar smoke (Edwin R. Lewinson, *John Purroy Mitchel: The Boy Mayor of New York* [New York: Astra Books, 1965], 61).

17. Quoted in Hays, "The Politics of Reform," 159.

18. According to Kenneth Finegold, in 1913–1914, the firm of J. P. Morgan "organized a syndicate of banks to market $80 million in bonds to meet the city's obligations. . . . The banks imposed a 'pay as you go' policy by which improvements that were not self-sustaining had to be financed from current revenues rather than bond issues" (*Experts and Politicians: Reform Challenges to Machine Politics in New York, Cleveland, and Chicago* [Princeton, N.J.: Princeton University Press, 1995], 61); see also Donald A. Ritchie, "The Gary Committee: Business, Progressives, and Unemployment in New York City, 1914–1915," *New York Historical Society Quarterly* 57 (1973): 330–31.

19. McCormick, *The Party Period,* 297; Hays, "The Politics of Reform," 160–61.

20. Teaford, *Unheralded Triumph,* 141.

21. Harold C. Syrett, ed., *The Gentleman and the Tiger: The Autobiography of George B. McClellan* (Philadelphia: J. B. Lippincott, 1956), 198. According to McGoldrick, New York City had no department of engineering as such; instead, more than 1,000 engineers were scattered through departments such as water supply, gas and electricity, docks, and plant and structures, as well as in the offices of the borough presidents ("The Board of Estimate and Apportionment," 133).

22. Teaford, *Unheralded Triumph,* 1–11; Kenneth Fox, *Better City Government: Innovation in American Urban Politics, 1850–1937* (Philadelphia: Temple University Press, 1977), 5; Peccorella, *Community Power,* 31–32.

23. Teaford, *Unheralded Triumph,* 268–79.

24. Samuel P. Hays, "The Social Analysis of American Political History, 1880–1920," *Political Science Quarterly* 80, no. 3 (September 1965): 373–94.

25. Delos F. Wilcox, "The Municipal Program," *The Commons* 9 (June 1904): 261.

26. Quoted in Richard C. Skolnick, "Civic Group Progressivism in New York City," *New York History* 51 (July 1970): 422.

27. Robert Muccigrosso, "The City Reform Club: A Study in Late Nineteenth Century Reform," *New York Historical Society Quarterly* 52 (1968): 240.

28. Fox, *Better City Government,* 46. Fox comments: "An . . . indication that unification of elite groups was the real purpose of these city reform organizations was their almost total exclusion of women. . . . The Baltimore League expressly excluded women. . . . Other groups . . . [let] it be known that women were not welcome to join."

29. Helene Silverberg, " 'A Government of Men': Gender, the City, and the New Science of Politics," in *Gender and American Social Science,* ed. Helene Silverberg (Princeton, N.J.: Princeton University Press, 1999), 171.

30. Samuel Haber, *Efficiency and Uplift: Scientific Management in the Progressive Era, 1890–1920* (Chicago: University of Chicago Press, 1964), 101.

31. Skolnick, "Civic Group Progressivism," 423.

32. Steven J. Diner, *A City and Its Universities: Public Policy in Chicago, 1892–1919* (Chapel Hill: University of North Carolina Press, 1980), 57.

33. Haber, *Efficiency and Uplift,* 107.

34. Peccorella, *Community Power,* 46–49.

35. Muccigrosso, "The City Reform Club," 247.

36. Hays, "The Social Analysis of American Political History," 387–88.

37. William Welch, "Sanitation in Relation to the Poor," *Charities* 5 (1900): 207.

38. Skolnick, "Civic Group Progressivism."

39. Quoted in ibid., 416.

40. Hays, "The Politics of Reform," 166.

41. Geoffrey Blodgett, "The Mugwump Reputation: 1870 to the Present," *Journal of American History* 66 (March 1980): 863–64.

42. Arnaldo Testi, "The Gender of Reform Politics: Theodore Roosevelt and the Culture of Masculinity," *Journal of American History* 81 (March 1995): 1526.

43. Rebecca Edwards, *Angels in the Machinery: Gender in American Party Politics from the Civil War to the Progressive Era* (New York and Oxford: Oxford University Press, 1997), 155.

44. Haber, *Efficiency and Uplift,* 46, 55, 59.

45. Syrett, *The Gentleman and the Tiger,* 284.

46. Fox, *Better City Government,* 16.

47. Syrett, *The Gentleman and the Tiger,* 284.

48. Ibid., 209–10; see also Lewinson, *John Purroy Mitchel.*

49. Jane S. Dahlberg, *The New York Bureau of Municipal Research: Pioneer in Government Administration* (New York: New York University Press, 1966), 11–12; John M. Gaus, *A Study of Research in Public Administration* (New York: Social Science Research Council, 1930), 8.

50. "William H. Allen, Civic Achiever," *Charities and the Commons* 18 (6 July 1907): 362–64.

51. New York Bureau of Municipal Research, "A National Program to Improve Methods of Government," *Municipal Research* 71 (March 1916): 2.

52. Dahlberg, *The New York Bureau,* 8–9.

53. Gaus, *A Study of Research,* 8. The question of who had the idea first became a bone of contention between Allen and Cleveland.

54. "City's Supply of Junk," *New York Evening Post,* 12 December 1908, IPA Archives. The newspaper stories referenced in this book were archived at the New York Bureau by Frederick Cleveland. They were clipped and pasted on cardboard, and no page numbers were preserved. They are available at the bureau's successor organization, the Institute of Public Administration (IPA).

55. At this time, faced with the growing power of unions, a number of corporations were setting up what were called "welfare programs" for their employees, instituting modest health and other benefits as well as morale-building efforts such as company picnics and employee clubs. See Edward D. Berkowitz and Kim McQuaid, *Creating the Welfare State: The Political Economy of 20th-Century Reform* (Lawrence: University Press of Kansas, 1988), 11–31.

56. Dahlberg, *The New York Bureau;* Bruere, *Reminiscences,* 17.

57. One of the assistants later recalled that a lot of time was spent standing around counting bags of cement (Dahlberg, *The New York Bureau,* 27–28, n. 23).

58. Bureau of City Betterment, "How Manhattan Is Governed" (New York: Citizens' Union, 1906), 10. See also Henry Bruere, "New York and the Bureau of City Betterment," *Charities and the Commons* 17 (10 November 1906): 223–25.

59. Syrett, *The Gentleman and the Tiger*, 207. Ahearn had held public office since 1882, when Mitchel was three years old.

60. McAneny, later elected president of the Board of Aldermen, helped reinvigorate that body. While in office, he led the Board of Estimate and Apportionment to initiate zoning, a move in which New York City led the nation (McGoldrick, "The Board of Estimate and Apportionment," 146).

61. Dahlberg, *The New York Bureau*, 19. Governor Hughes's ruling: "If there has been maladministration in matters seriously affecting the public welfare and gross breach of official obligation, the duty of removal is clear, albeit there is no proof of peculation or personal dishonesty" (Lewinson, *John Purroy Mitchel*, 42).

62. Bruere, "New York and the Bureau of City Betterment," 223.

63. New York Bureau of Municipal Research, *Making a Municipal Budget: Functional Accounts and Operative Statistics for the Department of Health of Greater New York* (New York: New York Bureau of Municipal Research, 1907), 6.

64. Ibid., 7.

65. Ibid., 34.

66. Frederick Cleveland, *Chapters on Municipal Administration and Accounting* (New York: Longmans, Green, 1909), 244–52.

67. Martin J. Schiesl, *The Politics of Efficiency: Municipal Administration and Reform in America, 1880–1920* (Berkeley: University of California Press, 1977), 113.

68. New York Bureau of Municipal Research, Articles of Incorporation, IPA Archives.

69. Henry Bruere, "The Bureau of Municipal Research," *Proceedings of the Fifth Annual Meeting of the American Political Science Association* (1909): 114.

70. Syrett, *The Gentleman and the Tiger*, 292. Bureau officials regularly insisted that they were not muckraking. Cleveland maintained that "many important reports aren't published so that officials can use the suggestions to correct problems—we let them take the credit for effectiveness measures" (*Chapters*, 352). But Bruere commented that the bureau "steadily employed publicity. It has constantly furnished the press with 'stories' in which are incorporated the results of its inquiries. . . . Its statements through the New York press are placed before several millions of readers" ("New York and the Bureau of City Betterment," 224).

71. "City's Supply of Junk."

72. "William H. Allen, Civic Achiever," 362.

73. William H. Allen, *Reminiscences* (1949; reprint, New York: Columbia University Oral History Project, 1972), 30.

74. Bruere, *Reminiscences*, 38, 41.

75. Ibid., 8–9, 12.

76. "A Servant to Public Servants: Henry Bruere, Appointed to Make New York's Government Efficient," *New York Independent*, 11 December 1914, 65, IPA Archives.

77. Barry Dean Karl, *Executive Reorganization and Reform in the New Deal: The Genesis of Administrative Management, 1900–1939* (Cambridge: Harvard University Press, 1963), 141.

78. Jonathan Kahn, *Budgeting Democracy* (Ithaca, N.Y.: Cornell University Press, 1997), 52.

79. Ibid., 39.

80. Eldon J. Eisenach, *The Lost Promise of Progressivism* (Lawrence: University Press of Kansas, 1994), 83.

81. Kahn, *Budgeting Democracy,* 51.

82. Dahlberg, *The New York Bureau,* 28, n. 27.

83. Irene S. Rubin, "Early Budget Reformers: Democracy, Efficiency, and Budget Reforms," *American Review of Public Administration* 24 (September 1994): 229–51.

84. William H. Allen, *Efficient Democracy* (New York: Dodd, Mead, 1907), viii.

85. Allen, *Reminiscences,* 159.

86. Bruere, "The Bureau of Municipal Research," 111.

87. Ibid., 121.

88. Henry Bruere, "Efficiency in Government," *Annals of the American Academy of Political and Social Science* 41 (May 1912): 3.

89. Ibid., 8.

90. Henry Bruere, *The New City Government: A Discussion of Municipal Administration Based on a Survey of Ten Commission Governed Cities* (New York and London: D. Appleton, 1912), 103.

91. Ibid., 108–9. In retrospect, Bruere put more emphasis on efficiency for its own sake in the bureau's founding vision. In his reminiscences, he characterized the bureau's aim as establishing "good methods of accountancy" and monitoring expenditures in city government (Bruere, *Reminiscences,* 41).

92. Frederick A. Cleveland, "The Need for Coordinating Municipal, State and National Activities," *Annals of the American Academy of Political and Social Science* 41 (May 1912): 27.

93. Rubin, "Early Budget Reformers," 240–41.

94. Frederick A. Cleveland, *Organized Democracy* (New York: Longmans, Green, 1913), 448.

95. Kahn, *Budgeting Democracy,* 53–58.

96. "The New York Bureau of Municipal Research," *Charities and the Commons* 18 (18 May 1907): 200.

97. New York Bureau of Municipal Research, "Six Years of Municipal Research for Greater New York" (New York: New York Bureau of Municipal Research, 1912), 10 ff.

98. Finegold, *Experts and Politicians,* 52.

99. New York Bureau, "Six Years of Municipal Research."

100. New York Bureau of Municipal Research minutes, IPA Archives.

101. Myrtile Cerf, "Bureaus of Public Efficiency: A Study of the Purpose and Methods of Organization," *National Municipal Review* 3 (January 1914): 41.

102. "How City Gets Bureau of Municipal Research," *Philadelphia Inquirer* (1911), IPA Archives.

103. "Finance Dept. of New York Changes System of Accounting," *Wall Street Journal,* 2 September 1909, IPA Archives.

104. *Tammany Times,* n.d., IPA Archives.

105. Metz had been elected in 1905 on the platform "A Business Man for a Business Office." He was responsible for organizing the city's Bureau of Municipal Investigation and Statistics, which was the principal avenue for Bureau of Municipal Research analysis of city expenditures in its campaign to institute a citywide budget. New York Bureau of Munic-

ipal Research, "Some Results and Limitations of Central Financial Control, as Shown by Nine Years' Experience in New York City," *Municipal Research* 81 (January 1917): 2–3.

106. " 'Shorter, Uglier' Word Applied to the Mayor by Comptroller," *New York American*, 23 January 1909, IPA Archives.

107. "Victory for New City Bookkeeping Plan," *New York World*, 4 February 1909, IPA Archives.

108. Richard S. Childs, review of *The New City Government*, by Henry Bruere, *National Municipal Review* 2 (January 1913): 186.

109. "The 'Besmirch' Society," *New York Times*, 9 February 1909, IPA Archives.

110. New York Bureau of Municipal Research, "A National Program to Improve Methods of Government," *Municipal Research* 71 (March 1916): 5–6.

111. Finegold, *Experts and Politicians*, 51.

112. New York Bureau of Municipal Research minutes, 22 April 1912, IPA Archives.

113. Gill, *Municipal Research Bureaus*, 138–39.

114. New York Bureau, "A National Program," 14.

115. Ibid., 15.

116. James T. Young, review of *Efficient Democracy*, by William H. Allen, *Charities and the Commons* 19 (12 October 1907): 877.

117. *The Survey* 22 (15 May 1909): 256–59.

118. Allen opposed the efforts of an elite coalition to centralize administration of the schools in order to reduce neighborhood power. For more on the controversy surrounding the investigation of the New York public school system, see Hindy Lauer Schachter, *Reinventing Government or Reinventing Ourselves: The Role of Citizen Owners in Making a Better Government* (Albany: State University of New York Press, 1997); Hammack, *Power and Society*. Hammack comments: "The [elite] reformers' chief objection was that the wrong sort of people managed the decentralized schools, and managed them in the wrong sort of way" (270).

119. "Dr. Allen Quits as Researcher, Making Charges," *New York Herald*, 6 October 1914, IPA Archives.

120. "Quits Research and Scores John D. Jr.," *Boston Travelers Evening Herald*, 6 October 1914, IPA Archives.

121. "Mrs. Harriman Halts Reply to Allen Charges," *New York American*, 7 October 1914, IPA Archives.

122. Frank P. Walsh, "The Great Foundations," n.d., quoted in James Weinstein, *The Corporate Ideal in the Liberal State, 1900–1918* (Boston: Beacon Press, 1968), 205.

123. Cutting himself was not above exerting such influence. After the investigation of Manhattan borough president Ahearn, John Purroy Mitchel was offered the fusion nomination for president of the Board of Aldermen, and Cutting pressured Mitchel to accept. He called Henry Bruere and told him to tell his friend Mitchel that if he did not accept, Cutting would cut off his support of the bureau. Mitchel felt that he owed the bureau too much to ignore Cutting's ultimatum (Lewinson, *John Purroy Mitchel*, 54–55).

124. "Talk in Secret to John D., Jr., Pleases Miners," *New York Tribune*, 29 January 1915, IPA Archives.

125. "Women Tell Horrors of Colorado Labor War," *New York Commercial*, 4 February 1915, IPA Archives.

126. "Industrial Board Called Unfair by Municipal Expert," *Washington Times*, 6 February 1915, IPA Archives.

127. "Hot Attack Is Made on Industrial Probe," *Cincinnati Post*, 6 February 1915, IPA Archives.

128. "Eliot Influenced by Rockefeller Charge," *Boston Traveler and Evening Herald*, 6 February 1915, IPA Archives.

129. Settlement houses faced the same dilemma. A survey of the Chicago stockyards performed by Mary McDowell's University Settlement found that inadequate wages were at the root of workers' problems. Packing company owners were major supporters of the settlement and of its sponsor, the University of Chicago. The university trustees' "offer to 'correct' true statements in the report that 'would carry a false impression' was a concession to the well-established limits of faculty activism" (Diner, *A City and Its Universities*, 127). Sklar notes that Hull House maintained comparative freedom of action because it was supported to a large extent by funds contributed by its founder-leader Jane Addams and by wealthy women who were personal friends of Addams (Kathryn Kish Sklar, "Who Funded Hull House?" in *Lady Bountiful Revisited: Women, Philanthropy, and Power*, ed. Kathleen D. McCarthy [New Brunswick, N.J.: Rutgers University Press, 1990], 94–118). Cyrus McCormick, Jr., head of the giant McCormick Works, where Henry Bruere briefly served as welfare secretary, gave only $1,500 between 1892 and 1914. As Sklar observes, McCormick and other industrialists were leery of Hull House because of its support for striking workers and for trade unions generally. In contrast, Louise DeKoven Bowen, whose family had made its fortune investing in downtown Chicago real estate, gave $542,282 to Hull House between 1898 and 1928, a figure that dwarfs Rockefeller's support of the New York Bureau. According to Sklar, Addams accepted only support that she was confident would have no strings attached. Of course, her own wealth made this approach feasible.

3. THE OTHER SIDE OF REFORM

1. Helen Campbell, "Social Settlements and the Civic Sense," *The Arena* 20 (November–December 1898): 593.

2. Helena Dudley, "Women's Work in Boston Settlements," *Municipal Affairs* 2 (September 1898): 494. Diner observes that, in Chicago, campaigns to improve public education brought together businessmen, clubwomen, and settlement workers. But they were motivated differently: businessmen by the desire for honest and efficient management, clubwomen and settlers by humanitarian and social welfare concerns (Steven J. Diner, *A City and Its Universities: Public Policy in Chicago, 1892–1919* [Chapel Hill: University of North Carolina Press, 1980], 77).

3. See Rebecca Edwards, *Angels in the Machinery: Gender in American Party Politics from the Civil War to the Progressive Era* (New York: Oxford University Press, 1997), 15–16.

4. Kathryn Kish Sklar, "The Historical Foundations of Women's Power in the Creation of the American Welfare State, 1830–1930," in *Mothers of a New World: Maternalist Policies and the Origins of Welfare States*, ed. Seth Koven and Sonya Mitchell (New York: Routledge, 1993), 43–93.

5. Barbara Welter, "The Cult of True Womanhood," in *Dimity Convictions: The American Woman in the 19th Century* (Athens: Ohio University Press, 1976), 21.

6. See Camilla Stivers, *Gender Images in Public Administration: Legitimacy and the Administrative State* (Newbury Park, Calif.: Sage Publications, 1993), chap. 5.

7. (Mrs.) Imogen B. Oakley, "The More Civic Work, the Less Need of Philanthropy," *American City* 6 (June 1912): 805–13.

8. Mary I. Wood, "Civic Activities of Women's Clubs," *Annals of the American Academy of Political and Social Science* 56 (November 1914): 79.

9. Quoted in Dorothy G. Becker, "Exit Lady Bountiful: The Volunteer and the Professional Social Worker," *Social Services Review* 38 (March 1964): 65.

10. Neva R. Deardorff, "Women in Municipal Activities," *Annals of the American Academy of Political and Social Science* 56 (November 1914): 72.

11. Wood, "Civic Activities," 79; Clinton Rogers Woodruff, "Women and Civics," *National Municipal Review* 3 (October 1914): 713–19.

12. Mary Ritter Beard, "Woman's Work for the City," *National Municipal Review* 4 (April 1915): 206.

13. C. M. Robinson, "Civic Improvement," *The Survey* 26 (26 August 1911): 725.

14. Richard T. Ely, *The Coming City* (New York: Thomas Y. Crowell, 1902), 105.

15. Deardorff, "Women in Municipal Activities," 73.

16. Ibid., 72.

17. Robinson, "Civic Improvement," 725.

18. Deardorff, "Women in Municipal Activities," 73.

19. Ibid., 75.

20. Darlene Clark Hine, " 'We Specialize in the Wholly Impossible': The Philanthropic Work of Black Women," in *Lady Bountiful Revisited: Women, Philanthropy, and Power*, ed. Kathleen D. McCarthy (New Brunswick, N.J.: Rutgers University Press, 1990), 70–93.

21. Linda Gordon, "Black and White Visions of Welfare: Women's Welfare Activism, 1890–1945," *Journal of American History* 78 (September 1991): 559–90. Gordon notes that by 1890, white women were campaigning to get governments to intervene to ameliorate urban problems; in contrast, African American women, disfranchised and with relatively little access to or influence over governments, until the New Deal, concentrated mainly on building private nonprofit institutions in their own segregated neighborhoods and communities.

22. See Evelyn Brooks-Higginbotham, *Righteous Discontent: The Women's Movement in the Black Baptist Church, 1880–1920* (Cambridge: Harvard University Press, 1993), 1–18.

23. Quoted in Sophonisba P. Breckinridge, *Women in the Twentieth Century: A Study of Their Political, Social and Economic Activities* (New York: McGraw-Hill, 1933), 19.

24. Ibid., 29.

25. Ibid., 30.

26. (Mrs.) T. J. Bowlker, "Woman's Home-making Function Applied to the Municipality," *American City* 6 (June 1912): 863.

27. (Mrs.) Frederick P. Bagley, "Relation of Women's Clubs to Public Charity Institutions," *The Commons* 10 (January 1904): 37–38.

28. (Mrs.) Bessie Leach Priddy, "The Woman Mind on Politics," *National Municipal Review* 10 (March 1921): 171.

29. Ely, *The Coming City*, 63.

30. Robert Wiebe, *Self-Rule: A Cultural History of American Democracy* (Chicago and London: University of Chicago Press, 1995), 171.

31. Lawrence Veiller, "The City Club of New York," *Charities and the Commons* 17 (10 November 1906): 212–13; Victor Elting, "The City Club of Chicago and Its Committee Plan," *Charities and the Commons* 17 (10 November 1906): 214–17.

32. Veiller, "The City Club of New York," 212.

33. Barry D. Karl, *Charles E. Merriam and the Study of Politics* (Chicago: University of Chicago Press, 1974), 53.

34. "Chicago City Club at Work," *Charities and the Commons* 16 (19 May 1906): 242.

35. "Women Organize in Boston," *Charities and the Commons* 22 (20 February 1909): 1012.

36. Arnaldo Testi, "The Gender of Reform Politics: Theodore Roosevelt and the Culture of Masculinity," *Journal of American History* 81 (March 1995): 1529.

37. Veiller, "The City Club of New York," 212.

38. Ibid., 213.

39. In Frankfurt, McDowell visited a sewage and garbage disposal plant adorned with a mural entitled "The Old Woman's Mill." According to *The Survey* of March 21, 1914: "The legend is that ugly old women through it are transformed into young and beautiful maidens. . . . [The larger] message [is] that the repulsive and ugly may, through science, be made over into something new and useful" (776). The imagery evokes the age-old vision of a female nature molded and shaped under the banner of science to suit purposes devised by men. See Carolyn Merchant, *The Death of Nature: Women, Ecology and the Science of Revolution* (New York: Harper and Row, 1980), 1–41.

40. Quoted in Maureen A. Flanagan, "Gender and Urban Political Reform: The City Club and the Woman's City Club of Chicago in the Progressive Era," *American Historical Review* 95 (October 1990): 1039.

41. On the role of women's clubs in social welfare policy development, see Theda Skocpol, *Protecting Soldiers and Mothers: The Political Origins of Social Policy in the United States* (Cambridge, Mass.: Belknap Press of Harvard University Press, 1992), 353–72, and Robyn Muncy, *Creating a Female Dominion in American Reform, 1890–1935* (New York: Oxford University Press, 1991), 57–62.

42. Beard, "Woman's Work for the City," 209 (emphasis in original).

43. Robert A. Woods and Albert J. Kennedy, *The Settlement Horizon: A National Estimate* (1922; reprint, New York: Arno Press, 1970), 49.

44. J. Ramsey McDonald, "American Social Settlements," *The Commons* 2 (February 1898): 3.

45. Woods and Kennedy, *The Settlement Horizon*, 22 ff.

46. Dudley, "Women's Work in Boston Settlements," 493–94; Katherine B. Davis, "Settlement Work as a Preparation for Civic Work," *College Settlements Association Quarterly* 1 (October 1916): 6–9.

47. Mary Kingsley Simkhovitch, *Neighborhood: My Story of Greenwich House* (New York: Norton, 1938), 84.

48. Joseph Lee, "Preventive Work," *Charities* 6 (6 April 1901): 305.

49. Julia C. Lathrop, "The Development of the Probation System in a Large City," *Charities and the Commons* 13 (7 January 1905): 344–49; Robyn Muncy, "Gender and Professionalization in the Origins of the U.S. Welfare State: The Careers of Sophonisba Breckinridge and Edith Abbott, 1890–1935," *Journal of Policy History* 2, no. 3 (1990): 290–315.

50. Jane Addams, *Twenty Years at Hull House* (1910; reprint, New York: Penguin Books Signet Classic, 1981), 163.

51. "Sanitary Ills Disclosed by Hull House Workers," *Charities and the Commons* 10 (13 June 1903): 587–88; "Lax Methods of the Chicago Sanitary Bureau," *Charities and*

the Commons 11 (1 August 1903): 1; "Chicago's Absurd Sanitary Bureau," *Charities and the Commons* 11 (17 October 1903): 353–54.

52. Allen J. Davis, *Spearheads for Reform: The Social Settlements and the Progressive Movement, 1890–1914,* 2d ed. (New Brunswick, N.J.: Rutgers University Press, 1984), 56.

53. Simkhovitch, *Neighborhood,* 155.

54. Mary Kingsley Simkhovitch, "Settlement Organization," *Charities and the Commons* 16 (1 September 1906): 568.

55. "Settlement Pioneers in City Government," *Charities and the Commons* (21 February 1914): 638.

56. Clarke A. Chambers, *Seedtime of Reform: American Social Service and Social Action, 1918–1933* (Ann Arbor: University of Michigan Press, 1963), 113–14.

57. Ibid.

58. Kathryn Kish Sklar, "Hull House in the 1890s: A Community of Women Reformers," *Signs: Journal of Women in Culture and Society* 10 (summer 1985): 658–77.

59. See Kathryn Kish Sklar, *Florence Kelley and the Nation's Work: The Rise of Women's Political Culture, 1830–1900* (New Haven, Conn., and London: Yale University Press, 1995), 228–29.

60. Walter I. Trattner, *From Poor Law to Welfare State: A History of Social Welfare in America* (New York: Free Press, 1979), 164–65.

61. Skocpol, *Protecting Soldiers and Mothers,* 347–49; John P. Rousmaniere, "Cultural Hybrid in the Slums: The College Woman and the Settlement House, 1889–1894," *American Quarterly* 22 (1970): 45–66.

62. Woods and Kennedy, *Settlement Horizon,* 437.

63. Trattner, *From Poor Law to Welfare State,* 164–65; Skocpol, *Protecting Soldiers and Mothers,* 347–49.

64. Stephen Kalberg, "The Commitment to Career Reform: The Settlement Movement Leaders," *Social Service Review* 49 (December 1975): 626 n. 13.

65. Quoted in Skocpol, *Protecting Soldiers and Mothers,* 347.

66. Quoted in Clarke A. Chambers, "Women in the Creation of the Profession of Social Work," *Social Service Review* 60 (March 1986): 18.

67. Quoted in Robert C. Reinders, "Toynbee Hall and the American Settlement Movement," *Social Service Review* 56 (March 1982): 45.

68. Sklar, "Historical Foundations," 67.

69. Chambers, *Seedtime of Reform,* 13.

70. Jane Addams, *My Friend Julia Lathrop* (New York: Macmillan, 1935), 74.

71. Sophonisba P. Breckinridge, ed., *Public Welfare Administration in the United States: Selected Documents* (Chicago: University of Chicago Press, 1927), 366–67.

72. Addams, *Twenty Years at Hull House,* 10.

73. Quoted in Elizabeth Ewan, *Immigrant Women in the Land of Dollars: Life and Culture on the Lower East Side, 1890–1925* (New York: Monthly Review Press, 1985), 82.

74. Quoted in Jacqueline K. Parker and Edward M. Carpenter, "Julia Lathrop and the Children's Bureau: The Emergence of an Institution," *Social Service Review* 55 (March 1981): 87.

75. Quoted in Barbara Sicherman, *Alice Hamilton: A Life in Letters* (Cambridge, Mass., and London: Commonwealth Fund/Harvard University Press, 1984), 152.

76. Gwendolyn Mink, "The Lady and the Tramp: Gender, Race, and the Origins of the American Welfare State," in *Women, the State, and Welfare*, ed. Linda Gordon (Madison: University of Wisconsin Press, 1990), 104; Elizabeth Lasch-Quinn, *Black Neighbors: Race and the Limits of Reform in the American Settlement Movement, 1890–1945* (Chapel Hill and London: University of North Carolina Press, 1993), 1; Ruth Hutchinson Crocker, *Social Work and Social Order: The Settlement Movement in Two Industrial Cities, 1889–1930* (Urbana and Chicago: University of Illinois Press, 1992), 5, 213. Also see Thomas Lee Philpott, *The Slum and the Ghetto: Immigrants, Blacks, and Reformers in Chicago, 1880–1930* (Belmont, Calif.: Wadsworth, 1991).

77. Davis, *Spearheads for Reform*, 173.

78. Diner argues that the turn-of-the-century urban reform movement differed from earlier crusades in blending the "traditional social reform concerns of women with the political and administrative interests of businessmen and lawyers" (*A City and Its Universities*, 63).

79. Davis, *Spearheads for Reform*, 173–74.

80. "Notes and Comments," *Charities* 6 (20 April 1901): 340. Allen participated in the debating club at College Settlement in New York and spent time at a London settlement, but his University of Pennsylvania mentor Simon Patten "discouraged" him from living in a settlement (William H. Allen, *Reminiscences* [1949; reprint, New York: Columbia University Oral History Project, 1972], 21, 30, 41).

81. Davis, *Spearheads for Reform*, 170–71.

82. Ibid.

83. Karl, *Charles E. Merriam*, 31.

84. Davis, *Spearheads for Reform*, 183.

85. Ibid.

86. Henry Bruere, "The Bureau of Municipal Research," *Proceedings of the Fifth Annual Meeting of the American Political Science Association* (1909): 112.

87. "William H. Allen, Civic Achiever," *Charities and the Commons* 18 (6 July 1907): 362.

88. William H. Allen, *Women's Part in Government Whether She Votes or Not* (New York: Dodd, Mead, 1913), 95.

89. H. M. Dermitt, review of *Women's Part in Government*, by William H. Allen, *National Municipal Review* 1 (April 1912): 329.

90. Frederick A. Cleveland, *Organized Democracy* (New York: Longmans, Green, 1913), 157–58.

4. TWO PHILOSOPHIES

1. The U.S. Constitution says nothing about "administration"—it never uses the word—beyond a reference to the existence of a "principal Officer in each of the executive Departments" and the president's authority to vest appointment of "inferior Officers" in the "Heads of Departments" (Article III, sec. 2). The *Federalist Papers* (ed. Jacob E. Cooke [Middletown, Conn.: Wesleyan University Press, 1961]), particularly a series written by Alexander Hamilton (67–77), discuss a number of administrative questions and are still an indispensable source for the American philosophy of public administration. But by the time of the municipal research movement, more than 100 years after the *Federalist Papers* were

written, little attention had yet been paid to the implications for government of an increasingly large and complex society. Woodrow Wilson's "The Study of Administration," written in 1887, made exactly the point that the changing conditions with which governments had to deal required systematic study of administrative processes.

2. After the Progressive Era, Dwight Waldo's *The Administrative State* (New York: Ronald Press, 1948) was the first to characterize the work of the municipal research bureaus in these terms. H. S. Gilbertson, a contemporary of the bureau men, described the animating idea of municipal research as follows: "Efficiency is quite compatible with democracy, provided that the democracy is kept informed as to what is going on" (H. S. Gilbertson, "Public Administration—A New Profession," *American Review of Reviews* 47 [May 1913]: 599).

3. Peter Miller and Ted O'Leary, "Hierarchies and American Ideals, 1900–1940," *Academy of Management Review* 14, no. 2 (1989): 250–65.

4. Samuel P. Hays, "The Politics of Reform in Municipal Government in the Progressive Era," *Pacific Northwest Quarterly* 55 (October 1964): 157–69; James Weinstein, *The Corporate Ideal in the Liberal State, 1900–1918* (Boston: Beacon Press, 1968); Kenneth Fox, *Better City Government: Innovation in American Urban Politics 1850–1937* (Philadelphia: Temple University Press, 1977).

5. Quoted in Weinstein, *Corporate Ideal*, 93.

6. Frederick A. Cleveland, *Chapters on Municipal Administration and Accounting* (New York: Longmans, Green, 1909), 207.

7. Ibid., 107.

8. Ibid., 357. Cleveland's views were echoed by Jesse Burks of the Philadelphia Bureau: "In the performance of a large proportion of its functions, a municipality must meet precisely the same technical problems that a private enterprise meets in the discharge of similar functions" (Jesse D. Burks, "Efficiency Standards in Municipal Management," *National Municipal Review* 1 [July 1912]: 367).

9. Henry Bruere, *The New City Government* (New York and London: D. Appleton, 1912), 1. William Allen's *Efficient Democracy* (New York: Dodd, Mead, 1907) is based throughout on the idea that governments should be like charitable organizations in adopting business practices.

10. Cleveland, *Chapters*, 349.

11. Ibid., 346.

12. See, for example, Frederick A. Cleveland, "The Need for Coordinating Municipal, State and National Activities," *Annals of the American Academy of Political and Social Science* 41 (May 1912): 23–39; and Frederick A. Cleveland, *Organized Democracy* (New York: Longmans, Green, 1913).

13. Cleveland, "The Need for Coordinating," 25–27.

14. Cleveland, *Chapters*, 1.

15. Cleveland, *Organized Democracy*, 112.

16. Ibid., 104.

17. Ibid.

18. Cleveland, *Chapters*, 467.

19. Cleveland, *Organized Democracy*, 111.

20. Ibid., 126–27.

21. Cleveland, *Chapters*, 17. For a view of the New York Bureau as an organization oriented toward involving average citizens in government, see Hindy Lauer Schachter, *Rein-*

venting Government or Reinventing Ourselves: The Role of Citizen Owners in Making a Better Government (Albany: State University of New York Press, 1997).

22. Henry Bruere, "Efficiency in City Government," *Annals of the American Academy of Political and Social Science* 41 (May 1912): 1–22.

23. Alan G. Dawley, *The Struggle for Justice* (Cambridge, Mass.: Belknap Press of Harvard University Press, 1991), 154.

24. "Notes of the Week," *Charities and the Commons* 10 (28 February 1903): 191.

25. See Paul Boyer, *Urban Masses and Moral Order in America, 1820–1920* (Cambridge: Harvard University Press, 1978); Michael B. Katz, *In the Shadow of the Poorhouse: A Social History of Welfare in America* (New York: Basic Books, 1986).

26. David Montgomery, *Citizen Worker: The Experience of Workers in the United States with Democracy and the Free Market during the Nineteenth Century* (Cambridge: Cambridge University Press, 1993), 68, 77–78.

27. Roy Lubove, *The Professional Altruist: The Emergence of Social Work as a Career 1880–1930* (Cambridge: Harvard University Press, 1965), 3–6. Bremner's milestone account calls Hartley "the most important single figure in American charity in the middle third of the nineteenth century." See Robert H. Bremner, *The Discovery of Poverty in the United States* [formerly *From the Depths*] (1956; reprint, New Brunswick, N.J.: Transaction Publishers, 1992), 35.

28. Katz, *In the Shadow of the Poorhouse,* 75.

29. Boyer, *Urban Masses and Moral Order,* 90–91.

30. Allen, *Efficient Democracy,* 143.

31. Chapter 5 discusses in more detail the likely impact of the scientific charity movement on bureau men and its significance for the professionalization of both public administration and social work.

32. Allen, *Efficient Democracy,* 181–82.

33. Bruere, *New City Government,* 121.

34. William H. Allen, "Boston and the Open Public Eye," *The Survey* 23 (2 October 1909): 14.

35. Burks, "Efficiency Standards in Municipal Management," 370.

36. William H. Allen, *Universal Training for Citizenship and Public Service* (New York: Macmillan, 1917), 87.

37. Cleveland, *Chapters,* 100–101.

38. Bruere, *New City Government,* 122–23.

39. Under Cleveland's leadership, the Taft Commission articulated a view of the federal government much like the one the men of the New York Bureau had set forth for municipal government. The commission's recommendations bore fruit with the passage of the Budget and Accounting Act of 1921, which marked "a fundamental shift in the theory and practice of federal governance," one that largely transferred oversight of the administrative apparatus from the legislative to the executive branch (Jonathan Kahn, *Budgeting Democracy* [Ithaca, N.Y.: Cornell University Press, 1997], 164 ff.).

40. Edward T. Fitzpatrick, "What Is Civic Education?" *National Municipal Review* 5 (April 1916): 279.

41. Frederick Cleveland, "What Is Civic Education?" *National Municipal Review* 5 (October 1916): 653.

42. Edward Fitzpatrick, "What Is Civic Education?" [rejoinder], *National Municipal Review* 5 (October 1916): 655.

43. Henry Bruere, "The Bureau of Municipal Research," *Proceedings of the Fifth Annual Meeting of the American Political Science Association* (1909): 111.

44. Cleveland, *Chapters,* 42.

45. Ibid., 175.

46. Allen, "Boston and the Open Public Eye," 15.

47. Cleveland, *Chapters,* 176–79.

48. Cleveland, *Organized Democracy,* 103.

49. For a discussion of the meaning of "volunteer" in American life, see Barry D. Karl, "Lo, the Poor Volunteer: An Essay on the Relation between History and Myth," *Social Service Review* 58 (December 1984): 493–521.

50. Bruere, *New City Government,* 12, 100.

51. Samuel Haber, *Efficiency and Uplift: Scientific Management in the Progressive Era, 1890–1920* (Chicago: University of Chicago Press, 1964), 11–12.

52. John Allder Dunaway, "Some Efficiency Methods of City Administration," *Annals of the American Academy of Political and Social Science* 64 (March 1916): 90.

53. James T. Young, review of *Efficient Democracy,* by William H. Allen, *Charities and the Commons* 19 (12 October 1907): 877.

54. Burks, "Efficiency Standards in Municipal Management," 368.

55. Cleveland, *Chapters,* 70.

56. William H. Allen, *Woman's Part in Government Whether She Votes or Not* (New York: Dodd, Mead, 1913), 87 (emphasis in original).

57. Cleveland, "The Need for Coordinating," 27.

58. George B. Hopkins, "The New York Bureau of Municipal Research," *Annals of the American Academy of Political and Social Science* 41 (May 1912): 237. The ideal type of this mode of fact-finding was the casework performed by friendly visitors associated with organizations such as the charity organization societies and the Association for Improving the Conditions of the Poor. See Lubove, *The Professional Altruist,* 11–18.

59. Allen, "Boston and the Open Public Eye," 15.

60. Ibid.

61. William H. Allen, *Civics and Health* (Boston: Ginn and Co., 1909), 321.

62. Bruere, "Efficiency in City Government," 8.

63. Donald C. Stone and Alice B. Stone, "Early Development of Education in Public Administration," in *American Public Administration: Past, Present, Future,* ed. Frederick C. Mosher (University: University of Alabama Press, 1975), 17.

64. Luther Gulick, *The National Institute of Public Administration: A Progress Report* (New York: National Institute of Public Administration, 1928), 31.

65. Kathryn Kish Sklar, "Hull House Maps and Papers: Social Science as Women's Work in the 1890s," in *The Social Survey in Historical Perspective, 1880–1930,* ed. Martin Bulmer, Kevin Bales, and Kathryn Kish Sklar (Cambridge: Cambridge University Press, 1991), 111–42.

66. Ibid.

67. "Spread of the Survey Idea," *The Survey* 30 (3 May 1913): 157.

68. Paul U. Kellogg, "The Pittsburgh Survey," *Charities and the Commons* 21 (2 January 1909): 517.

69. Colleagues in the Field Work, "The Pittsburgh Survey of the National Publications Committee of *Charities and the Commons," Charities and the Commons* 19 (7 March 1908): 1669.

70. Ibid., 1666.

71. Henry Bruere, *Reminiscences* (1950; reprint, New York: Columbia University Oral History Project, 1972), 44.

72. Murray Gross, "Civic and Social Surveys and Community Efficiency," *National Municipal Review* 3 (October 1914): 726.

73. Ibid.

74. The inclusion of Pittsburgh on this list is interesting in light of the mention, in minutes of the board of directors of the New York Bureau, that *Charities and the Commons,* the coordinator of the Pittsburgh Survey, invited the New Yorkers to participate in the survey, in particular to study the efficiency of the Pittsburgh government (New York Bureau of Municipal Research minutes, 7 October 1907, IPA Archives). But the meeting that day adjourned for lack of a quorum, and no further mention is made of joining the work in Pittsburgh.

75. Cleveland, *Chapters,* 356.

76. Frederick A. Cleveland, "Evolution of the Budget Idea in the United States," *Annals of the American Academy of Political and Social Science* 62 (November 1915): 15.

77. Cleveland, *Chapters,* 179. Jonathan Kahn has an interesting discussion of Cleveland's view of municipal accounting as a common language of public life (*Budgeting Democracy,* 70). One is also reminded of Vaclav Havel's play *The Memorandum,* a satire of bureaucratic life based on the premise that, for efficiency's sake, the government had created a new language in which the length of words was determined by how often they were used. The longest word in the new language was the term for "aardvark."

78. Kahn, *Budgeting Democracy,* 97.

79. Bruere, "Efficiency in City Government," 19.

80. William R. Patterson, "Some Problems of Social Research," *Charities and the Commons* 20 (23 May 1908): 247.

81. Allen, *Universal Training,* 130. It may be significant that Allen made this assertion after he had resigned from the New York Bureau. The subtext of his critical view of expertise here may have a tinge of sour grapes to it, since he now spoke as one who had been forced out of the preeminent organ of municipal research.

82. William A. Prendergast, "Efficiency through Accounting," *Annals of the American Academy of Political and Social Science* 41 (May 1912): 43.

83. Edwin R. Lewinson, *John Purroy Mitchel: The Boy Mayor of New York* (New York: Astra Books, 1965), 110.

84. Ibid., 106.

85. William H. Allen, "Mr. Rockefeller's Greatest Gift," *The Survey* 22 (15 May 1909): 256–59.

86. "The New York Bureau of Municipal Research," *Charities and the Commons* 18 (18 May 1907): 201.

87. New York Bureau of Municipal Research, *Making a Municipal Budget* (New York: New York Bureau of Municipal Research, 1907), 5.

88. Cleveland, "Evolution of the Budget Idea," 22.

89. Bremner, *Discovery of Poverty in the United States,* 149–51.

90. "New York's Budget Exhibit," *Charities and the Commons* 21 (10 October 1908).

91. Kahn, *Budgeting Democracy,* 104–16. Kahn is an indispensable source on the New York Bureau's advocacy of budgeting. He notes that the 1911 exhibit included not just graphs and charts but also a model milk station, a new jail cell, and "Brentwood," a twenty-one-year-old fire department horse. I relied heavily on Kahn's work to tell this part of the story.

92. "Budget Day in New York City," *The Survey* 22 (15 May 1909): 267.

93. Jane S. Dahlberg, *The New York Bureau of Municipal Research: Pioneer in Government Administration* (New York: New York University Press, 1966), 167–68.

94. Lawrence Veiller, "New York City as a Social Worker: The 1910 Budget and Social Needs," *The Survey* 23 (6 November 1909): 212.

95. "The Common Welfare: Father Knickerbocker and His Cash Register," *The Survey* 22 (1 May 1909): 160.

96. Veiller, "New York City as a Social Worker," 211.

97. John Martin, "New York's Budget for Permanent Betterment," *The Survey* 24 (24 August 1910): 739.

98. Kahn, *Budgeting Democracy,* 103–4.

99. Ibid., 156.

100. Of the thirty-four issues of *Municipal Research* published between January 1915 and November 1917, eighteen had to do with government budgeting and financial management. Dahlberg notes, however, that the principle of executive management was asserted as early as the bureau's 1907 *Report of the Charter Revision Commission* for New York City (*The New York Bureau,* 73–77).

101. Henry Bruere, "The Budget as an Administrative Program," *Annals of the American Academy of Political and Social Science* 62 (November 1915): 181, 185, 191.

102. Cleveland, "Evolution of the Budget Idea," 15.

103. New York Bureau of Municipal Research, "The Elements of State Budget Making," *Municipal Research* 80 (December 1916): 3.

104. New York Bureau of Municipal Research, "Some Results and Limitations of Central Financial Control as Shown by Nine Years' Experience in New York City," *Municipal Research* 81 (January 1917): 8.

105. Finegold notes that Mitchel depended heavily on the bureau for policy proposals. Bruere commented that Mitchel pretty much adopted a campaign platform written by the bureau as the basis for his administration (Kenneth Finegold, *Experts and Politicians: Reform Challenges to Machine Politics in New York, Cleveland, and Chicago* [Princeton, N.J.: Princeton University Press, 1995], 55).

106. New York Bureau of Municipal Research minutes, 8 December 1917, IPA Archives.

107. Finegold, *Experts and Politicians,* 64.

108. Quoted in Dahlberg, *The New York Bureau,* 93.

109. Kahn, *Budgeting Democracy,* 123.

110. New York Bureau of Municipal Research, "Constitution and Government of the State of New York," *Municipal Research* 61 (May 1915).

111. Kahn comments that the bureau men used budget reform to try to update James Madison's theories to the requirements of a complex industrial society: "Budget reform would relegate factions to the private sphere and harmonize all public action through adherence to rational assessment of scientifically obtained data" (*Budgeting Democracy,* 124).

112. "Real Reform," *New York Sun,* 28 June 1915, IPA Archives.

113. "Undismayed in His Research Effort," *New York Herald,* 31 March 1916, IPA Archives.

114. "Research Bureau Issues 'Samples from Pork Barrel,'" *New York Herald,* 1 April 1916, IPA Archives.

115. Quoted in Arnaldo Testi, "The Gender of Reform Politics: Theodore Roosevelt and the Culture of Masculinity," *Journal of American History* 82 (March 1995): 1511.

116. Grace Abbott, review of *Woman's Work in Municipalities*, by Mary Ritter Beard, *National Municipal Review* 4 (July 1915): 683.

117. Helen Campbell, "Social Settlements and the Civic Sense," *The Arena* 20 (November–December 1898): 592.

118. Kathryn Kish Sklar, "Two Political Cultures in the Progressive Era: The National Consumers' League and the American Association for Labor Legislation," in *U.S. History as Women's History: New Feminist Essays*, ed. Linda K. Kerber, Alice Kessler-Harris, and Kathryn Kish Sklar (Chapel Hill and London: University of North Carolina Press, 1995), 36–62.

119. (Mrs.) Frederick P. Bagley, "Relation of Women's Clubs to Public Charity Institutions," *The Commons* 10 (January 1904): 41.

120. Caroline Danielson, "Figuring Citizens: Gilman and Addams on Women's Citizenship" (paper presented at the annual meeting of the American Political Science Association, Chicago, September 1995), 8.

121. Quoted in Carol Nackenoff, "Gendered Citizenship: Alternative Narratives of Political Incorporation in the United States, 1875–1925" (paper presented at the annual meeting of the American Political Science Association, San Francisco, September 1996), 10. Used with the permission of the author.

122. Nearly a century later, a female candidate for mayor of the District of Columbia campaigned holding a broom, promising to sweep the D.C. government clean.

123. Quoted in Nackenoff, "Gendered Citizenship," 9.

124. Ibid., 10.

125. Robert A. Woods and Albert J. Kennedy, *The Settlement Horizon: A National Estimate* (1922; reprint, New York: Arno Press, 1970).

126. John Haynes Holmes, "Of New Ideals and the City," *The Survey* 25 (24 December 1910): 500–501. Lori D. Ginzberg argues that the scientific charity work in which late-nineteenth-century elite white women were a major force specifically modeled itself on corporate business values and practices (*Women and the Work of Benevolence: Morality, Politics, and Class in the Nineteenth Century United States* [New Haven, Conn.: Yale University Press, 1990]). See chapter 5 of the present work for a discussion of the influence of scientific charity on the professionalization of social work.

127. Jane Addams, *Democracy and Social Ethics* (New York: Macmillan, 1902), 222–23.

128. Woods and Kennedy, *Settlement Horizon*, 227.

129. Ibid., 229.

130. Addams, *Democracy and Social Ethics*, 229.

131. Mary Kingsbury Simkhovitch, *Neighborhood: My Story of Greenwich House* (New York: Norton, 1938), 176–77. Theda Skocpol argues that elite women were able to make common cause with their working-class sisters because the rhetoric of motherhood was a class-bridging language. In contrast, elite men never figured out how to surmount the class divide separating them from male workers (*Protecting Soldiers and Mothers* [Cambridge, Mass.: Belknap Press of Harvard University Press, 1992], 368).

132. Howard E. Wilson, *Mary McDowell: Neighbor* (Chicago: University of Chicago Press, 1928), 25 (emphasis in original).

133. Quoted in Robert C. Reinders, "Toynbee Hall and the American Settlement Movement," *Social Service Review* 56 (March 1982): 47.

134. (Mrs.) T. J. Bowlker, "Woman's Home-making Function Applied to the Municipality," *American City* 6 (June 1912): 869.

135. Addams, *Democracy and Social Ethics*, 16.

136. Bowlker, "Women's Home-making Function," 863.

137. Bagley, "Relations of Women's Clubs," 37.

138. Jane Addams, *Twenty Years at Hull House* (1910; reprint, New York: Penguin Books Signet Classic, 1981), 100.

139. Addams, *Democracy and Social Ethics,* 25–26.

140. Granted, there was a structural factor promoting this interpretation of citizenship—women's lack of the vote. Barred from casting their ballots, women had few other options than civic work if they were to have any impact in the public sphere.

141. See Camilla Stivers, "The Public Agency as Polis: Active Citizenship in the Administrative State," *Administration and Society* 22 (May 1990): 86–105; Camilla Stivers, "Citizenship Ethics in Public Administration," in *Handbook of Administrative Ethics,* ed. Terry L. Cooper (New York: Marcel Dekker, 1994), 435–455.

142. Jane Addams, *My Friend Julia Lathrop* (New York: Macmillan, 1935), 49.

143. Riva Shpak Lissak, *Pluralism and Progressives: Hull House and the New Immigrants, 1890–1919* (Chicago and London: University of Chicago Press, 1989), 1–9.

144. Skocpol, *Protecting Soldiers and Mothers,* 353–55.

145. Mary Jo Deegan, *Jane Addams and the Men of the Chicago School, 1882–1918* (New Brunswick, N.J.: Transaction Books, 1990), 34–39.

146. Quoted in ibid., 35.

147. Ibid., 38.

148. Lela B. Costin, *Two Sisters for Social Justice: A Biography of Grace and Edith Abbott* (Urbana and Chicago: University of Illinois Press, 1983), 45.

149. Simkhovitch, *Neighborhood,* 39.

150. Woods and Kennedy, *Settlement Horizon,* 59.

151. Katherine Bement Davis, "Settlement Work as a Preparation for Civic Work," *College Settlements Association Quarterly* 1 (October 1916): 6–7.

152. Herman F. Hegner, "Scientific Value of the Social Settlements," *American Journal of Sociology* 3 (September 1897): 175 ff.

153. Barbara Sicherman, *Alice Hamilton: A Life in Letters* (Cambridge, Mass., and London: Commonwealth Fund/Harvard University Press, 1984), 166–67.

154. Quoted in Addams, *My Friend Julia Lathrop,* 69.

155. Simkhovitch, *Neighborhood,* 100.

156. Mary Kingsbury Simkhovitch, "Settlement Organization," *Charities and the Commons* 16 (1 September 1906): 569.

157. Simkhovitch, *Neighborhood,* 101.

158. Quoted in Hegner, "Scientific Value of the Social Settlements," 174.

159. Simkhovitch, "Settlement Organization," 566–67.

160. Foreword to Wilson, *Mary McDowell: Neighbor,* x.

161. Woods and Kennedy, *Settlement Horizon,* 58.

162. Simkhovitch, *Neighborhood,* 71.

163. Davis, "Settlement Work as a Preparation for Civic Work," 8–9.

164. Wilson, *Mary McDowell: Neighbor,* 151.

165. Public administration theorist Marshall Dimock wrote, in a memorial to Grace Abbott: "The liberal disciplines himself to see all sides; the humanitarian feels a deep bond of sympathy and helpfulness for human kind; the progressive does both and adds to it a hardheaded program of action" ("The Inner Substance of a Progressive," *Social Services Review* 13 [December 1939]: 574).

166. Quoted in Addams, *My Friend Julia Lathrop*, 302.

167. Ibid., 70–71.

168. Quoted in Jane Addams, "Julia Lathrop's Services to the State of Illinois," *Social Service Review* 9 (June 1935): 192–93. Admittedly, in this instance, Lathrop's impact on the asylum superintendent was probably strengthened by her official status as a member of the State Board of Charities.

169. Jane Addams, "Problems of Municipal Administration," *American Journal of Sociology* 10 (January 1905): 425–44.

170. Press coverage of Lathrop's selection included bits of humor occasioned by her sex. For example, an article in *The Survey* commented: "The head of a bureau of the federal government is called a 'chief' [and addressed in writing] as 'Dear Mr. Chief.' Consequently, official Washington was thrown into consternation at the announcement that Julia Lathrop had been placed in charge of the new children's bureau, for there seemed no escape from the salutation, 'Dear Miss Chief' " ["Immediate Work," *The Survey* 29, no. 7 (1912): 189].

171. Julia C. Lathrop, "The Children's Bureau," *American Journal of Sociology* 18 (November 1912): 318–20.

172. Jacqueline K. Parker and Edward M. Carpenter, "Julia Lathrop and the Children's Bureau: The Emergence of an Institution," *Social Service Review* 55 (March 1981): 61–62.

173. Robyn Muncy, "Gender and Professionalization in the Origins of the U.S. Welfare State: The Careers of Sophonisba Breckinridge and Edith Abbott, 1890–1935," *Journal of Policy History* 2, no. 3 (1990): 290–315.

174. Parker and Carpenter, "Julia Lathrop," 73.

175. Edith Abbott, "Grace Abbott: A Sister's Memories," *Social Service Review* 13 (September 1939): 357.

176. Simkhovitch, *Neighborhood*, 177.

177. Robyn Muncy, *Creating a Female Dominion in American Reform, 1890–1935* (New York: Oxford University Press, 1991), 133.

178. Sara Deutsch, "Learning to Talk More Like a Man: Boston Women's Class-bridging Organizations, 1870–1940," *American Historical Review* 97 (April 1992): 379–404.

179. "Trained Social Workers Take Charge of New York City Government," *The Survey* 31 (10 January 1914): 431.

5. PROFESSIONALIZING PUBLIC SERVICE

1. Bryn Mawr's Dr. Marion Parris wrote: "Students don't dare squint at a microbe with less than three years' graduate biology. Yet we turn people loose on the social fabric without any other doctorate than a kind heart" (quoted in William H. Allen, "Training Men and Women for Public Service," *Annals of the American Academy of Political and Social Science* 41 [May 1912]: 309).

2. William H. Allen, *Reminiscences* (1949; reprint, New York: Columbia University Oral History Project, 1972), 206; Woodrow Wilson, "The Study of Administration," *Political Science Quarterly* 2 (June 1887): 197–222.

3. "School of Public Business," *New York Sun*, 13 November 1911, IPA Archives.

4. The minutes indicate that although Mrs. Harriman initially declined the offer, she was elected again in 1914 and served until her death in 1932 (New York Bureau of Municipal Research minutes, 14 December 1910, IPA Archives).

5. Quoted in Jonathan Kahn, *Budgeting Democracy* (Ithaca, N.Y.: Cornell University Press, 1997), 127.

6. William H. Allen, "Instruction in Municipal Affairs," *National Municipal Review* 1 (July 1912): 306.

7. "An Experiment in Training Men till They Become Expert in Municipal Government," *New York Tribune,* 19 November 1911, IPA Archives.

8. Ibid.

9. Allen, "Training Men and Women for Public Service," 307.

10. New York Bureau of Municipal Research minutes, 8 April 1912, IPA Archives.

11. Quoted in Kahn, *Budgeting Democracy,* 128. Beard was pressured to resign after he tried to intercede in defense of colleagues who had opposed the United States' entrance into World War I (Dorothy Ross, *The Origins of American Social Science* [Cambridge: Cambridge University Press, 1991], 325).

12. "Public Service Training and the Universities," *The Survey* 32 (25 April 1914): 91; "Universities and the Public Service," *The Survey* 32 (23 May 1914). See also Helene Silverberg, " 'A Government of Men': Gender, the City, and the New Science of Politics," in *Gender and American Social Science,* ed. Helene Silverberg (Princeton, N.J.: Princeton University Press, 1999), 175.

13. "Training School for Public Service Annual Report 1913," *Efficient Citizenship* 670 (18 March 1914): 37.

14. Ibid.

15. Charles A. Beard, "Training for Efficient Public Service," *Annals of the American Academy of Political and Social Science* 64 (March 1916): 221.

16. Jane S. Dahlberg, *The New York Bureau of Municipal Research: Pioneer in Government Administration* (New York: New York University Press, 1966), 129; Dwight Waldo, *The Administrative State* (New York: Ronald Press, 1948), 54.

17. Beard, "Training for Efficient Public Service," 221.

18. Magali Sarfatti Larsen, *The Rise of Professionalism: A Sociological Analysis* (Berkeley: University of California Press, 1977), 137. There is a sizable literature on the emergence of new professions in the late nineteenth and early twentieth centuries. This account has been influenced not only by Larsen but also by Robert Wiebe, *The Search for Order, 1877–1920* (New York: Hill and Wang, 1967); Burton J. Bledstein, *The Culture of Professionalism: The Middle Class and the Development of Higher Education in America* (New York and London: W. W. Norton, 1976); Ross, *The Origins of American Social Science;* Don S. Kirschner, *The Paradox of Professionalism: Reform and Public Service in Urban America, 1900–1940* (New York: Greenwood Press, 1986); Walter I. Trattner, *From Poor Law to Welfare State: A History of Social Welfare in America* (New York: Free Press, 1979); and Clarke A. Chambers, "Women in the Creation of the Profession of Social Work," *Social Service Review* 60, no. 1 (March 1986): 1–33.

19. Robert A. Woods and Albert J. Kennedy, *The Settlement Horizon: A National Estimate* (New York: Russell Sage, 1922; reprint, New York: Arno Press, 1970).

20. Robert A. Woods, "Social Work: A New Profession," *Charities and the Commons* 15 (16 January 1906): 469–76. Woods originally read his paper before the Harvard Ethical Society and published it in the *International Journal of Ethics* in 1905. In neither of those venues would the argument have had the wide audience of reformers that *Charities and the Commons* ensured it.

21. Edward T. Devine, *When Social Work Was Young* (1939) and "The Dominant Note

162   BUREAU MEN, SETTLEMENT WOMEN

of Modern Philanthropy" (1906), quoted in Kathleen Woodroofe, *From Charity to Social Work in England and the United States* (Toronto: University of Toronto Press, 1971), 93, 95.

22. Quoted in Arlien Johnson, "Her Contribution to the Professional Schools of Social Work," *Social Service Review* 22 (December 1948): 443, 445.

23. Henry Bruere, "The Bureau of Municipal Research," *Proceedings of the Fifth Annual Meeting of the American Political Science Association* (1909): 121.

24. Henry Bruere, "Efficiency in City Government," *Annals of the American Academy of Political and Social Science* 41 (May 1912): 3.

25. William H. Allen, *Efficient Democracy* (New York: Dodd, Mead, 1907), 263–78.

26. Bruere, "Efficiency in City Government," 3.

27. Lori D. Ginzberg, *Women and the Work of Benevolence: Morality, Politics, and Class in the Nineteenth-Century United States* (New Haven, Conn.: Yale University Press, 1990), 133–73.

28. Roy Lubove, *The Professional Altruist: The Emergence of Social Work as a Career, 1880–1930* (Cambridge: Harvard University Press, 1965), 5–7.

29. Robert H. Bremner, *The Discovery of Poverty in the United States* [formerly *From the Depths*] (1950; reprint, New Brunswick, N.J.: Transaction Publishers, 1992), 52.

30. Quoted in Lubove, *The Professional Altruist,* 50.

31. Ibid., 85.

32. Ibid., 35.

33. Miss Richmond's better-known paper was not the first appeal for social work training. In 1893, Anna L. Dawes read a paper before the International Congress of Charities, Corrections and Philanthropy in Chicago entitled "The Need for Training Schools for a New Profession."

34. David M. Austin, "The Flexner Myth and the History of Social Work," *Social Service Review* 57 (September 1983): 357–77. My discussion is indebted to Austin's analysis.

35. Ibid.

36. Lela B. Costin, "Edith Abbott and the Chicago Influence on Social Work Education," *Social Service Review* 57 (March 1983): 104.

37. Simon Patten, "Who Is the Good Neighbor?" *Charities and the Commons* 19 (29 February 1908): 1645.

38. Edith Abbott and Sophonisba Breckinridge emphasized social welfare policy in their groundbreaking graduate curriculum, but the practical orientation typical of settlement leaders, toward solving or ameliorating problems by means of intimate association with those afflicted by them, has failed to find a place at the center of the professional social work identity.

39. Austin, "The Flexner Myth," 361.

40. Chambers, "Women in the Creation of the Profession of Social Work," 1–33.

41. Frederick A. Cleveland, *Organized Democracy* (New York: Longmans, Green, 1913), 103.

42. Quoted in Waldo, *The Administrative State,* 33n.

43. Hindy Lauer Schachter, *Reinventing Government or Reinventing Ourselves: The Role of Citizen Owners in Making a Better Government* (Albany: State University of New York Press, 1997), 43–54.

44. Abraham Flexner, "The Educational Activities of the Bureau of Municipal Research of New York" (report to the General Education Board, February 1914), 16, 26. Photocopy furnished by the Rockefeller Archives.

45. The first graduate degree in public administration was a one-year master's program in municipal administration conceived and launched by the chairman of the political science department at the University of Michigan. Stone and Stone note that the program "never gained full control over its curriculum and budget until 1950" (Donald C. Stone and Alice B. Stone, "Early Development of Education in Public Administration," in *American Public Administration: Past, Present, Future*, ed. Frederick C. Mosher [University: University of Alabama Press, 1975], 273). Whether because of its association with political science or because of its later permutation into an institute for policy analysis, the Michigan program has never been accorded full status among public administrationists as the founding professional degree in the field.

46. "A Town Meeting Method of Making up Budgets," *Brooklyn Standard*, 27 January 1916, IPA Archives.

47. "Investigate Them!" *Brooklyn Eagle*, 31 March 1916, IPA Archives.

48. "W. B. Holton Replies to Biggs's Criticism," *New York Times*, 18 May 1916, IPA Archives.

49. "Undismayed in his Research Effort," *New York Herald*, 31 March 1916, IPA Archives.

50. New York Bureau of Municipal Research minutes, 14 April 1916, IPA Archives.

51. Ibid., 22 May 1917.

52. Beard's book, *The Economic Basis of the Constitution* (1913), painted the framers as self-interested men of wealth who crafted a governmental system aimed at preserving their economic privilege.

53. Charles T. Goodsell, "Charles A. Beard, Prophet for Public Administration," *Public Administration Review* 46 (March–April 1986): 106.

54. Barry Dean Karl, *Executive Reorganization and Reform in the New Deal: The Genesis of Administrative Management, 1900–1939* (Cambridge: Harvard University Press, 1963), 151.

55. Ibid., 150.

56. Luther Gulick, *The National Institute of Public Administration: A Progress Report* (New York: National Institute of Public Administration, 1928), 94.

57. Karl, *Executive Reorganization*, 145.

58. In late 1922, Fulton Cutting said that "an organic relationship with one of the larger universities would not be to the advantage of the work of the institute for the time being" (New York Bureau of Municipal Research minutes, 7 December 1922, IPA Archives).

59. Peter J. Johnson, "The Progressive Movement, Municipal Reform, and the Founding of the Maxwell School" (Syracuse, N.Y.: Maxwell School of Syracuse University, 1975), 9. Photocopy in IPA Archives.

60. Typescript memorandum (1924), box 2133, William E. Mosher Papers, Syracuse University.

61. Waldo, *The Administrative State*, 24.

62. Ibid., 54.

63. "Maxwell Graduate School, 1924–1945," box 5496, Mosher Papers.

64. William E. Mosher, "Training for Public Service," *Public Management* (April 1928): 325–28, 336, in box 2133, Mosher Papers.

65. Quoted in Waldo, *The Administrative State*, 70n.

66. Frederick M. Davenport, "A Training School for Politicians," *The Outlook* 21 (October 1925): 282, in box 2133, Mosher Papers.

67. Johnson, "Founding of the Maxwell School," 12.

68. Robyn Muncy, "Gender and Professionalization in the Origins of the U.S. Welfare State: The Careers of Sophonisba Breckinridge and Edith Abbott, 1890–1935," *Journal of Policy History* 2, no. 3 (1990): 290–315.

69. Costin, "Edith Abbott," 96.

70. Lela B. Costin, *Two Sisters for Social Justice: A Biography of Grace and Edith Abbott* (Urbana and Chicago: University of Illinois Press, 1983), 63–67.

71. Muncy, "Gender and Professionalization," 299.

72. Regina G. Kunzel, *Fallen Women, Problem Girls: Unmarried Mothers and the Professionalization of Social Work, 1890–1945* (New Haven, Conn., and London: Yale University Press, 1993), 48.

73. Quoted in ibid., 45.

74. Quoted in Costin, "Edith Abbott," 107.

75. Muncy, "Gender and Professionalization," 305.

76. Quoted in Costin, "Edith Abbott," 108.

77. Frank Bruno, "Twenty-five Years of Schools of Social Work," *Social Service Review* 18 (1944): 156.

78. Wiebe, *The Search for Order,* 286–302.

6. CONSTRUCTING PUBLIC ADMINISTRATION

1. Dwight Waldo, *The Administrative State: A Study of the Political Theory of American Public Administration* (New York: Ronald Press, 1948), 3.

2. Ibid., 44.

3. Ibid., 45.

4. Herbert Simon, "The Proverbs of Administration" [1947], in *Classics of Public Administration,* 4th ed., ed. Jay M. Shafritz and Albert C. Hyde (Fort Worth, Tex.: Harcourt Brace, 1997). See also Herbert Simon, *Administrative Behavior* (New York: Free Press, 1945).

5. George A. Graham, "Trends in the Teaching of Public Administration," *Public Administration Review* 10 (January–February 1950): 74.

6. G. David Garson argues that the work of Harold D. Lasswell, the father of policy science, reflected a concern for historical context and the application of knowledge to fundamental human problems, one that came to be obscured by the fervor for empirical method inherent in Lasswell's own behavioralism. See "From Policy Science to Policy Analysis: A Quarter Century of Progress," *Policy Studies Journal,* special issue 2 (1980–1981): 535–44.

7. See Laurence E. Lynn, Jr., "Public Management Research: The Triumph of Art over Science," *Journal of Policy Analysis and Management* 13, no. 2 (1994): 231–59; Mark E. Moore, "Policy Managers Need Policy Analysts," *Journal of Policy Analysis and Management* 1, no. 3 (1982): 413–18; John M. Quigley and Suzanne Scotchmer, "What Counts? Analysis Counts," *Journal of Policy Analysis and Management* 8, no. 3 (1989): 483–89.

8. John J. DiIulio, Jr., "Leadership and Social Science," *Journal of Policy Analysis and Management* 9, no. 1 (1990): 116–26.

9. For example, see Eugene Bardach, review of *Creating Public Value: Strategic Management in Government,* by Mark E. Moore, *American Political Science Review* 91 (June 1997): 463–64.

10. Fred Thompson, review of *The State of Public Management*, ed. Donald F. Kettl and H. Brinton Milward, *Journal of Policy Analysis and Management* 16, no. 3 (1997): 484–89.

11. Howard E. McCurdy and Robert E. Cleary, "Why Can't We Resolve the Research Issue in Public Administration?" *Public Administration Review* 45 (January–February 1984): 49–55.

12. A number of important pieces were reprinted in Jay D. White and Guy B. Adams, eds., *Research in Public Administration: Reflections on Theory and Practice* (Thousand Oaks, Calif.: Sage Publications, 1994).

13. See Guy B. Adams and Jay D. White, "Dissertation Research in Public Administration and Cognate Fields: An Assessment of Methods and Quality," *Public Administration Review* 54 (November–December 1994): 565–74; Jay D. White, Guy B. Adams, and John P. Forrester, "Knowledge and Theory Development in Public Administration: The Role of Doctoral Education and Research," *Public Administration Review* 56 (September–October 1996): 441–52.

14. Linda Kaboolian, "The New Public Management: Challenging the Boundaries of the Management vs. Administration Debate," *Public Administration Review* 58 (May–June 1998): 192.

15. Larry D. Terry, editor's introduction [untitled], *Public Administration Review* 58 (May–June 1998): 189.

16. Frank J. Thompson, Michael Brintnall, Robert F. Durant, Donald F. Kettl, Beryl A. Radin, and Lois Recasino Wise, "Report of the APSA-NASPAA Committee on the Advancement of Public Administration" (paper presented at the annual meeting of the American Political Science Association, Boston, 3–6 September 1998), 1, 4.

17. As the noted sociologist Anthony Giddens has argued, the problem with bringing social science firmly under a natural science approach is that the subject matter of social science—namely, human beings—is unlike the material of natural science. Because people are capable of taking study results and applying them, the next time a given situation is examined, it is likely to have been transformed by the knowledgeable actions of the people involved. See *Central Problems in Social Theory: Action, Structure and Contradiction in Social Analysis* (Berkeley: University of California Press, 1979).

18. Leonard D. White, "Introduction to the Study of Public Administration" [1926], in Shafritz and Hyde, *Classics*, 44, 45.

19. Paul Appleby, "Government Is Different" [excerpt from *Big Democracy*, 1945], in Shafritz and Hyde, *Classics*, 123.

20. Graham Allison, "Public and Private Management: Are They Fundamentally Alike in All Unimportant Respects?" in *Proceedings of the Public Management Research Conference*, OPM Document 127-53-1 (Washington, D.C.: Office of Personnel Management, February 1980).

21. The tables of contents of the four editions of Jay Shafritz and Albert Hyde's collection of public administration classics give an overview of the passing parade of business-minded reforms. The first edition in 1978 included Allan Schick on PPBS, Peter F. Drucker on management by objectives (MBO), and Peter Pyhrr on zero-based budgeting. The second edition (1987) kept PPBS and zero-based budgeting, dropped MBO, and included Graham Allison's essay on public and private management (see note 20). In the third edition, a 1995 essay on public management was included, reflecting the growing importance of that perspective in the study of government agencies. PPBS was still included, but zero-based

budgeting had disappeared. An essay by Ronald Moe on "privatization" reflected the Reagan-era emphasis not just on modeling government on business but also on divesting government responsibilities to the private sector. The most recent edition (1997) preserves the essays on PPBS and privatization and adds a spate of articles reflecting the business approach in government, including Michael Barzelay on customer-driven service, Philip Joyce on performance measures, and two pieces on "reinventing government" at the federal level. See Jay M. Shafritz and Albert C. Hyde, eds., *Classics of Public Administration,* 1st ed. (Oak Park, Ill.: Moore, 1978); 2d ed. (Chicago: Dorsey Press, 1987); 3d ed. (Belmont, Calif.: Wadsworth, 1992); 4th ed. (Fort Worth, Tex.: Harcourt Brace, 1997).

22. David Osborne and Ted Gaebler, *Reinventing Government: How the Entrepreneurial Spirit Is Transforming the Public Sector* (Reading, Mass.: Addison-Wesley, 1992); Executive Office of the President, "National Performance Review" [Gore report], in Shafritz and Hyde, *Classics,* 4th ed., 536.

23. Waldo, *The Administrative State,* p. 206.

24. Ibid.

25. Hannah Arendt, *Between Past and Future: Eight Exercises in Political Thought* (New York: Viking, 1968), 227–64.

26. Woodrow Wilson, "The Study of Administration." *Political Science Quarterly* 2 (June 1887): 220–21.

27. Norman N. Gill, *Municipal Research Bureaus* (Washington, D.C.: American Council on Public Affairs, 1944), 138–39.

Bibliography

The following list is organized into original and secondary sources. In addition to the documents listed, my research drew on a number of useful archives. The Social Welfare History Archives at the University of Minnesota houses complete collections of important journals of the period, including *Charities, The Commons,* the merged *Charities and the Commons,* and its successor *The Survey.* The William E. Mosher Papers at Syracuse University were a helpful source on the transfer of the Training School for Public Service to the Maxwell School for Citizenship and Public Affairs. The collection of documents at the Institute of Public Administration (IPA), formerly the New York Bureau of Municipal Research, is an invaluable resource to anyone interested in the early history of American public administration. Particularly useful were minutes of board of directors meetings, research reports, publications such as *Efficient Citizenship* and *Municipal Research,* training school files, and the newspaper clipping file maintained by Frederick Cleveland.

ORIGINAL SOURCES

Abbott, Edith. "Grace Abbott: A Sister's Memories." *Social Service Review* 13 (September 1939): 351–407.

Abbott, Grace. Review of *Woman's Work in Municipalities,* by Mary Ritter Beard. *National Municipal Review* 4 (July 1915): 683.

Addams, Jane. *Democracy and Social Ethics.* New York: Macmillan, 1902.

———. "Problems of Municipal Administration." *American Journal of Sociology* 10 (January 1905): 425–44.

———. *Twenty Years at Hull House.* 1910. Reprint, New York: Penguin Books Signet Classic, 1981.

———. "Julia Lathrop and Outdoor Relief in Chicago, 1893–94." *Social Service Review* 9 (March 1935): 24–33.

———. "Julia Lathrop's Services to the State of Illinois." *Social Service Review* 9 (June 1935): 191–211.

————. *My Friend Julia Lathrop.* New York: Macmillan, 1935.

Allen, William H. *Efficient Democracy.* New York: Dodd, Mead, 1907.

————. "Boston and the Open Public Eye." *The Survey* 23 (2 October 1909): 14–15.

————. "The Business of Citizenship in New York City." *American Review of Reviews* 40 (November 1909): 594–601.

————. *Civics and Health.* Boston: Ginn and Co., 1909.

————. "Mr. Rockefeller's Greatest Gift." *The Survey* 22 (15 May 1909): 256–59.

————. "Training Men and Women for Public Service." *Annals of the American Academy of Political and Social Science* 41 (May 1912): 307–12.

————. "Instruction in Municipal Affairs." *National Municipal Review* 1 (July 1912): 305–6.

————. *Woman's Part in Government Whether She Votes or Not.* New York: Dodd, Mead, 1913.

————. *Universal Training for Citizenship and Public Service.* New York: Macmillan, 1917.

————. *Reminiscences.* 1949. Reprint, New York: Columbia University Oral History Project, 1972.

Bagley, (Mrs.) Frederick P. "Relation of Women's Clubs to Public Charity Institutions." *The Commons* 10 (January 1904): 37–41.

Beard, Charles A. *American City Government: A Survey of Newer Tendencies.* New York: Century Co., 1912.

————. "Training for Efficient Public Service." *Annals of the American Academy of Political and Social Science* 64 (March 1916): 215–26.

Beard, Mary Ritter. "The Legislative Influence of Unenfranchised Women." *Annals of the American Academy of Political and Social Science* 41 (May 1914): 54–61.

————. "Woman's Work for the City." *National Municipal Review* 4 (April 1915): 204–10.

Bowlker, (Mrs.) T. J. "Woman's Home-making Function Applied to the Municipality." *American City* 6 (June 1912): 863–69.

Braddock, J. Harold. "Efficiency Value of the Budget Exhibit." *Annals of the American Academy of Political and Social Science* 41 (May 1912): 151–57.

Breckinridge, Sophonisba P., ed. *Public Welfare Administration in the United States: Selected Documents.* Chicago: University of Chicago Press, 1927.

————. *Women in the Twentieth Century: A Study of Their Political, Social, and Economic Activities.* New York: McGraw-Hill, 1933.

Bruere, Henry. "Public Utilities Regulation in New York." *Annals of the American Academy of Political and Social Science* 31 (May 1905): 1–17.

————. "New York and the Bureau of City Betterment." *Charities and the Commons* 17 (10 November 1906): 223–25.

————. "The Bureau of Municipal Research." *Proceedings of the Fifth Annual Meeting of the American Political Science Association* (1909): 111–21.

————. "Efficiency in City Government." *Annals of the American Academy of Political and Social Science* 41 (May 1912): 1–22.

————. *The New City Government: A Discussion of Municipal Administration Based on a Survey of Ten Commission Governed Cities.* New York and London: D. Appleton, 1912.

————. "The Budget as an Administrative Program." *Annals of the American Academy of Political and Social Science* 62 (November 1915): 176–91.

————. *Reminiscences.* 1950. Reprint, New York: Columbia University Oral History Project, 1972.

Bryce, James G. *The American Commonwealth*. Vol. 1. 1893. Reprint, New York: Macmillan, 1931.

Buck, A. E. "The Development of the Budget Idea in the United States." *Annals of the American Academy of Political and Social Science* 113 (May 1924): 31–39.

Bureau of City Betterment. *How Manhattan Is Governed*. New York: Bureau of City Betterment, 1906.

Burks, Jesse D. "Efficiency Standards in Municipal Management." *National Municipal Review* 1 (July 1912): 364–71.

Campbell, Helen. "Social Settlements and the Civic Sense." *The Arena* 20 (November–December 1898): 589–603.

Cerf, Myrtile. "Bureaus of Public Efficiency: A Study of the Purpose and Methods of Organization." *National Municipal Review* 3 (January 1914): 39–47.

"Chicago's Struggle for Scientific Garbage Collection and Disposal." *The Survey* 31 (21 March 1914): 776–77.

Childs, Richard S. Review of *The New City Government*, by Henry Bruere. *National Municipal Review* 2 (January 1913): 185–87.

Cleveland, Frederick A. "The Relation of Auditing to Public Control." *Annals of the American Academy of Political and Social Science* 26 (November 1905): 665–80.

———. *Chapters on Municipal Administration and Accounting*. New York: Longmans, Green, 1909.

———. "The Application of Scientific Management to the Activities of the State" [1911]. In *Addresses and Discussions at the Conference on Scientific Management Held October 12-13-14, 1911*. Tuck School of Business Management, Dartmouth College. Easton, Pa.: Hove Publishing, 1972.

———. "The Need for Coordinating Municipal, State and National Activities." *Annals of the American Academy of Political and Social Science* 41 (May 1912): 23–39.

———. *Organized Democracy*. New York: Longmans, Green, 1913.

———. "Evolution of the Budget Idea in the United States." *Annals of the American Academy of Political and Social Science* 62 (November 1915): 15–35.

———. "What Is Civic Education?" *National Municipal Review* 5 (October 1916): 652–54.

Coit, Stanton. *Neighborhood Guilds: An Instrument of Social Reform*. London: Swan Sonnenschein, 1891.

Colleagues in the Field Work. "The Pittsburgh Survey of the National Publications Committee of *Charities and the Commons*." *Charities and the Commons* 19 (7 March 1908): 1665–70.

"The Common Welfare: Father Knickerbocker and His Cash Register." *The Survey* 22 (1 May 1909): 159–61.

Croly, Herbert. *The Promise of American Life*. 1909. Reprint, New York: E. P. Dutton, 1963.

Davis, Katherine Bement. "Settlement Work as a Preparation for Civic Work." *College Settlements Association Quarterly* 1 (October 1916): 6–9.

Dawson, Edgar. "The Invisible Government and Administrative Efficiency." *Annals of the American Academy of Political and Social Science* 44 (March 1916): 11–21.

Deardorff, Neva R. "Women in Municipal Activities." *Annals of the American Academy of Political and Social Science* 56 (November 1914): 71–77.

Dermitt, H. M. Review of *Woman's Part in Government*, by William H. Allen. *National Municipal Review* 1 (April 1912): 329–30.

Dudley, Helena. "Women's Work in Boston Settlements." *Municipal Affairs* 2 (September 1898): 493–96.

Dunaway, John Allder. "Some Efficiency Methods of City Administration." *Annals of the American Academy of Political and Social Science* 64 (March 1916): 89–102.

Elting, Victor. "The City Club of Chicago and Its Committee Plan." *Charities and the Commons* 17 (10 November 1906): 214–17.

Ely, Richard T. *The Coming City.* New York: Thomas Y. Crowell, 1902.

Fitzpatrick, Edward T. "What Is Civic Education?" *National Municipal Review* 5 (April 1916): 278–82.

———. "What Is Civic Education?" [rejoinder]. *National Municipal Review* 5 (October 1916): 654–55.

———. *Experts in City Government.* New York: D. Appleton, 1919.

Flexner, Abraham. *The Educational Activities of the Bureau of Municipal Research of New York.* Report to the General Education Board, February 1914. Rockefeller Archives.

Gaus, John M. "The Politics of the City Neighborhood." *The Public* 21 (15 June 1918): 758–62.

———. *A Study of Research in Public Administration.* New York: Social Science Research Council, 1930.

Gilbertson, H. S. "Public Administration—A New Profession." *American Review of Reviews* 47 (May 1913): 599–602.

Gross, Murray. "Civic and Social Surveys and Community Efficiency." *National Municipal Review* 3 (October 1914): 726–30.

Gulick, Luther. *The National Institute of Public Administration: A Progress Report.* New York: National Institute of Public Administration, 1928.

Hegner, Herman F. "Scientific Value of the Social Settlements." *American Journal of Sociology* 3 (September 1897): 171–82.

Holmes, John Haynes. "Of New Ideals and the City." *The Survey* 25 (24 December 1910): 499–501.

Hopkins, George B. "The New York Bureau of Municipal Research." *Annals of the American Academy of Political and Social Science* 41 (May 1912): 235–44.

Johnson, Alexander. "Training for Public Service." *The Survey* 26 (26 August 1911): 755–57.

Kelley, Florence. "Children in the Cities." *National Municipal Review* 4 (April 1915): 197–203.

Kellogg, Paul U. "The Pittsburgh Survey." *Charities and the Commons* 21 (2 January 1909): 517–26.

Lathrop, Julia C. "The Development of the Probation System in a Large City." *Charities and the Commons* 13 (7 January 1905): 344–49.

———. "The Children's Bureau." *American Journal of Sociology* 18 (November 1912): 318–30.

Lee, Joseph. "Preventive Work." *Charities* 6 (6 April 1901): 303–9.

Martin, John. "New York's Budget for Permanent Betterment." *The Survey* 24 (24 August 1910): 737–39.

McDonald, J. Ramsey. "American Social Settlements." *The Commons* 2 (February 1898): 3.

Mitchel, John Purroy. "The Office of Mayor." *Proceedings of the Academy of Political Science* 5 (April 1915): 479–94.

Munro, William Bennett. "Instruction in Municipal Government in the Universities and Colleges of the United States." *National Municipal Review* 5 (October 1916): 565–73.

New York Bureau of Municipal Research. *Making a Municipal Budget: Functional Accounts and Operative Statistics for the Department of Health of Greater New York*. New York: New York Bureau of Municipal Research, 1907.

——. "Training School for Public Service Annual Report, 1913." *Efficient Citizenship* 670 (18 March 1914).

——. "Constitution and Government of the State of New York." *Municipal Research* 61 (May 1915).

——. "A National Program to Improve Methods of Government." *Municipal Research* 71 (March 1916).

——. "The Elements of State Budget Making." *Municipal Research* 80 (December 1916).

——. "Some Results and Limitations of Central Financial Control, as Shown by Nine Years' Experience in New York City." *Municipal Research* 81 (January 1917).

——. "The State Movement for Efficiency and Economy." *Municipal Research* 90 (October 1917).

——. "The Recent Movement for State Budget Reform: 1911–1917." *Municipal Research* 91 (November 1917).

"The New York Bureau of Municipal Research." *Charities and the Commons* 18 (18 May 1907): 200–201.

"Notes and Comment—Florence Kelley, a Modern Crusader." *Social Service Review* 6 (1932): 306–10.

"Notes and Comment—Julia Lathrop and the Public Social Services." *Social Service Review* 6 (1932): 301–6.

Oakley, (Mrs.) Imogen B. "The More Civic Work, the Less Need of Philanthropy." *American City* 6 (June 1912): 805–13.

Patten, Simon. "Who Is the Good Neighbor?" *Charities and the Commons* 19 (29 February 1908): 1642–47.

Patterson, William R. "Some Problems of Social Research." *Charities and the Commons* 20 (23 May 1908): 247–48.

Perrine, Frederick A. C. "The Scientific Aspect of the University Settlement Movement." *Science* 21 (17 February 1893): 91–92.

Prendergast, William A. "Efficiency through Accounting." *Annals of the American Academy of Political and Social Science* 41 (May 1912): 43–56.

Priddy, (Mrs.) Bessie Leach. "The Woman Mind on Politics." *National Municipal Review* 10 (March 1921): 171–76.

Riis, Jacob. *How the Other Half Lives: Studies among the Tenements of New York*. 1901 [1890]. Reprint, New York: Dover Publications, 1971.

Roberts, (Dr.) John B. "Real Causes of Municipal Corruption." *The Commons* 16 (October 1905): 537–40.

Robinson, C. M. "Civic Improvement." *The Survey* 26 (26 August 1911): 724–25.

Sait, Edward M. "Research and Reference Bureaus." *National Municipal Review* 2 (February 1913): 48–56.

Sands, Herbert R., and Fred W. Lindars. "Efficiency in Budget-making." *Annals of the American Academy of Political and Social Science* 41 (May 1912): 138–50.

Simkhovitch, Mary Kingsbury. "Settlement Organization." *Charities and the Commons* 16 (1 September 1906): 566–69.

——. *Neighborhood: My Story of Greenwich House*. New York: Norton, 1938.

"Spread of the Survey Idea." *The Survey* 30 (3 May 1913): 157.

"Trained Social Workers Take Charge of New York City Government." *The Survey* 31 (10 January 1914): 430–33.

"Traveling Exhibit for City Welfare." *The Survey* 28 (6 April 1912): 6–8.

Veiller, Lawrence. "The City Club of New York." *Charities and the Commons* 17 (10 November 1906): 212–13.

———. "New York City as a Social Worker: The 1910 Budget and Social Needs." *The Survey* 23 (16 November 1909): 211–16.

Wald, Lillian. *The House on Henry Street*. 1915. Reprint, New York: Dover Publications, 1971.

Welch, William. "Sanitation in Relation to the Poor." *Charities* 5 (1900): 207.

Wilcox, Delos F. "The Municipal Program." *The Commons* 9 (June 1904): 261–65.

"William H. Allen, Civic Achiever." *Charities and the Commons* 18 (6 July 1907): 362–64.

Wilson, Woodrow. "The Study of Administration." *Political Science Quarterly* 2 (June 1887): 197–222.

"Women in Municipal Research." *National Municipal Review* 8 (March 1919): 199–200.

Wood, Mary I. "Civic Activities of Women's Clubs." *Annals of the American Academy of Political and Social Science* 56 (November 1914): 78–87.

Woodruff, Clinton Rogers. "Women and Civics." *National Municipal Review* 3 (October 1914): 713–19.

Woods, Robert A. "Social Work: A New Profession." *Charities and the Commons* 15 (16 January 1906): 469–76.

Woods, Robert A., and Albert J. Kennedy. *The Settlement Horizon: A National Estimate*. 1922. Reprint, New York: Arno Press, 1970.

Young, James T. Review of *Efficient Democracy,* by William H. Allen. *Charities and the Commons* 19 (12 October 1907): 877.

SECONDARY SOURCES

Adams, Guy B. "Enthralled with Modernity: The Historical Context of Knowledge and Theory Development in Public Administration." *Public Administration Review* 52 (July–August 1992): 363–73.

Adams, Guy B., Priscilla Bowerman, Kenneth M. Dolbeare, and Camilla Stivers. "Joining Purpose to Practice." In *Images and Identities in Public Administration,* edited by Henry B. Kass and Bayard L. Catron, 219–40. Newbury Park, Calif.: Sage Publications, 1990.

Adams, Guy B., and Jay D. White, "Dissertation Research in Public Administration and Cognate Fields: An Assessment of Methods and Quality." *Public Administration Review* 54 (November–December 1994): 565–74.

Allen, Oliver E. *The Tiger: The Rise and Fall of Tammany Hall*. Reading, Mass.: Addison-Wesley, 1993.

Allison, Graham. "Public and Private Management: Are They Fundamentally Alike in All Unimportant Respects?" In *Proceedings of the Public Management Research Conference*. OPM Document 127-53-1. Washington, D.C.: Office of Personnel Management, February 1980.

Appleby, Paul. "Government Is Different" [1945]. In *Classics of Public Administration,* 4th ed., edited by Jay M. Shafritz and Albert C. Hyde. Fort Worth, Tex.: Harcourt Brace, 1997.

Arendt, Hannah. *Between Past and Future: Eight Exercises in Political Thought.* New York: Viking, 1968.

Austin, David M. "The Flexner Myth and the History of Social Work." *Social Service Review* 57 (September 1983): 357–77.

Bardach, Eugene. Review of *Creating Public Value: Strategic Management in Government,* by Mark E. Moore. *American Political Science Review* 91 (June 1997): 463–64.

Becker, Dorothy G. "Exit Lady Bountiful: The Volunteer and the Professional Social Worker." *Social Service Review* 38 (March 1964): 57–72.

Berkowitz, Edward D., and Kim McQuaid. *Creating the Welfare State: The Political Economy of 20th-Century Reform.* Lawrence: University Press of Kansas, 1988.

Bledstein, Burton J. *The Culture of Professionalism: The Middle Class and the Development of Higher Education in America.* New York and London: W. W. Norton, 1976.

Blodgett, Geoffrey. "The Mugwump Reputation: 1870 to the Present." *Journal of American History* 66 (March 1980): 867–87.

Boyer, Paul. *Urban Masses and Moral Order in America, 1820–1920.* Cambridge: Harvard University Press, 1978.

Bremner, Robert H. *The Discovery of Poverty in the United States* [formerly *From the Depths*]. 1956. Reprint, New Brunswick, N.J.: Transaction Publishers, 1992.

Brooks-Higgenbotham, Evelyn. *Righteous Discontent: The Women's Movement in the Black Baptist Church, 1880–1920.* Cambridge: Harvard University Press, 1993.

Bruno, Frank. "Twenty-five Years of Schools of Social Work." *Social Service Review* 18 (1944): 152–64.

Brush, Lisa D. "Love, Toil, and Trouble: Motherhood and Feminist Politics." *Signs* 21 (winter 1996): 429–54.

Cerillo, Augustus, Jr. "The Impact of Reform Ideology: Early Twentieth Century Municipal Government in New York City." In *The Age of Urban Reform: New Perspectives on the Progressive Era,* edited by Michael H. Ebner and Eugene M. Tobin, 68–85. Port Washington, N.Y.: Kennikat Press, 1977.

Chambers, Clarke A. *Seedtime of Reform: American Social Service and Social Action, 1918–1933.* Ann Arbor: University of Michigan Press, 1963.

———. "Women in the Creation of the Profession of Social Work." *Social Service Review* 60, no. 1 (March 1986): 1–33.

———. "Toward a Redefinition of Welfare History." *Journal of American History* 73 (1986): 407–33.

Costin, Lela B. *Two Sisters for Social Justice: A Biography of Grace and Edith Abbott.* Urbana and Chicago: University of Illinois Press, 1983.

———. "Edith Abbott and the Chicago Influence on Social Work Education." *Social Service Review* 57 (March 1983): 94–111.

Crocker, Ruth Hutchinson. *Social Work and Social Order: The Settlement Movement in Two Industrial Cities, 1889–1930.* Urbana and Chicago: University of Illinois Press, 1992.

Dahlberg, Jane S. *The New York Bureau of Municipal Research: Pioneer in Government Administration.* New York: New York University Press, 1966.

Danbom, David B. *"The World of Hope": Progressives and the Struggle for an Ethical Public Life.* Philadelphia: Temple University Press, 1987.

Danielson, Caroline. "Figuring Citizens: Gilman and Addams on Women's Citizenship." Paper presented at the annual meeting of the American Political Science Association, Chicago, September 1995.

Davis, Allan J. *Spearheads for Reform: The Social Settlement and the Progressive Movement, 1890–1914*. 2d ed. New Brunswick, N.J.: Rutgers University Press, 1984.

Dawley, Alan G. *The Struggle for Justice*. Cambridge, Mass.: Belknap Press of Harvard University Press, 1991.

Deegan, Mary Jo. *Jane Addams and the Men of the Chicago School, 1882–1918*. New Brunswick, N.J.: Transaction Books, 1990.

Deutsch, Sarah. "Learning to Talk More Like a Man: Boston Women's Class-bridging Organizations, 1870–1940." *American Historical Review* 97 (April 1992): 379–404.

DiIulio, John J., Jr. "Leadership and Social Science." *Journal of Policy Analysis and Management* 9, no. 1 (1990): 116–26.

Dimock, Marshall E. "The Inner Substance of a Progressive." *Social Service Review* 13 (December 1939): 573–78.

Diner, Steven J. *A City and Its Universities: Public Policy in Chicago, 1892–1919*. Chapel Hill: University of North Carolina Press, 1980.

Edwards, Rebecca. *Angels in the Machinery: Gender in American Party Politics from the Civil War to the Progressive Era*. New York: Oxford University Press, 1997.

Ehrenreich, John H. *The Altruistic Imagination: A History of Social Work and Social Policy in the United States*. Ithaca, N.Y.: Cornell University Press, 1985.

Eisenach, Eldon J. "Reconstituting the Study of American Political Thought in a Regime-Change Perspective." In *Studies in American Political Development*, vol. 4, edited by Karen Orren and Stephen Skowronek, 169–228. New Haven, Conn.: Yale University Press, 1990.

———. *The Lost Promise of Progressivism*. Lawrence: University Press of Kansas, 1994.

Ewen, Elizabeth. *Immigrant Women in the Land of Dollars: Life and Culture on the Lower East Side, 1890–1925*. New York: Monthly Review Press, 1985.

Executive Office of the President. "National Performance Review." In *Classics of Public Administration*, 4th ed., edited by Jay M. Shafritz and Albert C. Hyde. Fort Worth, Tex.: Harcourt Brace, 1997.

Finegold, Kenneth. *Experts and Politicians: Reform Challenges to Machine Politics in New York, Cleveland, and Chicago*. Princeton, N.J.: Princeton University Press, 1995.

Flanagan, Maureen. "Gender and Urban Political Reform: The City Club and the Woman's City Club of Chicago in the Progressive Era." *American Historical Review* 95 (October 1990): 1032–50.

Fox, Kenneth. *Better City Government: Innovation in American Urban Politics, 1850–1937*. Philadelphia: Temple University Press, 1977.

Garson, G. David. "From Policy Science to Policy Analysis: A Quarter Century of Progress." *Policy Studies Journal*, special issue 2 (1980–1981): 535–44.

Giddens, Anthony. *Central Problems in Social Theory: Action, Structure and Contradiction in Social Analysis*. Berkeley: University of California Press, 1979.

Gill, Norman N. *Municipal Research Bureaus*. Washington, D.C.: American Council on Public Affairs, 1944.

Ginzberg, Lori D. *Women and the Work of Benevolence: Morality, Politics, and Class in the Nineteenth Century United States*. New Haven, Conn.: Yale University Press, 1990.

Goodsell, Charles T. "Charles A. Beard, Prophet for Public Administration." *Public Administration Review* 46 (March–April 1986): 105–7.

Gordon, Linda. "Black and White Visions of Welfare: Women's Welfare Activism, 1890–1945." *Journal of American History* 78 (September 1991): 559–90.

Graham, George. "Trends in the Teaching of Public Administration." *Public Administration Review* 10 (January–February 1950): 69–77.

Haber, Samuel. *Efficiency and Uplift: Scientific Management in the Progressive Era, 1890–1920.* Chicago: University of Chicago Press, 1964.

Hammack, David C. *Power and Society: Greater New York at the Turn of the Century.* New York: Russell Sage, 1982.

Harding, Sandra. *The Science Question in Feminism.* Ithaca, N.Y., and London: Cornell University Press, 1986.

Harding, Sandra, and Jean F. O'Barr, eds. *Sex and Scientific Inquiry.* Chicago and London: University of Chicago Press, 1987.

Hays, Samuel P. "The Politics of Reform in Municipal Government in the Progressive Era." *Pacific Northwest Quarterly* 55 (October 1964): 157–69.

———. "The Social Analysis of American Political History, 1880–1920." *Political Science Quarterly* 80, no. 3 (September 1965): 373–94.

Hill, Caroline Miles. *Mary McDowell and Municipal Housekeeping: A Symposium.* Chicago: Millar, 1937.

Hine, Darlene Clark. " 'We Specialize in the Wholly Impossible': The Philanthropic Work of Black Women." In *Lady Bountiful Revisited: Women, Philanthropy, and Power,* edited by Kathleen D. McCarthy, 70–93. New Brunswick, N.J.: Rutgers University Press, 1990.

Hofstadter, Richard. *The Age of Reform: From Bryan to F.D.R.* New York: Vintage Books, 1957.

———. *Anti-Intellectualism in American Life.* New York: Alfred A. Knopf, 1963.

Holli, Melvin G. *Reform in Detroit: Hazen S. Pingree and Urban Politics.* New York: Oxford University Press, 1969.

Johnson, Arlien. "Her Contribution to the Professional Schools of Social Work." *Social Service Review* 22 (December 1948): 442–47.

Johnson, Peter. "The Progressive Movement, Municipal Reform, and the Founding of the Maxwell School." Syracuse, N.Y.: Maxwell School of Syracuse University, 1975. Photocopy, Institute for Public Administration Archives.

Kaboolian, Linda. "The New Public Management: Challenging the Boundaries of the Management vs. Administration Debate." *Public Administration Review* 58 (May–June 1998): 189–93.

Kahn, Jonathan. *Budgeting Democracy.* Ithaca, N.Y.: Cornell University Press, 1997.

Kalberg, Stephen. "The Commitment to Career Reform: The Settlement Movement Leaders." *Social Service Review* 49 (December 1975): 608–28.

Kann, Mark E. "Individualism, Civic Virtue, and Gender." In *Studies in American Political Development,* vol. 4, edited by Karen Orren and Stephen Skowronek, 46–81. New Haven, Conn.: Yale University Press, 1990.

Karl, Barry Dean. *Executive Reorganization and Reform in the New Deal: The Genesis of Administrative Management, 1900–1939.* Cambridge: Harvard University Press, 1963.

———. *Charles E. Merriam and the Study of Politics.* Chicago: University of Chicago Press, 1974.

———. "Public Administration and American History: A Century of Professionalism." *Public Administration Review* 36 (September–October 1976): 489–503.

———. "Lo, the Poor Volunteer: An Essay on the Relation between History and Myth." *Social Service Review* 58 (December 1984): 493–521.

Katz, Michael B. *In the Shadow of the Poorhouse: A Social History of Welfare in America.* New York: Basic Books, 1986.

Keller, Evelyn Fox. *Reflections on Gender and Science.* New Haven, Conn., and London: Yale University Press, 1985.

Kerber, Linda K. *Women of the Republic: Intellect and Ideology in Revolutionary America.* New York: W. W. Norton, 1980.

————. "A Constitutional Right to Be Treated Like American Ladies: Women and the Obligations of Citizenship." In *U.S. History as Women's History,* edited by Linda K. Kerber, Alice Kessler-Harris, and Kathryn Kish Sklar. Chapel Hill and London: University of North Carolina Press, 1995.

Kirschner, Don S. *The Paradox of Professionalism: Reform and Public Service in Urban America, 1900–1940.* New York: Greenwood Press, 1986.

Kunzel, Regina. *Fallen Women, Problem Girls: Unmarried Mothers and the Professionalization of Social Work, 1890–1945.* New Haven, Conn., and London: Yale University Press, 1993.

Larsen, Magali Sarfatti. *The Rise of Professionalism: A Sociological Analysis.* Berkeley: University of California Press, 1977.

Lasch-Quinn, Elizabeth. *Black Neighbors: Race and the Limits of Reform in the American Settlement Movement, 1890–1945.* Chapel Hill and London: University of North Carolina Press, 1993.

Lears, T. Jackson. *No Place of Grace: Anti-modernism and the Transformation of American Culture 1880–1920.* 1982. Reprint, Chicago: University of Chicago Press, 1994.

Lewinson, Edwin R. *John Purroy Mitchel: The Boy Mayor of New York.* New York: Astra Books, 1965.

Lissak, Riva Shpak. *Pluralism and Progressives: Hull House and the New Immigrants, 1890–1919.* Chicago and London: University of Chicago Press, 1989.

Lubove, Roy. *The Professional Altruist: The Emergence of Social Work as a Career, 1880–1930.* Cambridge: Harvard University Press, 1965.

Lynn, Laurence E., Jr. "Public Management Research: The Triumph of Art over Science." *Journal of Policy Analysis and Management* 13, no. 2 (1994): 231–59.

McCormick, Richard L. *The Party Period and Public Policy: American Politics from the Age of Jackson to the Progressive Era.* New York and Oxford: Oxford University Press, 1986.

McCurdy, Howard E., and Robert E. Cleary. "Why Can't We Resolve the Research Issue in Public Administration?" *Public Administration Review* 45 (January–February 1984): 49–55.

McGerr, Michael E. *The Decline of Popular Politics: The American North, 1865–1928.* New York and Oxford: Oxford University Press, 1986.

McGoldrick, Joseph. "The Board of Estimate and Apportionment of New York City." *National Municipal Review Supplement* (February 1929): 125–52.

Merchant, Carolyn. *The Death of Nature: Women, Ecology and the Scientific Revolution.* New York: Harper and Row, 1980.

Miller, Peter, and Ted O'Leary. "Hierarchies and American Ideals, 1900–1940." *Academy of Management Review* 14, no. 2 (1989): 250–65.

Mink, Gwendolyn. "The Lady and the Tramp." In *Women, the State, and Welfare,* edited by Linda Gordon, 92–122. Madison: University of Wisconsin Press, 1990.

Montgomery, David. *Citizen Worker: The Experience of Workers in the United States with*

Democracy and the Free Market during the Nineteenth Century. Cambridge: Cambridge University Press, 1993.

Moore, Mark E. "Policy Managers Need Policy Analysts." *Journal of Policy Analysis and Management* 1, no. 3 (1982): 413–18.

Mosher, Frederick C. "Research in Public Administration: Some Notes and Suggestions." *Public Administration Review* 16 (summer 1956): 169–78.

Muccigrosso, Robert. "The City Reform Club: A Study in Late Nineteenth Century Reform." *New York Historical Society Quarterly* 52 (1968): 235–54.

Muncy, Robyn. "Gender and Professionalization in the Origins of the U.S. Welfare State: The Careers of Sophonisba Breckinridge and Edith Abbott, 1890–1935." *Journal of Policy History* 2, no. 3 (1990): 290–315.

———. *Creating a Female Dominion in American Reform, 1890–1935.* New York: Oxford University Press, 1991.

Nackenoff, Carol. "Gendered Citizenship: Alternative Narratives of Political Incorporation in the United States, 1875–1925." Paper presented at the annual meeting of the American Political Science Association, San Francisco, 1996.

Noble, David F. *A World without Women: The Christian Clerical Culture of Western Science.* New York and Oxford: Oxford University Press, 1992.

Painter, Nell Irvin. *Standing at Armageddon: The United States, 1877–1919.* New York: W. W. Norton, 1987.

Parker, Jacqueline K., and Edward M. Carpenter. "Julia Lathrop and the Children's Bureau: The Emergence of an Institution." *Social Service Review* 55 (March 1981): 60–77.

Pease, Otis A. "Urban Reformers in the Progressive Era: A Reassessment." *Pacific Northwest Quarterly* 62 (April 1971): 49–58.

Peccorella, Robert F. *Community Power in a Post-Reform City: Politics in New York City.* Armonk, N.Y.: M. E. Sharpe, 1994.

Philpott, Thomas Lee. *The Slum and the Ghetto: Immigrants, Blacks, and Reformers in Chicago, 1880–1930.* Belmont, Calif.: Wadsworth, 1991.

Quigley, John M., and Suzanne Scotchmer. "What Counts? Analysis Counts." *Journal of Policy Analysis and Management* 8, no. 3 (1989): 483–89.

Reinders, Robert C. "Toynbee Hall and the American Settlement Movement." *Social Service Review* 56 (March 1982): 39–54.

Ritchie, Donald A. "The Gary Committee: Business, Progressives, and Unemployment in New York City, 1914–1915." *New York Historical Society Quarterly* 57 (1973): 330–31.

Ross, Dorothy G. *The Origins of American Social Science.* Cambridge: Cambridge University Press, 1991.

Rousmaniere, John P. "Cultural Hybrid in the Slums: The College Woman and the Settlement House, 1889–1894." *American Quarterly* 22 (1970): 45–66.

Rubin, Irene S. "Early Budget Reformers: Democracy, Efficiency, and Budget Reforms." *American Review of Public Administration* 24 (September 1994): 229–51.

Schachter, Hindy Lauer. *Reinventing Government or Reinventing Ourselves: The Role of Citizen Owners in Making a Better Government.* Albany: State University of New York Press, 1997.

———. "Settlement Women and Bureau Men: Did They Share a Usable Past?" *Public Administration Review* 57 (January–February 1997): 93–94.

Schiesl, Martin J. *The Politics of Efficiency: Municipal Administration and Reform in America, 1880–1920.* Berkeley: University of California Press, 1977.

Scott, Joan Wallach. *Gender and the Politics of History.* New York: Columbia University Press, 1988.

Sicherman, Barbara. *Alice Hamilton: A Life in Letters.* Cambridge, Mass., and London: Commonwealth Fund/Harvard University Press, 1984.

———. "Gender Professionalism and Reform in the Career of Alice Hamilton." In *Gender, Class, Race, and Reform in the Progressive Era,* edited by Noralee Frankel and Nancy Schrom Dye, xx–xx. Lexington: University of Kentucky Press, 1991.

Silverberg, Helene. " 'A Government of Men': Gender, the City and the New Science of Politics." In *Gender and American Social Science,* edited by Helene Silverberg, 156–84. Princeton, N.J.: Princeton University Press, 1999.

Simon, Herbert. *Administrative Behavior.* New York: Free Press, 1945.

———. "The Proverbs of Administration" [1947]. In *Classics of Public Administration,* 4th ed., edited by Jay M. Shafritz and Albert C. Hyde. Fort Worth, Tex.: Harcourt Brace, 1997.

Sklar, Kathryn Kish. "Hull House in the 1890s: A Community of Women Reformers." *Signs: Journal of Women in Culture and Society* 10 (summer 1985): 658–77.

———. "Who Funded Hull House?" In *Lady Bountiful Revisited: Women, Philanthropy, and Power,* edited by Kathleen D. McCarthy, 94–115. New Brunswick, N.J.: Rutgers University Press, 1990.

———. "Hull House Maps and Papers: Social Science as Women's Work in the 1890s." In *The Social Survey in Historical Perspective, 1880–1930,* edited by Martin Bulmer, Kevin Bales, and Kathryn Kish Sklar, 111–42. Cambridge: Cambridge University Press, 1991.

———. "The Historical Foundations of Women's Power in the Creation of the American Welfare State, 1830–1930." In *Mothers of a New World: Maternalist Politics and the Origins of Welfare States,* edited by Seth Koren and Sonya Mitchell, 43–93. New York: Routledge, 1993.

———. *Florence Kelley and the Nation's Work: The Rise of Women's Political Culture, 1830–1900.* New Haven, Conn., and London: Yale University Press, 1995.

———. "Two Political Cultures in the Progressive Era: The National Consumers' League and the American Association for Labor Legislation." In *U.S. History as Women's History: New Feminist Essays,* edited by Linda K. Kerber, Alice Kessler-Harris, and Kathryn Kish Sklar, 36–52. Chapel Hill and London: University of North Carolina Press, 1995.

Skocpol, Theda. *Protecting Soldiers and Mothers: The Political Origins of Social Policy in the United States.* Cambridge, Mass.: Belknap Press of Harvard University Press, 1992.

Skolnick, Richard C. "Civic Group Progressivism in New York City." *New York History* 51 (July 1970): 411–39.

Skowronek, Stephen. *Building a New American State: The Expansion of National Administrative Capacities, 1877–1920.* Cambridge: Cambridge University Press, 1982.

Stivers, Camilla. "The Public Agency as Polis: Active Citizenship in the Administrative State." *Administration and Society* 22 (May 1990): 86–105.

———. *Gender Images in Public Administration: Legitimacy and the Administrative State.* Newbury Park, Calif.: Sage Publications, 1993.

———. "Citizenship Ethics in Public Administration." In *Handbook of Administrative Ethics,* edited by Terry L. Cooper, 435–55. New York: Marcel Dekker, 1994.

———. "Settlement Women and Bureau Men: Constructing a Usable Past for Public Administration." *Public Administration Review* 55 (November–December 1995): 522–29.

———. "Settlement Women and Bureau Men: Rejoinder to Schachter." *Public Administration Review* 57 (July–August 1997): 370.

———. "Translating Out of Time: Public Administration and Its History." Review of *Budgeting Democracy,* by Jonathan Kahn, and *Reinventing Government or Reinventing
Ourselves,* by Hindy Lauer Schachter. *Public Administration Review* 59 (July–August
1999): 362–66.

Stone, Donald C., and Alice B. Stone. "Early Development of Education in Public Administration." In *American Public Administration: Past, Present, Future,* edited by Frederick C. Mosher, 11–48. University: University of Alabama Press, 1975.

Strom, Sharon Hartman. *Beyond the Typewriter: Gender, Class, and the Origins of Modern
American Office Work, 1900–1930.* Urbana and Chicago: University of Illinois Press,
1992.

Syrett, Harold C., ed. *The Gentleman and the Tiger: The Autobiography of George B.
McClellan.* Philadelphia: J. B. Lippincott, 1956.

Taylor, Lea D. "The Social Settlement and Civic Responsibility: The Life Work of Mary
McDowell and Graham Taylor." *Social Service Review* 28 (March 1954): 31–40.

Teaford, Jon C. *The Unheralded Triumph: City Government in America, 1870–1900.* Baltimore: Johns Hopkins University Press, 1984.

Testi, Arnaldo. "The Gender of Reform Politics: Theodore Roosevelt and the Culture of
Masculinity." *Journal of American History* 81 (March 1995): 1509–33.

Thompson, Frank J., Michael Brintnall, Robert F. Durant, Donald J. Kettl, Beryl A. Radin,
and Lois Recasino Wise. "Report of the APSA-NASPAA Committee on the Advancement of Public Administration." Presented at the annual meeting of the American Political Science Association, Boston, September 1998.

Thompson, Fred. Review of *The State of Public Management,* edited by Donald F. Kettl and
H. Brinton Milward. *Journal of Policy Analysis and Management* 16, no. 3 (1997):
484–89.

Toulmin, Stephen. *Cosmopolis.* New York: Free Press, 1990.

Trattner, Walter I. *From Poor Law to Welfare State: A History of Social Welfare in America.*
New York: Free Press, 1979.

Waldo, Dwight. *The Administrative State: A Study of the Political Theory of American Public Administration.* New York: Ronald Press, 1948.

Weinstein, James. *The Corporate Ideal in the Liberal State, 1900–1918.* Boston: Beacon
Press, 1968.

Welter, Barbara. "The Cult of True Womanhood." In *Dimity Convictions: The American
Woman in the 19th Century.* Athens: Ohio University Press, 1976.

White, Jay D., Guy B. Adams, and John P. Forrester. "Knowledge and Theory Development
in Public Administration: The Role of Doctoral Education and Research." *Public
Administration Review* 56 (September–October 1996): 441–52.

White, Jay D., and Guy B. Adams, eds. *Research in Public Administration: Reflections on
Theory and Practice.* Thousand Oaks, Calif.: Sage Publications, 1994.

White, Leonard D. "Introduction to the Study of Public Administration" [1926]. In *Classics of Public Administration,* 4th ed., edited by Jay M. Shafritz and Albert C. Hyde.
Fort Worth, Tex.: Harcourt Brace, 1997.

Wiebe, Robert H. *The Search for Order, 1877–1920*. New York: Hill and Wang, 1967.
———. *Self-Rule: A Cultural History of American Democracy*. Chicago and London: University of Chicago Press, 1995.
Wilson, Howard E. *Mary McDowell: Neighbor*. Chicago: University of Chicago Press, 1928.
Woodroofe, Kathleen. *From Charity to Social Work in England and the United States*. Toronto: University of Toronto Press, 1971.

Index